SOONER
CITIZEN

Lillian D. Miller

CONTENTS

Course and Chapter Connections

Course Objective	Chapter	Content
Cognitive Development *Stimulate Cognitive and Intellectual Development*	Chapter 2 Chapter 3 Chapter 4	**Academic Skills** **Executive Functions** **Multiple Intelligence** **Learning Styles** **Critical Thinking**
Campus Engagement *Promote Campus Engagment and Connection*	All Chapters	**OU History and Traditions** **University Resources** **Campus Involvement** **Serving the Campus Community**
Citizenship Skills *Encourage Community Responsibility and Active Citizenship*	Chapter 6 Chapter 7 Chapter 10	**Cultural Competence** **Civility and Respect** **Community Service** **Community Engagement** **Active Citizenship**
Social Interaction *Foster Positive Social Interaction Among Students*	Chapter 3 Chapter 6 Chapter 7	**Collaborative Learning** **Communication and Relationships** **Cultural Competence** **Campus Involvement**
Educational & Professional Planning *Support Educational and Professional Planning*	Chapter 1 Chapter 5	**Members of the Academic Community** **Courses, Majors, and Degrees** **Careers**
University Policy *Present Academic and other University Policies*	Chapter 1 Chapter 2 Chapter 3 Chapter 5	**Degree Requirements** **GPA Requirements** **Academic Integrity** **Academic Policies and FERPA**
Life Management Skills *Introduce Necessary Skills for Life Long Well-Being*	Chapter 2 Chapter 5 Chapter 6 Chapter 8 Chapter 9 Chapter 10	**Executive Functions** **Career Development** **Interpersonal Skills** **Health and Wellness** **Financial Management** **Active Citizenship**
Faculty/Staff Interaction *Facilitate Meaningful Interaction with Faculty and Staff*	Chapter 1 Chapter 5 Chapter 6	**Members of the Academic Community** **Advisor Interaction** **Proper Faculty/Staff Communication**

REI Cycle of Activities

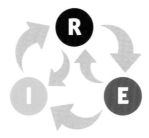

This textbook will provide you with a framework for achieving meaningful learning outcomes inside and outside of the classroom. A continuous process, known as the **REI Cycle of Activities**, will guide you to make sense of past experiences, interact with new information, and integrate old and new knowledge to impact your future decisions, actions, and outcomes.

R Reflect

This stage will allow you to process past experiences and previous learning. During reflection, you should recall past failures, successes, reactions, and established beliefs. From this recollection, you should determine what is needed for additional growth. Reflection is essential to learning and should be revisited periodically throughout the process. As you reflect, you should assess your current understanding and any limitations you may have. Some activities that promote reflection are journaling, self-assesment, and responsive writing.

E Engage

This stage will encourage you to engage in purposeful activities that broaden your understanding. It also involves you interacting with advanced material, engaging in new activities, and performing more complicated exercises. This stage promotes involvement, participation, and practice. The primary focus of this stage is participating in activities that will further your knowledge and skills. There are many ways for you to effectively engage in these activities. Engagement can range from joining an organization, forming a study group, working problems, reading course material, volunteering, becoming involved in classroom discussions, participating in research, or involving yourself in any other activity that will promote growth.

I Impact

This stage will allow you to integrate your previous learning with the new knowledge you gained through your recent engagement in order to establish competence, achieve goals, and make future contributions. The primary focus of this stage is to utilize all knowledge and experiences to benefit yourself and others. This stage allows you to create new ideas, contribute knowledge, and improve processes. Impact can extend from having the ability to navigate the institution, effectively communicate in the classroom, and improve issues in your spheres of influence through service and leadership.

Throughout each chapter, you will be encouraged to take time to participate in activities related to each of these stages.

You are beginning your first week at OU! You can expect this time to be filled with excitement and some anxieties about the unknown. Fortunately, you have chosen a university that has a strong sense of community and a friendly atmosphere. Anyone you meet will be happy to help you get the answers you need. Here is a guide to help you get started, but do not be afraid to also ask for help when needed.

Here are some things you should know about to help make your transition a smooth one:

1. **Sooner Card – Your Campus Identification Card**
2. **Campus DIning**
3. **Parking**
4. **Buying Books**
5. **oZone**
6. **Desire2Learn (D2L) and Canvas**
7. **Advising and Add/Drop Process**
8. **Bursar and Financial Aid**
9. **Athletic Tickets**

1. Sooner Card – Your Campus Identification Card

The Sooner card is the official identification card for the University of Oklahoma. It is the card you will use for the following university services:

- Using your meal plan to eat at on-campus restaurants
- Checking a book out at the library
- Unlocking various doors on campus to which you have been given access
- Entering the Huston Huffman Fitness Center
- Attending many athletic events
- Using your Sooner Sense debit account

On the Norman Campus, the Sooner card is issued at the Sooner Card office in the Oklahoma Memorial Union, room 127. To receive your Sooner card, present your driver's license, military ID card, passport, or other government-issued photo ID. The cost of obtaining or replacing your Sooner card is $20. This cost is subject to change. Your Sooner card is valid for the entire time you are enrolled at the university.

Sooner Sense is the debit account that all Sooner card holders may utilize for conducting business at various locations at the University of Oklahoma. Your Sooner Sense balance can be used at all on-campus restaurants, bookstores, laundry facilities and select vending and copy machines. You can activate your Sooner Sense account simply by making a deposit. This can be done online at *ou.edu/soonercard* or in person at the Sooner Card office in the Oklahoma Memorial Union, room 127.

Sooner Sense funds never expire and are available as long as you are enrolled at the university. Balances over $10 can be refunded when you officially leave the University by submitting a written request at the Sooner Card office.

2. Campus Dining

Planning to eat while you're here? You can take advantage of any of the 20 dining options on campus, but first you need to understand your meal plan. There are four basic freshman meal plans. Each plan is made up of a combination of "Meals" and "Meal Plan Points."

Meals are used most often at Couch Restaurants, our all-you-care-to-eat restaurant that is centrally located near the residence halls. Meals typically have a value of $12.50 when used in Couch Restaurants. Meals are numbered per week, meaning that you have a limited number to utilize in a given week. Meals reset every Sunday morning at 12:01 a.m. and unused meals do not roll over from week to week.

Meal Points are a debit-card system loaded onto your Sooner OneCard that may be used at all campus dining locations. Each Meal Point equals $1.00. Each time you use the card, the amount of your purchase is deducted from your balance. Meal Plan Points are easily confused with Sooner Sense; remember -- meal plan points cannot be used at the Bookstore, copiers, vending machines, laundry rooms, or at off-campus merchants.

Meals can be converted into Meal Points through a Meal exchange. There are various rules about when you can use a meal exchange where, but they give you additional flexibility to use up your meals before they expire at the end of the week. One meal converts to $8 worth of points. Meal exchanges can be used at the following times in the Union:

- Monday-Friday: After 2 p.m. at all operations that accept meal exchanges. Including - Starbucks, Chick-fil-A, Quiznos, Laughing Tomato, and Union Market.
- Saturday and Sunday: Anytime
- At Crossroads Restaurant all day, seven days a week.

You have two weeks to change your meal plan. If you find that none of the basic meal plans work for you, you can purchase enhanced plans for an additional cost. Visit Housing and Food Services in Walker, room 126 for help.

3. Parking

You can purchase a parking permit either in person or online. Parking and Transportation Services is located at 1107 Elm Ave. in the Stubbeman Place area. It is open 8 a.m. to 5 p.m. Monday through Friday. Permits can also be securely purchased online at *ou.edu/parking*. Look for the "Purchase Permit" link in the menu on the right hand side. Student parking permits are available for $249 and are valid from August until May for both the fall and spring semesters.

Permits are required to park on the University of Oklahoma Norman campus from 7 a.m. until 9 p.m. Monday through Friday. Students who live in university housing are eligible to park near the residence halls. Although there are just under 15,000 parking spaces on campus, about two-thirds of which are for students, it will not always be necessary to take the time to look for a parking spot. Many students choose to walk or bike to class or to take the bus (the CART) around campus.

For more about parking, go to *ou.edu/parking*.

4. Buying Books

After you enroll for your classes, your Ozone page will feature a link to the books and other materials you need for the classes in which you are enrolled. The University Bookstore is located in the Stadium.

Book vouchers are a pre-set financial allowance to charge your books and required supplies to your Bursar bill. Book vouchers are only given if your financial aid package is not yet available for disbursement or if you do not have the financial resources (summer savings, money from parents, etc.) to buy books at the start of the semester. A book voucher is not an additional source of financial aid; when your financial aid package becomes available, it will "repay" your debt to the bookstore in your Bursar account. If you obtain your financial aid refund before classes start, you must use that to purchase your books.

Book vouchers are available for those who need them approximately one week before classes start in the fall and spring semesters. If you're unsure of the actual dates, click on the "Ask the Sooners" widget at the bottom of your "money" tab on oZone and the answer will be given to you. Once vouchers become available, go to Financial Aid Services in Buchanan Hall Room 216 (Mon.-Fri. 8am-5pm) with your OU Sooner ID card. There you will sign a Financial Aid Book Voucher Form which includes Book Voucher Payment Authorization before book voucher privileges can be assigned.

For more details about book vouchers, visit the Financial Aid Office homepage at *financialaid.ou.edu*.

5. oZone

oZone (*ozone.ou.edu*) is OU's main online system designed for you to manage your information with the University. Anything you want to do – enroll, pay your bursar bill, access your grades, and manage your courses, can be done through this system. You can access oZone by using your 4x4 and password.

At the top of your cutstomized homepage is a menu of tabs that will take you directly to "Money," "Academics," "Libraries," and other pages of pertinent information. Quick links will take you to commonly visited pages, like your Bursar account, the Campus Map, and other resources. You can customize your oZone homepage to feature the tools you use the most often.

For more on oZone, like information on your academic profile and Degree Navigator, see the "Sooner Intro and Enrollment" section of your Graduation Planner.

What is my student number? This is the nine-digit number you were assigned when accepted to the University. It starts with a 112 or a 113. You won't need it every day, but it is handy to know it for when you do.

What is my "4x4"?
Your "4x4" ("four-by-four") is made up of the first four letters of your last name and the last four digits of your student number. It is used in combination with a password to access oZone, D2L, campus and other campus resources.

6. Desire2Learn (D2L) and Canvas

Currently, the University of Oklahoma is in the process of migrating courses from a former learning management system, OU Desire2Learn or D2L to Canvas. You may have some courses this year that will still be using OU D2L and others that will use Canvas to make course information accessible.

Desire2Learn (D2L)

When you log in to D2L (learn.ou.edu) with your 4x4 and password, you will see courses listed by semester. Clicking on the course title will lead you to a homepage for that course. Some professors list course announcements ("Class is canceled on Tuesday, but remember to meet in the library on Thursday," for example) on this main page, so it is important to check in with each course often.

Many course homepages will include:
- Content (the syllabus, readings, links, etc.)
- Grades (by assignment, plus other information, at professor's discretion)
- Roster (names and emails of your professor, any teaching assistants, and other students)
- Assignments including discussion boards for online conversations, a link to quizzes, and a "Dropbox" for turning in assignments. The dropbox and quiz feature includes a

timestamp that records when you submit these assignments.

In a similiar way, Canvas will provide you with syllabi, assignment details, and grade information for your courses in this system. Instructors may also require you to submit your assignments through the tool. You can access Canvas by logging into *oklahoma.instructure.com* using your 4x4 and password.

Need Help with Canvas?
Receive technical assistance from OU IT via:

- Call: 325-HELP
- Email: canvas@ou.edu
- Self-Help: askit.ou.edu

7. Advising and Add/Drop Process

If you are reading this, you have already been advised for the current semester, but it isn't too early to start planning for spring. For the first few weeks of the semester, however, you only have one concern: your current classes and whether or not you need to add or drop any. For the first week of any semester, you may add any courses without having to seek instructor approval; during the second week, you may be able to add a course, but only if the professor approves. During these first two weeks, you may also drop courses without additional charges or grading penalties. No grades will be recorded for dropped courses during this period of time.

Beginning the third week, you will need to manage any changes in your enrollment at Enrollment Services in Buchanan Hall, room 203. There are also different financial and grade-related rules and penalties for dropping or adding after the second week of the semester; for these, visit *ou.edu/enrollment/home* to learn more.

8. Bursar and Financial Aid – paying tuition and accessing financial aid

As mentioned above, you have access to your Bursar bill on your homepage of oZone. This bill will include any owed tuition, fees, or fines. You've probably already delved into the confusing world of paying for college, but for the basics, see the "Money Matters" section in your Graduation Planner. Remember, for any question you have, simply log in to oZone and go to the "Money" tab. There you will find links to the Financial Aid Office, your accounts and balances, and more. You will also see the "Ask the Sooners" (ATS) box at the bottom of the page where you can make inquiries about any information you cannot find.

Financial Aid Speak for Beginners

ATS - Ask the Sooners – a great search function for funding answers about your OU finances

FAFSA - Free Application for Federal Student Aid

FAS - OU Financial Aid Services department

OU-FAN – Financial Aid Notification (online awards notification)

SAP – Satisfactory Academic Progress for financial aid recipients

9. Athletic Tickets

Ah, now for the fun stuff!

As an OU student, you are are admitted free to all sports events, except football and men's basketball. Just show up, show your Sooner Card ID, and support your Sooner family. Take the time to support your peers on the field, the mat, and on the water.

For football and men's basketball tickets, go to *SoonerSports.com* and follow links for Student Tickets. There you can also buy or sell tickets on StubHub via the Sooner Sports website.

Chapter 1

Understanding Your University: *OU in the World*

Cornelia Lambert, Ph.D., former Adjunct Lecturer, Freshman Programs
Lillian Miller, M.Ed., Director, Freshman Programs

In this chapter, you will:

- Become familiar with the Spheres of Influence and the meaning of a Sooner Citizen.
- Learn about the virtues of a well-rounded person.
- Recognize OU's status as a research university and the different members of the OU academic community.
- Learn about University College and degree-granting colleges.
- Discover some of OU's most important history and traditions.

"The University of Oklahoma is truly an extraordinary institution, known for its academic excellence and strong sense of community ."

- President David Boren

Welcome to the University of Oklahoma. It is no mistake that your path has led you here, and we are excited that you have joined the many students, faculty and administrators who have also chosen this great institution.

One thing you will notice about OU is that we often refer to ourselves as "the OU community." We also speak of ourselves as a family, a close interconnected group united around our shared experiences and rich traditions. Even though you might instantly appreciate being a part of this engaging environment, you might also see the University of Oklahoma as a world of its own. You will notice many overlapping realms of human activity which involve people of all ages, of all levels of education and training, and from a diversity of backgrounds. On any given day, you may attend a lecture by a retired professor who has returned to campus to teach, eat lunch with a graduate student from another country, or play with the dog belonging to your residence hall's Faculty-In-Residence. So, when we welcome you to the University of Oklahoma, we are welcoming you to a group composed of many different types of people who have come together to share experiences and knowledge.

Acclimating to this new environment will not happen overnight. After all, this is a big transition. In a way, coming to college is much like the mental adjustment people had to make, many years ago, when Nicolas Copernicus, a scholar living in what is now Poland, presented his argument that the sun, not the earth, stood at the center of the known universe. As historians have noted, Copernicus' bold argument took the earth out of its central location at the center of the solar system, and relegated it to a position among all of the other planets.

Similarly, you have left a part of the universe where you were a central focus for one in which you may feel less significant. You will, however, soon feel at home. Your OU family members – your hall-mates, professors, and RAs – all know that you are transitioning during this first semester. Furthermore, your Gateway instructor, PTA, and other University College professionals are enthusiastic and ready to share with you all that OU has to offer. We are here to help.

Welcome to Gateway

Discovering your new place in the universe starts here, with *Gateway to College Learning*. In this course you will learn about an array of topics that have been carefully selected to

The Oxford English Dictionary defines "University" as: An institution of higher education offering tuition in mainly non-vocational subjects and typically having the power to confer degrees. The term comes from the French "univers" dating to the 1400's which means: the whole of creation, the inhabited world, and the spheres of human activity.

Figure 1.1

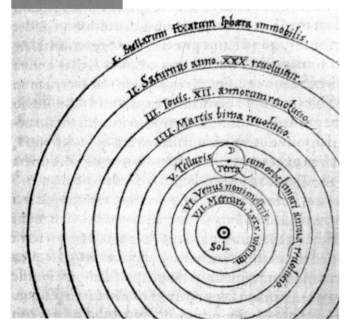

Copernicus's controversial theory was published in 1543 in De revolutionibus orbium coelestium, or On the Revolutions of the Celestial Spheres. *This picture is from OU's copy of this rare text, located in the History of Science Collections in the Bizzell Memorial Library.*

help you become accustomed to your new role. The *Gateway to College Learning* course objectives are to:

- Stimulate cognitive and intellectual development
- Foster positive social interaction among students
- Introduce necessary skills for life long well-being
- Promote campus engagement and connection
- Support educational and professional planning
- Facilitate meaningful interaction with faculty and staff
- Encourage community responsibility and active citizenship
- Present academic and other university policies

Perhaps the best way to understand the *Gateway to College Learning* curriculum is to visualize yourself as the center of ever-widening spheres of influence. These *spheres of influence* include your campus community, your local and national communities, and the global community as a whole. The topics in this course were selected to help you develop your relationship to these communities and to awaken you to the impact you can have within each community. Some readings will concern your personal growth into adulthood, while others will be broader in scope.

But, all of them are part of what we believe to be the most useful tools for success in college and beyond. These are the tools of "Sooner Citizenship," the idea we use to em-

body the standards and strengths of the University of Oklahoma graduate.

As a student, and later as a graduate, you will continue to develop as a Sooner Citizen. A *Sooner Citizen* is a person who exemplifies the University of Oklahoma's tradition of excellence by actively contributing creativity, knowledge, and service to his or her communities. Becoming an active member of the OU community will connect you to people and resources that will equip you to make contributions to the other communities you are a part of as well.

The OU community will provide many amazing opportunities for you to learn, grow, and succeed in a quickly changing and increasingly global society. This book and your Gateway experience will help you jump-start that development.

A Well-Rounded Person

John Adams, one of the principal Founding Fathers, believed that "the end of study is to make you a good man and a useful citizen." As you embark on your journey at the University of Oklahoma, reflect on the people you admire. What do you admire about them? Your college years provide you with the time and opportunity to cultivate within yourself the qualities you admire in others. These sorts of qualities that you admire are called virtues, and not only do you have the opportunity to develop them within yourself, but doing so is essential to your success at the University and in life after graduation.

Consider three categories of virtue: intellectual, executive, and civic. The *intellectual virtues* are those qualities that we admire in a person who has an excellent mind. They include:

Love of learning - In your first year at OU, you will explore history and politics, language and culture, the fine arts and the natural sciences. Maybe you will study the way that weather systems form, or the chemical basis of DNA, or how entrepreneurs decide when to take chances. Or maybe you will explore how intercultural conflict supports innovation in work teams or be inspired to investigate the role of social media, fine arts, community activism and public relations. You have before you a menu of intellectual riches that no other generation before you has had. Love of learning includes both the desire to get new knowledge and the delight in achieving it. It includes curiosity about the world and a proper regard for the difficulty in achieving genuine knowledge (thus it is connected to intellectual humility). It leads to a desire to expand the fields of knowledge one has already acquired.

Intellectual humility

Intellectual humility - Humility in general is the virtue of facing up to the truth about oneself, neither over-evaluating nor under-evaluating one's abilities and accomplishments. Intellectual humility is facing up to the truth about one's intellectual abilities and accomplishments, and admitting the limits of one's epistemic perspective. The intellectually humble person does not deny her accomplishments, but shows a lack of concern about intellectual status, and is sensitive to the ways in which one's beliefs can go wrong even though they seem right. Don't be afraid to go to your professor's office hours to ask for an explanation – that's what office hours are for!

Open-mindedness

Open-mindedness - Open-mindedness is the readiness to step outside one's own point of view to consider the merits of alternative perspectives, with a willingness to change one's beliefs when that is warranted. Open-mindedness follows from a genuine love of truth, and the humility to admit that one might be mistaken in one's beliefs. Whether it's a calculus problem, a philosophical debate, or a chemistry experiment, an open mind is ready to test different hypotheses and to do so fairly.

Not all virtues are virtues of the mind. There are also *executive virtues*, the qualities of flourishing individuals. These qualities will be essential as you transition to the responsibilities of college life, where you will be barraged with choices and forced to make decisions that will impact your short- and long-term future. Executive virtues include:

Self-control

Self-control - Self-control is one of the most basic virtues, in the sense that some degree of self-control is necessary for the acquisition of any other virtue. The ancient Greeks tried to live by the motto "nothing in excess." It is the capacity to regulate and restrain one's thoughts, emotions, and behaviors for the sake of achieving good ends. Self-control especially includes the ability to regulate the desires, and it includes the ability to direct one's thoughts and attention to one's goals.

Perseverance

Perseverance - Perseverance is the ability to stay on the path to one's goals despite the presence of obstacles, the discouragement of failure, and the distracting effect of temptations. It is crucial for the achievement of long-term goals, the pursuit of which presents so many opportunities to veer off-course or abandon one's aims. The persevering person does not lose sight of her purpose even when it takes a considerable amount of time to reach it, and they do not give up easily. Inevitably, you will fall short of some goal. But, failure is one of the greatest teachers, if you will learn from your experiences and use them to motivate you to succeed next time. When Thomas Edison struggled to make his light bulb work, he remarked, "I have not failed. I've just found 10,000 ways that won't work." It's that spirit that made him one of the great inventors in history.

Honesty

Honesty - Honesty is not just an executive virtue; it is also a basic intellectual and civic virtue. Most generally, honesty is a deep and pervasive commitment to truth - seeking it out, acknowledging it, holding oneself (and others) accountable to it, and conforming one's conduct to it. Honesty is closely related to integrity, which is the virtue of being true to oneself, of having one's beliefs, feelings, and behavior in harmony. A person of integrity does not say one thing and do another, so other people can count on him to do his part in following and upholding the rules of the community. Honesty is therefore also closely connected to respecting others in the community. To excel in academic life, you will need honesty. But, honesty is about more than not cheating or not plagiarizing. It's about having the type of integrity that will lead you to avoid grey areas, to want to be proud of your own work, and to do what's right whether you think anyone is watching or not.

Finally, college life will allow you to cultivate *civic virtues* – those qualities which are essential to a healthy community. These include:

Civility - Civility is a social virtue that is indispensable to open political discourse and reasoned disagreement. A civil person is willing to engage others in respectful dialogue, without scorn or insult, even when the issues are intensely important or disagreement runs deep. Civility has especially strong connections with intellectual humility and self-control. It means treating others with respect and caring about others, regardless of their background. The University is a wonderfully diverse place. You will interact with people of different religious and political beliefs. Indeed, many of your classes will engage your most deeply-held beliefs about the world. You will confront others whose deepest beliefs are irreconcilably different from your own. Yet, civil conversation is one of the most enriching experiences of university life, because it will allow you to reflect on your own beliefs, enriching your understanding and leaving you with a deeper sense of who you are as a person.

Compassion - Compassion is the ability to feel sorrow over another person's suffering, and to express that sorrow in a way that is intended to alleviate the suffering. Unlike pity, compassion does not suggest any feeling of superiority to the suffering person, but is instead a virtue that forms a bond with the sufferer. It is a quality you can cultivate in your relationships and in your academic experiences. It means the ability to use your mind to see the world through someone else's eyes.

Fairness - Fairness is a central virtue both of individuals and social institutions. Fairness is characterized by impartiality (a lack of favoritism). When people exhibit fairness, they consistently apply standards and rules to everyone and insist that others do the same, regardless of people's prestige, and whatever consequences for the self or preferred group. Fairness is thus an essential element of justice.

In his autobiography (one of the most remarkable books ever written), Benjamin Franklin wrote out thirteen virtues that he believed were fundamental, and he dedicated

himself to trying to achieve them. Consider writing out the qualities that you admire in others and that you'd like to see in yourself. Then, come back to the list periodically during your time at the University to measure how you've developed or how your goals have changed.

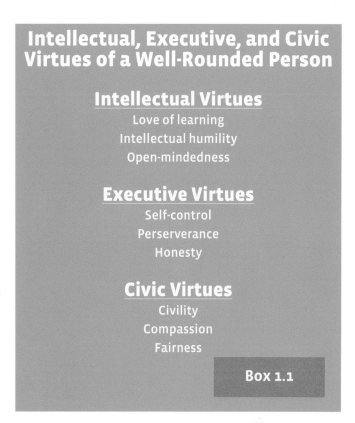

Intellectual, Executive, and Civic Virtues of a Well-Rounded Person

Intellectual Virtues
Love of learning
Intellectual humility
Open-mindedness

Executive Virtues
Self-control
Perserverance
Honesty

Civic Virtues
Civility
Compassion
Fairness

Box 1.1

OU in History: A Quick Look Back

The University of Oklahoma has a unique history. Established when this land was just a territory, OU began in 1890, almost twenty years before statehood. From its beginning, OU's leaders forged a university out of two guiding values: respect for tradition and education for citizenship. They also had the will to keep working despite setbacks, which is an example of the virtue, *perseverance*.

Like many of the universities established in the Progressive Era, the University of Oklahoma employed highly-trained professionals and entrepreneurs, in order to promote learning and regional economic growth. But, OU's early leaders also looked to older university traditions, such as "Ivy League" private colleges of New England, for more inspiration. For example, David Ross Boyd, the University's first president, landscaped the new campus with trees, even before construction began on campus buildings. According to one historian, Boyd "could not conceive of a treeless campus" (Gumprecht, 2007, p. 97). Boyd and other early founders of our university, such as Vernon Louis Parrington, were familiar with the rich histories and traditions of higher learning in both America and abroad, and they saw OU as part of that tradition.

Their vision for this university reflected not only the attention to quality and beauty shared by our early leaders, but also implied that OU could rival the more established, ivy-covered campuses that had served Americans since colonial times.

The Seed Sower symbolizes the efforts of our first president, David Ross Boyd. Boyd planted many trees and sowed seeds of knowledge. The Seed Sower emblem is a reminder that the Sooner community continues to sow important seeds that will blossom for generations to come.

Members of the Academic Community

By joining this university community, you are participating in exercises that date back to the learning communities of the Middle Ages. From the beginning, the European university was an institution of rank and order. Learned scholars were divided into faculties based on their disciplines, or fields of study. A few years of study would earn a young scholar (always male, in those days), a Bachelor of Arts degree; more years would earn a Master of Arts. Devoted students studying the higher subjects of law, of medicine, or of theology could earn the degrees which conferred upon them the title "doctor". Professors oversaw teaching, but masters were tasked with reading and commenting upon texts. And, all students learned by studying and by teaching other students.

President Boren is the first person in state history to serve as Governor of Oklahoma, U.S. Senator, and President of the University of Oklahoma.

Today's university looks almost the same. OU's academic community is made up of students, administrators, faculty, and professional staff. While your day-to-day experiences will largely concern faculty, staff, and other students, it is also important to understand how the university functions as a whole. Getting to know other members of the OU community will help you understand and appreciate the many layers that must function to keep our campus operating.

The University of Oklahoma is structured hierarchically, with a *president* who presides over senior administrators and establishes the visions and goals for the university. The *provost* reports to the president, and serves as the "chief" academic officer, overseeing the academic functions of the university that are carried out by the various colleges on campus. Colleges are comprised of academic departments and programs. A *dean* has the responsibility of overseeing a given college. Academic departments house the specific discipline in which students earn their degrees.

For example, the College of Arts and Sciences, the largest college at the University of Oklahoma, houses the Chemistry, Psychology, English, and History departments, among many others. A *department chair* (sometimes just called the "chair") is the faculty member responsible for a given academic department. Department chairs are usually tenured scholars who assume this administrative duty in addition to their scholarly and teaching responsibilities.

Tenure is an academic status guaranteeing a faculty member's job security. In order to "make tenure," junior faculty members must meet requirements such as a certain number and quality of

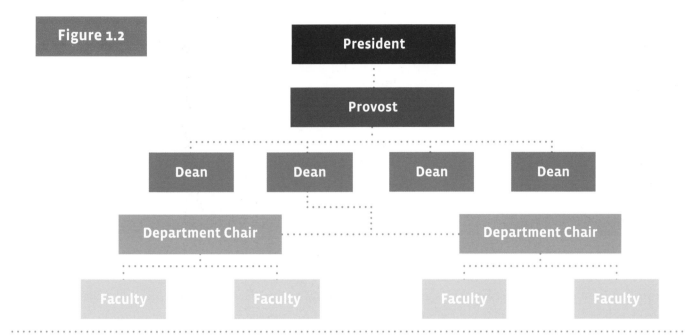

Figure 1.2

publications, service to the University and to their disciplines, teaching, and other contributions. Tenure exists in order to protect the academic freedom of professors and researchers; in other words, it guards them from being fired on the basis of their research findings or professional or personal opinions. *Full professors* are seasoned, tenured professors with years of research, publication, and teaching experience. Although the rules for advancement vary, *associate professors* are usually those mid-level professors who have earned tenure, and *assistant professors* are untenured.

Additionally, there are others who teach on campus. On occasion you may have an instructor who is part-time; these are often called *adjunct lecturers* (if they have Ph.D.'s) or *adjunct instructors*. In any institution of higher learning, the faculty is composed of those members who pass knowledge to the incoming generation of learners.

Undergraduate students are at the university to receive bachelor's degrees. At most universities, professors teach not only students coming directly from high school, but also post-graduate learners, and/or *graduate students,* students who are continuing their studies beyond a bachelor's degree to learn the fundamentals of their disciplines or master the tools needed to establish their careers. As part of their training, graduate students sometimes take on research and teaching roles in support of their major professors. You may have labs, discussion sections, or even whole courses taught by these graduate teaching assistants. Though they have not completed their full professional training, these scholars are trained and qualified to instruct the courses they teach.

At a *research university* such as OU, faculty members also have the task of engaging in extensive research activity and contributing new knowledge in their specialized fields. They conduct their own research, publish papers and books, contribute to conferences and symposia, and belong to professional organizations composed of people who study similar areas. In other words, professors are not only engaged in teaching students like you what they know – they are also actively engaged in expanding the boundaries of human knowledge.

A *research university* is an institution of higher learning in which faculty are charged with contributing actively to their academic fields. Research universities feature graduate and professional schools in addition to undergraduate colleges.

University College

As you learned earlier, universities are made up of colleges and departments. At our institution, incoming students begin in University College, which was founded in 1942 and serves as the academic front door to the university. *The mission of University College is to assist new students in making a successful transition to the university and in building a solid foundation for further academic success.* University College is comprised of six primary student service departments, mostly located in Lissa and Cy Wagner Hall.

The *Academic Advising Office* serves first-year, pre-health,

undecided, and non degree-seeking students. Professional academic counselors are available throughout the year to help students decide on majors and become acquainted with the university policies and resources they need to succeed at the University of Oklahoma.

The *Assessment Center* provides assessment of student knowledge and educational experiences by determining students' skill levels using Math, English, and Reading placement testing.

The *Center for Major and Career Exploration* provides advising for undecided students and additional services that help students explore majors, minors, and career paths. Using interest assessment tests and expert knowledge of OU majors and careers, a Major Exploration Coach can help you discover your options.

The *Center for Student Advancement* provides resources to motivate and equip students with the skills they need to succeed at OU. CSA coordinates the course, *Strategies for Success*, for University College students on academic probation or notice. The course is designed to help students improve their grade point averages and to help them begin to focus on success in the classroom.

The *Freshman Programs Office* assists students in making a successful transition from high school to university learning. This department provides two types of academic courses, the theme-based *Gateway to College Learning* (UCOL 1002) courses and the topic-based *University College Seminar* (UCOL 1022) courses. Both of these courses provide a small, interactive learning environment for first-year students. The Freshman Programs Office also advises the national freshman honor society, Alpha Lambda Delta.

The *Student Learning Center* promotes students' academic achievement, critical thinking skills, and positive study habits. This is accomplished through free, certified academic assistance (UC Action), computer software tutorials, *Student Success Seminars*, resource materials, and learning consultations.

Students remain at University College until they:
- complete first academic year,
- declare a major, and
- attain the minimum GPA to enter the degree-granting college of their declared major.

Once these three criteria are met, most students will automatically transfer from University College to their specific degree-granting college. Pre-professional health majors remain in University College for advising until admitted to their specific program at OU Health Science Center.

Degree-Granting Colleges

OU has 13 degree-granting colleges and offers over 150 majors at the baccalaureate level on the Norman campus. Across its three campuses, OU also offers many programs at the master's level, doctoral level, and doctoral professional level. Among OU's most popular undergraduate majors are Psychology, Business, Management, Marketing, Communication, and Multi-Disciplinary Studies. You may find undergraduate degree requirements online at ***checksheets.ou.edu.*** From this site, students may access electronic degree sheets for every major on the OU Norman campus. General education and major requirements are listed on each of the degree sheets.

The requirements for health programs at OU Health Science Center may be found at the University College link: ***http://www.ou.edu/content/univcoll/majors/degree_requirements.html***

General Education Requirements

OU is special in that, as a research institution, it requires of its undergraduates a preparation in the liberal arts. *Liberal arts* courses are distinct from the professional and technical training that may be a student's major and include a combination of courses, such as English, history, government, science, and philosophy. These courses are also known as *general education* (gen-ed) courses. Most are usually taken in the first two years of college. Liberal arts courses constitute a minimum of 40 credit hours of your total 120 (or more) required credit hours for graduation. While you may feel some of these classes are similar to those you took in high school, understand that these courses will be taught very differently by requiring more active learning and fostering open-mindedness. For example, your history classes may not just focus on memorizing dates and names, but will concern important issues and big ideas. This, alone, makes the liberal arts education more interesting in the college setting. But, the university has even more reasons – both traditional and modern – to require the liberal arts.

> *Liberal arts* is a curriculum distinct from the professional and technical training that may be required by your major and include courses such as English, history, government, science, and philosophy courses.

First, these courses teach you the skills necessary to succeed in the classes of your chosen major and your future career. As one group of scholars put it, these skills are "durable and transferable," meaning that they are lasting skills and that they apply to whatever subject or career you pursue (Cuseo, Fecas, & Thompson, 2007, p. 34). In other words, these courses contribute to the development of a well-rounded person. No matter what direction you take with your career, the skills you learn in these courses constitute the building blocks of your future success.

Perhaps more importantly, studying the liberal arts connects you to a historical tradition of education for citizenship. The word "liberal" comes from the Latin term for "free" and "freeing" and refers to the liberating effects of having access to knowledge. In Colonial days, America's founding fathers and mothers established schools and colleges in hopes that children and young adults would be educated in the ways of democracy and liberty. They focused on these "basic" courses

in order to train thinkers for the new American Republic, eventually established in 1776. Now, over 225 years later, you are part of the same tradition.

Also, by requiring courses over a wide range of disciplines, the university enables you to acquire a breadth of knowledge and to explore outside your comfort zone. In your general education courses, you will meet students from a wide range of majors and will be introduced to people and topics you might not otherwise experience. In this way, you begin to become a member of the wider community that is the University of Oklahoma, and you will gain education for citizenship in this community and others. Citizens trained in the liberal arts are able to weigh options critically and to make informed decisions in the voting booth. They are also able to recognize their own power to make changes through active engagement in their communities. In sum, OU requires a firm foundation in the liberal arts because it will tie you to your shared past, and will prepare you for your unique future.

University of Oklahoma Traditions

Just as a liberal arts education is a tradition at OU, community is an integral part of the university. The University of Oklahoma is a vast community spread out through time and space. The campus is an environment that will bring you together with students from across all fifty states and from more than one hundred twenty countries around the world. Becoming a member of the OU community connects you to the past, as well as to the future, and offers you an opportunity to share in a rich tradition. The University of Oklahoma has established many traditions that inspire a sense of community. Some of these traditions include:

OU Colors
May Overstreet, the only woman on the OU faculty in 1895, was asked to chair a committee to select the university's colors. The colors crimson and corn were adopted; however, they evolved to crimson and cream after local merchants could not continue to supply the demand.

OU Chant
The OU Chant was written by Jessie Lone Clarkson Gilkey, the director of the OU women's glee club, in 1936. As the OU Chant plays, Sooners stand and raise one index finger in

looking both forward and backward: by charting a path that maintains its reputation for excellence, while holding fast to the traditions that make it a truly special place. In recent years, OU has been named one of *Princeton Review's* top public universities in the nation in terms of academic excellence and cost for students. OU is a leader among all American universities in international exchange and study abroad programs. OU has also produced outstanding research and has achieved the Carnegie Foundation's highest tier of research activity classification (Carnegie Foundation for the Advancement of Teaching, n.d.).

As you will learn, there are many more activities happening across campus that give OU distinction as a world class university. Its founders would be proud, just as you will be, when you contribute to OU's good standing in the years ahead.

Now, OU's history is part of your history, and its values will become part of you: commitment to learning, respect for history and beauty, and the spirit of triumph that has defined the Sooner spirit from the beginning. You are ready to learn more about your new environment, access the resources available, practice responsibility, cultivate vital life skills, and share in traditions and campus culture at the University of Oklahoma. The exposure you are about to gain will help you to find your niche. Welcome to your new home!

the air as a symbol of unity and pride. (The lyrics of the OU Chant can be found on Page 6 of the Graduation Planner.)

OU Fight Song

"Boomer Sooner", OU's fight song, was written in 1905 by Arthur M. Alden. The tune was inspired by Yale's "Boola-Boola." A year later, additions were made from North Carolina's "I'm a Tarheel Born." This song is a favorite among OU fans!

OU Seal

The OU Seal was designed by George Bucklin and was inspired by President David Ross Boyd's chapel talk on the parable of a man sowing seeds.

OU in the World

Through the years, OU has made its mark in the world by

Boomer Sooner

Boomer Sooner, Boomer Sooner, Boomer Sooner, Boomer Sooner
Boomer Sooner, Boomer Sooner, Boomer Sooner, OKU
Oklahoma, Oklahoma, Oklahoma, Oklahoma
Oklahoma, Oklahoma, Oklahoma, OKU
I'm a Sooner born and a Sooner bred
And when I die, I'll be a Sooner dead!
Rah Oklahoma, Rah Oklahoma, Rah Oklahoma, OKU!

Academic Regalia

At university convocations and graduation ceremonies, faculty, administrators, and select students don special clothing, colloquially called "caps and gowns," in a style that dates back to Europe's medieval universities. Academic regalia includes academic robes, which are usually black and differ in form according to the rank of scholarship. The gowns worn by bachelor's degree recipients have long, pointed sleeves, for example, while those worn by students receiving master's degrees feature sleeves with oblong, hollow pockets on the bottom. In the medieval university, masters were required to carry books, food, and other items, hence the pockets in the sleeves. Although masters are no longer required to carry these supplies, the pockets remain. As the level of degree would suggest, the doctoral robe is the most ornate. It often features details in materials like velvet or fur in the colors of the degree-granting school and in the colors associated with the discipline of the degree earned. Headwear varies from the flat-topped mortarboard, typically associated with graduations for bachelor's and master's degrees, to the more elaborate velvet caps or tams worn by doctors. These vary widely from institution to institution, but all feature tassels in colors symbolic of the university, the discipline, or other specific honors. (Note: See page 82 for more information on degrees.) In addition to robes, graduate scholars also wear hoods that rest at the front of the neck and drape down the back. When a scholar earns his or her master's or doctorate, the ceremony includes a "hooding," when the major professor places the hood over the head of the new graduate.

University of Oklahoma Timeline

The Early Years 1892 - 1929

1895

OU FOOTBALL BEGINS

1892

DAVID ROSS BOYD BECOMES FIRST OU PRESIDENT

1903

FIRST ADMINISTRATION BUILDING DESTROYED BY FIRE

1890

GOVERNOR OF TERRITORY OF OKLAHOMA APPROVED A BILL FOR THE ESTABLISHMENT OF A UNIVERSITY IN NORMAN

1893

PRESIDENT BOYD BEGINS TREE PROJECT

THE FIRST "OKLAHOMA UNIVERSITY" ADMINISTRATION BUILDING OPENED. LOCATED WHERE EVANS HALL IS TODAY

1904

UNIVERSITY BAND WAS ORGANIZ

1898

FIRST BACHELOR OF ARTS DEGREE CONFERRED

FIRST GRADUATE STUDENTS ENROLLED

1905

BENJAMIN "BENNIE" GILBERT OWEN BECOMES FOOTBALL COACH - LONGEST STANDING FOOTBALL COACH

FIRST ANNUAL YEARBOOK CALLED THE "MISTLETOE" WAS PUBLISHED IN THE SPRING OF 1905

1912

STRATTON D. BROOKS BECOMES THIRD PRESIDENT

1929

OKLAHOMA MEMORIAL UNION OPENED DEDICATED IN HONOR OF THE OU STUDENTS WHO DIED IN WORLD WAR I; LATER REDEDICATED TO HONOR ALL

1907

SECOND MAJOR FIRE DESTROYED THE SECOND BUILDING BUILT WHERE EVANS HALL STANDS TODAY

A. GRANT EVANS BECOMES SECOND PRESIDENT

1923

JAMES S. BUCHANAN BECOMES FOURTH PRESIDENT

1915

RUF/NEKS ORGANIZED TO GATHER SUPPORT AT FOOT-BALL GAMES

MEX THE DOG BECAME THE FIRST OU MASCOT (1915-1928)

1905

SIDENT BOYD MOVES

BOYD HOUSE COM-ED ORIGINAL BOYD SE PICTURED ABOVE

1911

ADMINISTRATION HALL (NOW EVANS HALL) COMPLETED

1925

WILLIAM BENNETT BIZZELL BECOMES FIFTH PRESIDENT

Campus Highlights

Welcome to the University of Oklahoma!

Here are a few places we think you should explore while you are here. We hope you will discover the rich history and tradition of our beautiful campus.

. . . .

Boyd House

The Boyd House was built in 1906 by the first University of Oklahoma president, David Ross Boyd, as his family home. The Boyd House was later acquired by the University as the official presidential residence. This was its designation until 1969. The structure was reopened as the University House in 1970, occupied by the Office of Development Visitor Center, and in 1979, by the Office of Prospective Student Services. When President Boren came to the University of Oklahoma in 1994, he renamed the building to honor its builder and privately funded a renovation and expansion. In 1996, the Boyd House, again, became the official residence of the University's president. The large, northside addition contains the Cleo Cross Room, which accommodates approximately 60 guests for official University roundtable dinners.

. . . .

Oklahoma Memorial Union

The Oklahoma Memorial Union is commonly described as the 'living room of the OU community.' The Oklahoma Memorial Stadium and Oklahoma Memorial Union fundraising drive was the first organized event of the University of Oklahoma to solicit funds from private sources. Credit can be attributed to Bennie Owens, OU football coach for whom Owens Field is named after, for creation of such a program. The Union itself was built in memorial of the faculty, staff, and students who served and gave their lives for their country in World War I. Students played an integral role in the creation of this great facility. The Union was to be operated by students and for the students, with the vice chairman of the Student Council serving as the chair of the Union Committee.

The Union features the historic ballroom, Meacham Auditorium, Beaird Lounge, and Stuart Landing. Several important offices are located in the Union, such as Student Affairs, Center for Student Life, Career Services, Women's Outreach Center, the Leadership Development and Volunteerism Office, and the Alumni Association. The Archie-Dunham-Conoco Student Leadership Wing serves as the home of the Student Government Association (SGA), as well as many of the 400 active student organizations on campus.

Spoonholder

The current Spoonholder, located on the North Oval, was a combined gift from the classes of 1949 and 1999. It is a reproduction of the original Spoonholder, which was constructed by the class of 1910. Legend says if a young couple kisses in the Spoonholder, they are destined to be married. Parts of the old Spoonholder were actually kept and ground up to be included in the new Spoonholder.

Carl Albert Statue

Paul Moore's statue of Carl Albert, a gift from Wanda and Jack Bass of McAlester, is a larger- than-life bronze of one of the most innovative leaders in our state's political history. This memorial is found on the east side of the Oklahoma Memorial Union.

Winona

This statue, by R.C. Gorman, was of gift of Kathryn and Robert Simpson of Duncan. It depicts a reclining American Indian woman holding a bowl. You may find Winona on the west side of Ellison Hall.

Homeward Bound

This statue by Allan Houser is a gift of Fran and Earl Ziegler of Dallas. A bronze depiction of a Navajo woman following sheep and a dog across a bridge, this statue is found between Bizzell Memorial Library and Adams Hall.

Holmberg Hall

Constructed in 1918 to serve as a Grand Opera House, Holmberg Hall was first called "The Auditorium" and later named for OU's first Dean of Fine Arts (1913-1936), Frederick Holmberg. In 2002 construction began to restore Holmberg Hall to its former beauty, thanks to a grant from the Donald W. Reynolds Foundation. Before its current renovations, the hall served its original function of hosting concerts and theatrical productions. It is also the home to Sooner Scandals and University Sing, both student-led musical productions organized by the Campus Activities Council.

Buchanan Hall

From 1926 until after World War II, this building, named for OU's third president James S. 'Uncle Buck' Buchanan, served as the center for liberal arts instruction. Buchanan came to OU as a professor in 1895 and became the first Dean of College of Arts and Sciences. In 1923, he was appointed president and served for two years. Today, Buchanan Hall houses the offices of the Registrar, the Bursar, Admissions and Records, Registration, and Financial Aid.

North Arches

Donated by the classes of 1915 and 1917, the arches on the Parrington Oval provide an example of OU's unique campus flavor. On examining these arches in the 1940's, architect Frank Lloyd Wright coined a new architectural term to describe their style – Cherokee Gothic. OU's campus remains the largest collection of Cherokee Gothic architecture in the world. In fact, OU is one of the only universities in the world that has developed its own form of architecture. This style gives buildings an appearance similar to those at Harvard and Cambridge.

The Field House

Construction of the OU Field House was completed in 1928. It was originally designed as a physical education building because, at that time, all OU students were required to take a physical education course before graduating. However, from the time of its completion, it has served the University in numerous capacities and remains an important part of the University of Oklahoma's athletic program. Throughout its history, the OU Field House has been the home of both men's and women's basketball, swimming, volleyball and wrestling. Since 1975, when both basketball teams moved to Lloyd Noble, the Field House has functioned primarily as the home of men's wrestling and women's volleyball.

Bizzell Memorial Library

With an ever-expanding collection of over 5 million volumes, 75,000 serial subscriptions, and 300 databases, the University of Oklahoma OU Libraries constitute the largest research library system in the state of Oklahoma. Constructed in 1929 and named for the University's 5th president, William Bennett Bizzell, Bizzell Memorial Library serves as the main hub of the University of Oklahoma Libraries. The library contains numerous study areas, open to the OU community. In addition, state-of-the-art computers and equipment provide students with free Internet access. Lavishly furnished study rooms, collections of Native American paintings, and the Great Reading Room help create the unique atmosphere at the Bizzell Memorial Library.

Evans Hall

The site of the University's first building is home to many of the University's administrative offices today. OU's first president, David Ross Boyd, and his students occupied Evans Hall near the turn of the century. Unfortunately, that structure was destroyed in a tragic fire on January 6, 1903. The second building on campus, University Hall, was built in this same location only to burn down in 1907. The Cherokee Gothic building standing today was built in 1912 of brick and stone and was rumored to be absolutely fireproof. Known first as New University Hall, it later became the Administrative building. In 1924, it was renamed Evans Hall for Arthur Grant Evans, OU's second president.

Red Phone Booths

President David L. Boren brought six British-style, bright red telephone booths to campus in the 1990s to give the campus color and an international atmosphere. They were initially eqipped with coin operated phones, which helped pay for their upkeep. They are no longer coin operated or available for long-distance calls, but can be used free-of-charge to make local calls.

Booth locations:
- » Northwest side of Couch Cafeteria
- » Between Dale and Copeland Halls
- » Northwest side of Richards Hall
- » Southeast side of Oklahoma Memorial Union
- » Southwest side of Jacobson Hall
- » West side of Fred Jones Jr. Museum of Art

The top 10 things you should do during your freshman year at OU

1. **Visit a professor in office hours** - *Every professor has office hours, a time they set aside to meet with students outside of class. These office hours should be listed on the syllabus for each of your classes.*

2. **Visit Sam Noble Museum of Natural History** - *The Sam Noble Oklahoma Museum of Natural History has more than 7 million artifacts. The museum exhibits include the largest Apatosaurus on display in the world and the oldest work of art ever found in North America — a lightning bolt painted on an extinct bison skull.*

3. **Attend a sporting event** - *As a student, you are admitted free to all OU sports events, except football and men's basketball. For a schedule of upcoming events, visit SoonerSports.com.*

4. **Visit Fred Jones Museum of Art** - *Fred Jones Museum of Art contains nearly 16,000 art pieces in its permanent collection. Included is the Weitzenhoffer Collection of French Impressionism, one of the most important gifts of art ever given to a U.S. public university.*

5. **Attend a tutoring session** - *Action Tutoring, Action Centers and the Writing Center are all free tutoring services available to students. Visit the Graduation Office website ou.edu/graduatesooner for a comprehensive list of tutoring options available.*

6. **Attend a meeting for a student organization** - *There are currently over 400 active registered student organizations that cover a multitude of interests. If you can't find a student organization that interests you, you can even start your own! Visit Student Life for more information about getting involved.*

7. **Attend a campus theatre production** - *OU has one of the oldest comprehensive colleges of fine arts in the Great Plains states, with highly regarded schools of Music, Drama, Art and Dance, and with programs in opera, musical theater and sculpture.*

8. **Find a perfect study spot** - *There are many places designated for studying in Bizzell Memorial Library, including The Great Reading Room, which is a beautiful designated quiet area, located on the second floor.*

9. **Go to a musical performance at Catlett Music Center** - *Home to the School of Music, Catlett Music Center offers choir, band, and orchestra performances throughout the year. To view the calendar, visit music.ou.edu.*

10. **Visit the Barry Switzer Center** - *Visit the Barry Switzer Center on campus for more information about Oklahoma Football History and traditions.*

How OU is Developing Virtue in
Our Students

Institute for Human Flourishing

The Institute for the Study of Human Flourishing, made possible by a generous grant of the John Templeton Foundation and the support of the University of Oklahoma, is founded on the belief that humans flourish when they develop to their fullest potential as rational and moral creatures living in healthy communities.

The concept of flourishing can be approached through the discipline of philosophy, which helps us define, understand, and evaluate what it means to flourish. It can be approached through the discipline of psychology, which enables us to measure the traits that underlie the ideal of flourishing and to understand the nature of human well-being. It can be approached through the field of education, which teaches us how to cultivate the virtues in our students and in ourselves. Therefore, the Institute believes the study of flourishing lies at the intersection of philosophy, psychology, and education.

Student Initiatives and Programs:

1. Last Lecture Series

If you could give one last lecture before you die, what would you say? This is the premise of the Last Lecture. This idea gained international popularity when Randy Pausch, a professor at Carnegie Mellon who had been diagnosed with terminal pancreatic cancer, gave a lecture entitled "The Last Lecture: Really Achieving Your Childhood Dreams."

Our Last Lecture series gives OU leaders an opportunity to reflect deeply about what matters most to them, and to share those reflections with the OU community.

THE UNIVERSITY OF OKLAHOMA

CAMP IMPACT

2. Camp IMPACT

Camp IMPACT is designed to provide OU students with an opportunity for an in-depth exploration of the role of character in their lives. It includes three main components: volunteer/service opportunities; personal, cultural and social experiences; and civic exposures. Students will engage in these purposeful experiences for three days over Spring Break in downtown Oklahoma City as well as participate in pre- and post-camp activities.

3. Gateway and Common Read

OU's Gateway to College Learning course reaches thousands of first-year students, helping them to transition to college life. This course has integrated the nine virtues explicitly into the content and structure and is one of the programs that facilitates the common read program that allows students to read a book related to one or more virtues. Each year a public lecture will be held to further discuss this book.

This year's book, *This I Believe*, is a compilation of essays from both famous and everyday citizens who were encouraged to share the personal philosophies that have helped shape their lives.

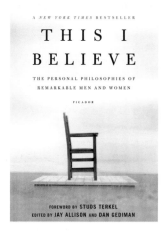

A *NEW YORK TIMES* BESTSELLER

THIS I
BELIEVE

THE PERSONAL PHILOSOPHIES OF
REMARKABLE MEN AND WOMEN

PICADOR

FOREWORD BY STUDS TERKEL
EDITED BY JAY ALLISON AND DAN GEDIMAN

Chapter 1 REI

Understanding Your University

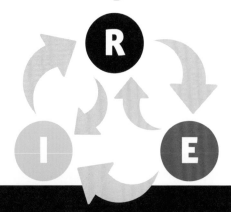

Reflect

You have been at OU for over a week now. During this brief time, you have probably noticed that many things in college are different than high school, including the campus environment and the various types of students, faculty, and staff. What is one thing that has positively stood out to you so far? Have you encountered any challenges? What is one thing that you have learned about OU since you have been here?

....

Engage

Review the descriptions of each of the virtues throughout the chapter.

....

Impact

In what ways do you anticipate the OU campus community will positively impact you during your time as an undergraduate student? Specifically, what virtue might you further develop from your interactions with students, faculty, and staff and your exposure to broad liberal arts coursework?

....

References

Brickman, W. W. (1972). American higher education in historical perspective. *Annals of the American Academy of Political and Social Science, 404,* 31-43.

Carnegie Foundation for the Advancement of Teaching (n.d.). Institution profile: University of Oklahoma Norman campus. Retrieved from carnegiefoundation.org.

Cuseo, J., Fecas, V., & Thompson, A. (2010). *Thriving in college and beyond* (2nd ed.). Dubuque, Iowa: Kendall Hunt.

Gumprecht, B. (2007). *The campus as a public space in the american college town. Journal of Historical Geography,* 33 72–103.

Smith, C., Turner, S. (2015). *The radical transformation of diversity and inclusion: The millennial influence.* Deloitte University Leadership Center for Inclusion. Billie Jean King Leadership Initiative.dention

U.S. Department of Education, National Center for Education Statistics. (2015). *Digest of Education Statistics, 2013* (2015-011)

Chapter 2

Mastering Executive Functions: *Goal Setting, Time Management, and Motivation*

Johnnie-Margaret McConnell, M.Ed., Director, Center for Student Advancement
Lisa Portwood, Ph.D., Assistant Dean, University College

In this chapter, you will:

- Set long-term, short-term, and immediate goals, using the S.M.A.R.T. method.
- Understand how to overcome obstacles.
- Manage your time by prioritizing your commitments.
- Discover habits for academic success.
- Define what motivates you.

"The man who moves a mountain begins by carrying away small stones."

- Chinese Proverb

Every fall, the University of Oklahoma welcomes a new class of dreamers. Some dream of becoming doctors, some want to become famous athletes, some hope to cure cancer one day, and a few may even aspire to be President of the United States. But, they each have in common with one another – and, now, with you – the dream of graduating from the University of Oklahoma. So, how do they make this dream a reality? This chapter is about the day-to-day steps necessary for you to achieve your dream of graduating from the University of Oklahoma.

No matter your ultimate goal, performing well in your classes is fundamental to earning a college degree. There is more to academic success, however, than understanding and remembering your course materials. In this chapter, you will learn about those practices that maximize your opportunities for success, including goal-setting, time-management, and maintaining motivation.

These skills are known as **executive functions**, the cognitive skills and habits that help you complete projects and achieve goals. Any one of these may seem like a trivial skill, but together they are some of the most important ingredients for your academic success. These skills relate directly to the Executive Virtues discussed in Chapter 1. By practicing the executive virtues of self-regulation and perseverance, these abilities can also be strengthened.

This chapter is a combination of years of research by educational psychologists and personal wisdom from a variety of campus leaders. Interwoven in sections on skills associated with various executive functions are notes about particular campus resources like Action Tutoring, Bizzell

Library, and others. Taken together, you will have the tools you need to achieve academic success at OU.

> Think of a time when you have set out to achieve a goal and have been successful.
>
> What steps did you take to reach your goal?
>
> Did you come across any obstacles along the way?
>
> What did you do to overcome these obstacles?
>
> What virtues were most helpful in your success?

Dreams and Goals

At their best, dreams are guiding passions, which can fuel hard work. But, without a strong dose of reality, a solid plan, and lots of hard work, dreams remain dreams and are never achieved. How does one translate a wishful fantasy into a practical plan of action? A dream only becomes real when it is translated into discrete, defined goals. Just like the quotation at the beginning of the chapter – "the man who moves a mountain begins by carrying away small stones" – any dream for the future can be divided into smaller tasks.

Dividing your dream into discrete goals helps you realize them: first, by tying them to reality, and second, by providing you with direction and focus. In many ways, life is like a river, always moving, always changing the terrain of the bank as it crests and flows. Unless you work to steer your boat to a specific location, you will arrive wherever the water carries you. However, if you focus your energy and effort on a destination, you significantly increase your chances of arriving there. Very few good things in life just happen; they usually come only after hard work and planning (Hopper, 2004).

Of course, your dreams and goals may change over time. What you want out of life is likely to transform as you grow older and as your needs and desires change. In fact, the ability to adjust your goals, as you gain experience and self-awareness, is an additional ingredient of success.

The best way to ensure that your goals will work for you is to follow a handy guide by Paul J. Meyer, known as "S.M.A.R.T." "S.M.A.R.T." is an acronym to help you remember the five characteristics of healthy goals (2006).

- First, you must define a _Specific_ goal on which to focus your energies. The goal of "I want to work with people" is so vague that it would be hard to predict what steps should be taken to achieve the goal. A goal should be defined precisely, so that it can give your "river trip" focus and so that the image of accomplishing it can be used for motivation. In what capacity do you wish to "work with people"? What kind of work? What kind of people? Aspiring to "plan social and educational programs for children and adolescents" is a more specific goal.

- Second, the goal needs to be _Measurable_. Deciding that you want to "make good grades" is a positive start, but how do you know if you have achieved your goal? Choosing, instead, to pursue a specific grade point average (GPA) makes the goal measurable so that, at the end of the semester, you can evaluate your success.

- Third, your goals should be realistic and _Attainable_. You are setting yourself up for disappointment if you set the bar for success so high that you are doomed to fail. Rather, you need to be honest with yourself and set goals that can be realistically met and lead you to success.

Figure 2.1

General Goals	⇨⇨⇨⇨⇨⇨⇨⇨⇨⇨	S.M.A.R.T. Goal
I want to work with people.	Specific. Define your goals specifically enough that you can focus your energies.	I want to plan social and educational programs for children and adolescents.
I want to do well in my class.	Measurable. Provide a yardstick for measuring outcomes.	I want to earn a 3.00 GPA this year, with no grade below "B."
I want to earn my law degree within one year of graduation.	Attainable. Draft realistic goals that challenge you, but that are not, by definition, out of reach.	I want to earn my law degree within 3 years of graduation.
I wish to thoroughly review each career listed in the Occupational Outlook Handbook.	Relevant. Make sure each goal is consistent with other goals you have established and fits with your immediate and long-range plans.	I will spend time in the Career Services Library researching careers associated with my Communication major.
I will graduate.	Time-bound. Give yourself time to achieve your goals.	I will graduate in four years by taking 15 hours per semester.

- Fourth, your goals should be _Relevant_ to your overall dream. Avoid wasting time on petty tasks that take time away from your defined goal. Self-control is a virtue that can help you stay focused on relevant goals and prevent distractions.

- Finally, your goals should be _Time-Bound_. Set realistic timetables for achieving the steps of your dream. Having an end date in mind will also give you something to look forward to when your work seems insurmountable (Meyer, 2006).

Following the S.M.A.R.T. model helps to make dreams less about wishes and more about reality. As life coach Diana Robinson warns, without precision and thoughtfulness, achieving a dream is merely a matter of luck. Instead, Robinson (1998) counsels, "You must clarify it, provide the details, and make it so clear that you can see it, feel it, know what you will feel like when you get there". Otherwise, you wager your dream on a gamble.

Just as dreams should be divided into goals, goals can also be categorized, in order to help you prioritize what to work on first. **Long-term goals** are goals that you plan to achieve in four years or longer. Perseverance is extremely important to achieve long-term goals. Examples of long-term goals include: graduating from college, finding a life partner, starting a business, etc. Intermediate goals are those that you hope to obtain within one-to-three years. Examples include: studying abroad, working an internship, or earning an invitation to an honor society in your major or college.

Short-term goals are those that you plan to achieve within the next year. You may know, for example, that you will need a summer job, and rather than waiting until May 31st to begin your job search, you can begin networking and scouting potential jobs now. **Immediate goals** are goals that are focused on the current week. For example, "I will review my notes for an hour, everyday, to prepare for my zoology test on Tuesday." Another example of an immediate goal would be planning to go to Chinese Action Tutoring for two hours this week.

Short-term and immediate goals serve as steps to the achievement of larger goals. The effort you put into accomplishing daily and weekly goals will build to a successful end of the semester. Then, each successful

Academic Goal Setting

Take time to explore some of the academic assistance opportunities available for your current courses by visiting the following link:

ou.edu/content/graduatesooner/resources/tutoring.html

What immediate goal can you create to utilize an appropriate service? (e.g. "My immediate goal is to attend the Action Center for BIOL 1114 this Monday from 6-8 pm to gain a better understanding of how amino acids form protein.")

"My challenges in college were always related to time management, as I was a student-athlete involved in lots of travel. When I reached my upper-level courses (Human Anatomy, Shakespeare, Chaucer, etc.), I found it increasingly difficult to prepare for exams, due to competition and travel. So, I began the practice of either re-writing or (more often) typing my notes each night. Fortunately, I had a great keyboarding teacher in high school and could type quickly, so it was not very labor-intensive! Each night, I would simply type all of the day's notes, thinking that they would then be in a neat, orderly form from which to study when exam time came. What I found was that I rarely needed to "study," when exam time came, because the recreation of the content helped me learn it. It moved me from rote memorization to true comprehension."

- Sherri Coale, OU Women's Basketball Coach

semester builds to a diploma and to a celebration of your graduation from the University of Oklahoma! Divide the mountains of your dreams into small stones, and slowly, but surely, your mountains can be moved.

"Remind yourself every single day of what it is you want. Write it down. Tell people. See it happening in your mind."
- Sherr Coale, OU Head Women's Basketball Coach

Overcoming Obstacles

Setting goals is a good first step, but remember: life does not always go according to plan. Obstacles can arise that make achieving your goals more challenging than expected. An **obstacle** is any barrier that hinders you from achieving your goals. External obstacles are barriers that result from circumstances, such as a family member's health issues or a financial need to work over twenty hours per week. Internal obstacles, on the other hand, stem from within you. These include mental obstructions, such as the following:

1. Trying to please someone else. – Most people like to please others, but in college, it is important to choose the goals that please you. College requires a lot of hard work, time, and energy, and it is challenging to devote yourself entirely, when you are pursuing someone else's dream - and not your own.

2. Not really wanting it. – All goals require effort, and if the goal is not something you feel strongly about, it can be challenging to summon the motivation to work toward the

goal. If you want a career that does not require a college degree, perhaps you should focus on that goal. Work toward what you really want to do.

3. Being a perfectionist. – College will quickly teach you that there is no such thing as perfect. If you were perfect and had nothing to learn, you would not be in college. The desire to be perfect leads to frustration and discouragement.

4. Trying to "go at it alone." – Few people can get through life without help or support from others. Many students believe that asking for help from professors, RA's, or other staff, is a sign of weakness. It is actually the opposite. One of the reasons you are at the University of Oklahoma is to utilize its many resources and support systems. Your goals are your own, but everyone needs moral and emotional support, so be willing to share your goals with others. Ask for help. OU has resources to assist you.

5. Resisting change. – Some people find change to be scary and disruptive. Yet, you have changed your entire life to attend college. All successful people share the attribute of adaptability. Being flexible and open to change allows you to try new things and to learn from these experiences. No healthy person remains the same throughout life, or even through college. New technologies, new cultural phenomena, new people, and new personal interests, tastes, and goals come into everyone's life. What marks a successful person is the ability to adapt to change.

Time-Management: Scheduling Your Life

Many of you are entering college directly from high school, where every day began with the school bell alerting you to go to class with everyone else. In most cases, every day was exactly the same. College works very differently. Every student has a different schedule. Classes are scattered all over campus and begin as early as 7 a.m. and finish as late as 10 p.m.. Further, each day may look different, due to once-a-week science labs, discussion groups, and varying work schedules. The first year of college is filled with too many transitions to count, but learning to become your own scheduler is one of the most critical skills needed to be successful both inside and outside the classroom. Developing a daily schedule that balances classes, work, campus and personal commitments can quickly become overwhelming.

In order to be a successful scheduler, you must: 1) prioritize your commitments, 2) make a calendar that reflects these priorities, 3) review your schedule daily, and 4) be flexible.

Prioritizing Commitments

Each of you have come to college with a goal in mind – to graduate! But, beyond that, each of you have varying commitments. Some of you must work. Some of you are here on scholarships through athletics or fine arts, and these scholarships have their own sets of requirements. Some of you are choosing to participate in lots of extracurricular campus activities. With so many commitments, it is important to take a few minutes to identify your priorities. Prioritizing commitments requires you to be honest with yourself about what is important and how long each task may take. It takes self-control and perseverance to work on the most important things before other tasks that might be more enjoyable.

The following exercise, formulated by the well-known businessman and educator, Stephen R. Covey (1994), is a great tool for analyzing priorities and for identifying a way forward when you are overwhelmed by things to do. This exercise will assist you in identifying your priorities and identifying how much time your should spend on each.

Step One: On a piece of paper, make a list of 15-20 items on your to-do list. This list may range from working out daily to finding a campus job.

Step Two: Identify each item in relation to your goal to graduate. Rate each as:
- Important / Not Important, and
- Urgent / Not Urgent

Step Three: See Figure 2.2 to create a personal graph with four quadrants.

Step Four: Plot your items on your graph, according to the level of importance and urgency.

Step Five: Analyze the results of the first three steps. In what quadrant do most of your activities fall?

Most people find that Quadrant I (Important/Urgent) and III (Urgent, but not Important) fill up pretty quickly.

Figure 2.2

Covey Time Management Quadrant

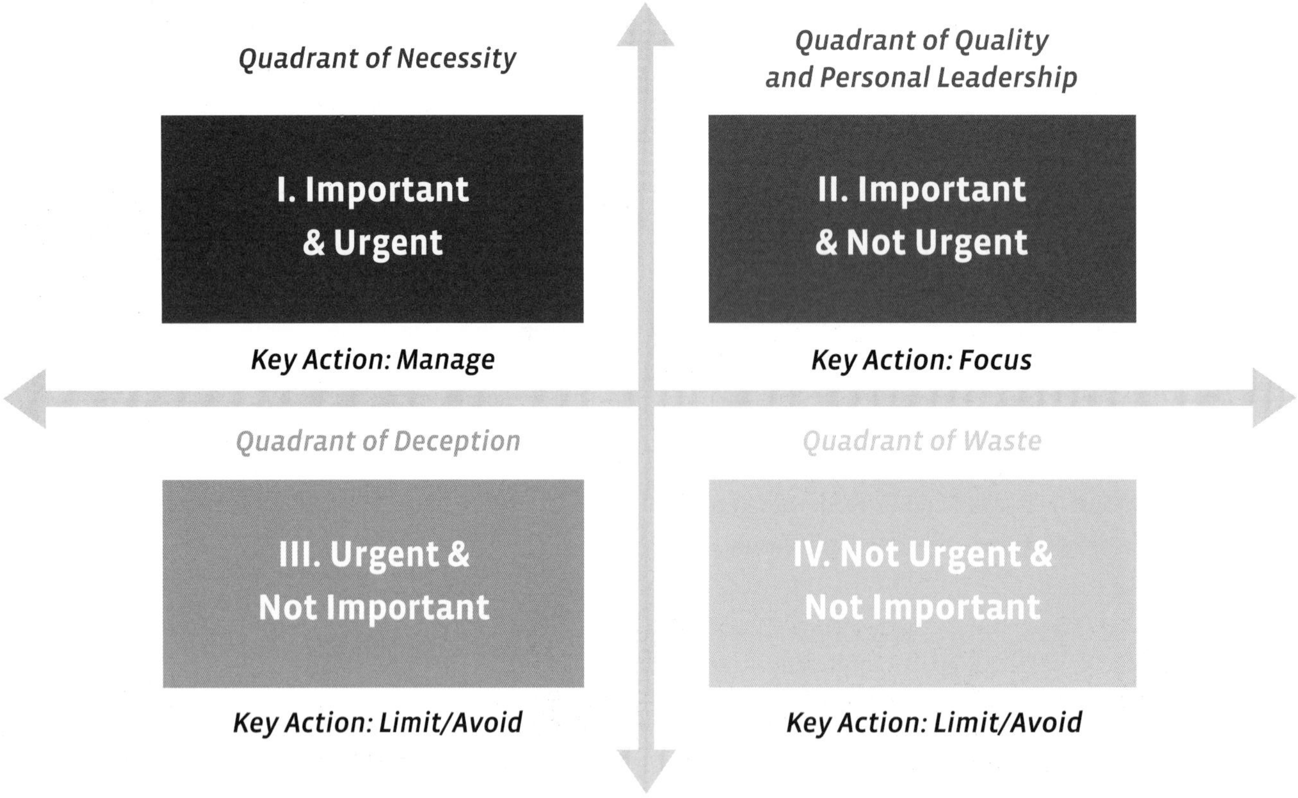

Quadrant of Necessity

Quadrant of Quality and Personal Leadership

I. Important & Urgent

II. Important & Not Urgent

Key Action: Manage

Key Action: Focus

Quadrant of Deception

Quadrant of Waste

III. Urgent & Not Important

IV. Not Urgent & Not Important

Key Action: Limit/Avoid

Key Action: Limit/Avoid

How much time would you save if you eliminated some of the activities from Quadrant III? How do you recognize if something belongs in this quadrant? Why is Quadrant III called the Quadrant of Deception?

Quadrant II is often empty. Quadrant II is for the habits and activities that relate to your long-term goals. This is where activities related to prevention, planning, and the search for new opportunities should be listed. Effective people churn through their Quadrant I tasks but keep a steady eye on Quadrant II's tasks, as well.

For further analysis:
- Challenge yourself to list all of your daily habits that fall into Quadrants III and IV. How much time can you save if you cut down on these type activities?
- Ask yourself: When should you allow yourself to indulge in Quadrant IV-type activities?

- Play through in your head how you will say "no" the next time a Quadrant III opportunity presents itself. What motivation do you need to say "no" to and stay on track with your larger goals?
- Use the Quadrant system if you are facing a big to-do list and do not know where to start.

Set Up a Calendar

Having determined your priorities, it is time to set up a calendar. There are a variety of planners to choose from. Many are available for free, from printable calendars from the web to calendars on your electronic device. The main idea is that you pick one method and make a commitment to stay with it through the entire semester. Your calendar should be easy-to-use and readily accessible.

Begin with developing the basic framework. Enter the times

Figure 2.3   *Sample Weekly Timetable*

TIME	MONDAY	TUESDAY	WEDNESDAY	THURSDAY	FRIDAY	SATURDAY	SUNDAY
8:00 AM							
8:30 AM	Breakfast	Breakfast	Breakfast	Breakfast	Breakfast		
9:00 AM		Prepare for Lecture		Prepare for Lecture			
9:30 AM	ENGL 1113		ENGL 1113		ENGL 1113		
10:00 AM						Study	
10:30 AM	PSY 1113	CHEM 1315	PSY 1113	CHEM 1315	PSY 1113		
11:00 AM							
11:30 AM	Lunch		Lunch		Lunch		
12:00 PM		Lunch		Lunch			
12:30 PM	MATH 1743		MATH 1743		MATH 1743		
1:00 PM							
1:30 PM		UCOL 1002		UCOL 1002			
2:00 PM						Study	Study
2:30 PM	CHEM 1315 Lab						
3:00 PM		Exercise	Exercise	Exercise		Exercise	
3:30 PM							
4:00 PM		Study	Study	Study			
4:30 PM							
5:00 PM							
5:30 PM							
6:00 PM	Dinner	Dinner	Dinner	Dinner	Dinner		Meeting
6:30 PM							
7:00 PM	Study	Meeting		Study			
7:30 PM			Meeting				
8:00 PM							
8:30 PM		Study					
9:00 PM							
9:30 PM							
10:00 PM	Sleep	Sleep	Sleep	Sleep			Sleep
10:30 PM							
11:00 PM							
11:30 PM							

█ MEALS   █ STUDY   █ CLASS   █ EXERCISE   █ MEETINGS   █ SLEEP

for all of your classes, labs and discussions. Next, add the required activities associated with your academic studies such as work, rehearsals, team practice, etc. Finally, add in at least 2-3 hours per class attended to study, as well as any additional personal commitments that you see as benefiting your overall college success. Some students find it beneficial to color-code and/or assign specific fonts to each commitment. If you are using a portable electronic device, consider setting your alarm for commitments that you might have trouble remembering.

Once you have developed a framework of your weekly schedule, you should be able to easily see where other essential life functions, such as working out, can fit. A completed framework also allows you to figure out when you have time to grab a bite with friends or catch a free movie in the Meacham Auditorium.

Review Daily and Weekly
Successful college students use their planners! It is not enough to develop a weekly schedule, and then, never review it. You must routinely check your schedule to ensure that you make the most of your time. Without using a schedule, you will not remember all of the due dates for assignments, projects, etc., as well as the variations associated with a daily college schedule. Managing all of your priorities is a daily commitment. It is also helpful to identify one day per week to sit down and review all pending assignments and activities. For example, you might plan to take 20 minutes on Sunday night or Monday morning to look ahead. It is said that for every 20 minutes you spend planning, you actually save yourself an hour.

College is full of distractions, ranging from weekend parties to hanging out and talking with new friends. It is up to you to follow your schedule. Saying "no" to others is difficult,

but in the end, hanging out with friends, when you really cannot afford to do so, will not earn you the grades to finish your degree.

Maintain flexibility
No two weeks are the same in college. While a weekly schedule will help to provide some structure, your schedule may change unexpectedly, when a professor cancels class, when the weather changes dramatically, or when unexpected life crises arises. This is when you should determine the level of urgency of your commitments.

Habits for Academic Success

1. Attend every class.
Going to every class session gives you a real advantage. In fact, cutting class is a predictor of how well you will *not* do. This is where most students make mistakes their first semester of college. It takes self-control and perseverence to attend class even when you're tired or attendance is not monitored, but it is important to think about the bigger picture.

Think about the tuition you are wasting when you cut class. Or, think of class attendance as preparation for a job. How many employers will keep an employee who never comes to work? Also, professors are not required to stick to the schedule on their syllabi. It is critical that you not rely on others to pass along information, but be there to hear it for yourself.

2. Read all assigned materials prior to attending class, and review notes and readings after each class.
Taking notes and developing questions helps you to stay focused and to prepare for class. Even if you cannot finish

Emailing Your Professor

...ition to visiting professors during office hours, it is perfectly appropriate to use e-mail to communicate with your professo... ...aching assistants. But, e-mail is also a minefield because it is tempting to be informal. Follow these rules to ensure your e-... ...are appropriate:

1. Use the e-mail address the professor provides on your syllabus. This is the one he or she expects students to use. Likewise, e-mail from your university address, as some professors will not open emails from other accounts.

2. Address the professor formally, e.g. "Dear Dr. Portwood," or "Professor Ziegler."

3. Provide a clear subject in the subject line ("Clarissa Smith's Make-up Exam"), and keep the message short and to-the-point.

4. Save any attachments in Microsoft Word or the form your professor specifies.

5. Proofread your e-mail. Misspelling does not give the professor a good impression of your ability to earn an "A" in the class.

6. Likewise, do not use slang or text-speak. Even if a professor can understand your language, it is not appropriate for professional communication.

7. Do not forget to sign the e-mail with your first and last names, preferably after closing with "Thank you," or "Sincerely."

8. Send a quick "thank-you" message if a professor has provided you with help in any way. If he or she sent you attached materials, let him or her know you received them.

9. Remember that emails never go away. They are a permanent record of your interaction with an instructor.

Box 2.1

...ted from Hyman & Jacobs (2010)

a reading assignment before class, you can still read the chapter's introduction and summary. The same goes for after class. Research has shown that students retain more information when they review their notes/readings on the same day they have class (Kiewra, 1985). For some students, rewriting notes or re-reading sections of assignments assists in deeper learning.

3. Engage with the material during class.

Take notes in every class – even if the professor is showing a movie – because anything said in class is "fair game" for tests. Ask questions. Most students are afraid that they will look stupid, but remember, if you already knew everything, you would not be in college. Professors appreciate when you ask questions because, often, you are not the only student who does not know or who is confused. Intellectual humility is a virtue that often leads true understanding and a love of learning.

4. Visit regularly with professors during office hours.

Many students see this strategy and immediately say, "But I don't have anything to talk to the professor about!" Yes, you do. You can discuss an upcoming test, ask for clarification about material from a confusing lecture, review the opening

to your upcoming mid-term paper, etc. Emailing your professor is also a great way to communicate. See Box 2.1 above for guidelines on emailing.

5. Use campus resources.

For every class you are taking there is at least one campus resource you can use to help your learning. OU's Writing Center is a clear resource for English class papers, but why would you not also use it for other class papers or even to review a scholarship application? Challenge yourself to identify a campus resource for every class you are taking this semester.

6. Don't overload yourself.

Some students think it is to their advantage to take as many classes as possible their first semesters – even if they are working full or part-time. Academic life at OU is a full-time job in itself and overloading can be more harmful than productive. Remember the tortoise and the hare: slow and steady wins the race!

7. Don't procrastinate.

Do you tell yourself you need the adrenaline rush to finish assignments? Waiting until the last minute to complete an assignment only leads to increased stress, and you will not have time to revise or correct assignments. Utilize self-control to plan ahead and give yourself enough time to properly complete the work.

8. Never pull an all-nighter.

There is really no reason any college student should pull an all-nighter to finish a paper or prepare for a test. While professors may alter their syllabus due dates, you should still have ample time to study for a test or complete a paper.

9. Find a study spot.

Everyone has a preferred study environment. It is important in the first few weeks of class to define the best setting for you. Ask yourself: Do you like complete silence or to have the radio playing? Do you like it to be bright or somewhat dark? Do you prefer to study in your residence hall room or maybe the Adams Center 24-hour study lounge located in Johnson Tower?

10. Beware of distractions!

The biggest concern for college educators today is continuous partial attention. We are all guilty of having our e-mail up, being logged into Facebook, and keeping our cell phone

Bizzell Memorial Library
Named after OU President William Bennett Bizzell, the library contains more than five million books. Among these are a collection of Bibles from the Renaissance and several early editions of works by Galileo Galilei, including one with his handwritten notes for corrections. The oldest section of the library was built in 1929, with a north wing added in 1958. The western wing was built in 1982, along with the clock tower and the Oklahoma Canyon Garden (accessible from the lowest level). Students know the Bizzell Library today as a great place for between-class naps on comfy couches. Don't miss the Great Reading Room on the second floor of the old wing!

next to us while we attempt to complete our work. You cannot engage in deep learning if your mind is constantly being interrupted from outside stimuli. People often claim they are multi-tasking, but in reality they are merely multi-stimulated. This overstimulation is actually detrimental to academic success because the brain begins to shut down when asked to take on too many different tasks. Use social media as a reward for when you have achieved your short-term goal for the day.

Motivation

College is tough. Doing well takes lots of effort and time, and while there will be moments when you want to give up, if you want to finish, you will have to put your head down and power through the work. One of the keys to staying on course to goal-completion during tough times like midterms or finals is to maintain your motivation. Motivation is the force that moves you to action, giving you energy, direction and persistence. Motivation moves you to the goals that you have set. Even in the face of obstacles, motivation can move you forward (Waitley, 2010). There are two forms of motivation: extrinsic motivation and intrinsic motivation.

Extrinsic (external) motivation refers to motivation that comes from sources outside of you. Extrinsic motivation includes the need to avoid trouble or punishment, the desire to please others, or the yearning to fit in socially. Extrinsic motivation can be positive if it moves you forward to a desired goal, but it can be negative if it is based on fear or avoidance. For example, if you are speeding down the interstate and suddenly slow down after seeing a police car, you have just responded to external motivation to drive within the speed limits (the threat of a ticket). If you go to your campus job each afternoon because you know you need the money, you are responding to external motivation (the paycheck you will receive).

Intrinsic (internal) motivation refers to drive that comes from within you. Intrinsic motivation is the most productive source of motivation. You must really want something for yourself to be motivated to attain it (Waitley, 2010). An example of internal motivation is spending an afternoon studying Spanish because you really want to speak a second language well. Intellectual humility can also be a great internal motivator because when you admit to yourself that you have much to learn, you are often more motivated to find understanding. When you tidy your dorm room just because you enjoy returning to a clean room, you are operating from internal motivation.

Before you came to OU, you likely received a great deal of external motivation on a regular basis. For example, your high school teachers carefully monitored whether you were doing your work, and your parents kept track of whether you cleaned your room, took care of your health, etc. If you did not do the things that were expected of you, they may have given punishments or consequences. Now that you are in college, however, you will encounter far less external motivation, and you will need to rely more upon your internal motivation. This shift in motivation is sometimes difficult for college students, but learning to rely upon internal motivation will make a significant difference in whether you are successful at OU and in life.

Academic Motivation – GPA and Degree Completion

What happens if you do not perform well at OU? For many students, grade point average (GPA) was not stressed in high school. However, GPA determines whether a student can stay at OU, move to the major of his/her choice, and whether or not he/she qualifies for financial aid. The University keeps track of three types of GPAs on your transcript. The first is the total institution GPA (your OU GPA), which is the GPA for all of the coursework you have taken at OU. The second is the total transfer GPA, (the hours and GPA of courses you have taken at other institutions total). Third, is the overall GPA which is the total of the OU/Institution GPA and the total transfer GPA. The Oklahoma State Regents of Higher Education, the governing body for all state public institutions have defined a minimum 2.0 overall GPA as "in good standing." If a student's overall GPA falls below a 2.0, the student is placed on academic probation or academic notice as follows:

Hours Attempted	GPA	Standing
below 30	1.70 to 1.99	academic notice
below 30	1.00 to 1.69	academic probation
30 and above	0.00 to 1.99	academic probation

Figure 2.4

A student is placed on academic probation the semester after the overall GPA falls below a 2.0. To remain at the University of Oklahoma, the student must make a 2.0 the semester they are placed on probation. The 2.0 GPA is the standard, regardless of the number of hours of enrollment – whether the student takes only one credit hour or more. This rule also applies to a student who has entered the University of Oklahoma on an admission contract; his or her continued enrollment requires that the student have a 2.0 overall GPA at the end of the second semester. In addition to a 2.0 overall GPA, all colleges at OU require that a student's OU/Total Institution GPA remain at a minimum of a 2.0 for continued enrollment. The GPA requirements of the degree-granting colleges vary, with some requiring higher than a 2.0 GPA. It is your responsibility to know the GPA requirements for the degree-granting college of which you are a part. You should be able to calculate your expected GPA at various points in the semester, based on your performance in your courses. This will enable you to gauge how you are doing academically at all times. Instructions for calculating your GPA may be found at the OU website: *ougradplanner.com/gpacalculator*.

Retention is the university's ability to keep a student from admission through graduation. The flip side of retention is persistence, or the "desire and action of a student to stay within the system of higher education from beginning through degree completion" (Seidman, 2005, p. 14). One of the reasons that Gateway to College Learning is offered to you by the University of Oklahoma is that statistics show that retention, or your ability to stay in college until you have earned your degree, is highest among those who get through the first year without major problems (Seidman, 2005, p. 14). This is the reason that it is so important to institute proper executive functions in order to maintain a desirable GPA and complete your degree at the University of Oklahoma.

The Graduation Office assists students in reaching their graduation goals. The staff of the Graduation Office works collaboratively with all areas of university life to increase opportunities for student achievement and to help students remove barriers which they may encounter along their path to graduation.

What Motivates You?
Motivation Quiz

1. You are offered a position as a lab assistant for a zoology course you took last semester. The first thought that comes to your mind is:

    A. I wonder if it will be fun to assist in lab.
    B. Will I be a good lab assistant? Will I perform well?
    C. Do I get paid to do this? How much?

2. Your roommate has become lazy about cleaning up after herself in your shared spaces. What are you likely to do?

    A. Talk to her about her choices to see what is going on.
    B. Yell at her the next time you find her wet towels on the floor.
    C. Remind her in a friendly tone to do her share of the cleaning.

3. You applied for a campus job and went to an interview a few weeks ago. When you get a letter in the mail stating that the position has been filled, you think:

    A. I didn't match what they were looking for.
    B. I'm not good enough for the job.
    C. I will have better luck getting a job when I have some network connections.

4. You are taking a class in a new discipline this semester. You are more concerned about:

    A. How interested you are in the subject matter.
    B. Whether you can do the work.
    C. Whether it will contribute to your career plans.

5. You are going to a large party tonight. As you look forward to it, you expect that you will:

    A. Be able to find people to relate to and will have a good time.
    B. Have a hard time fitting in and will probably feel isolated.
    C. Try to fit in; you don't want to look uncool.

6. Your supervisor at work has asked you to be an assistant manager for the summer. You will be in charge of making sure all of your employees get breaks, but they cannot break all at once. You will most likely:

    A. Ask your workers their schedules.
    B. Ask your supervisor for the best way to schedule breaks.
    C. Assign break times without input from anyone else.

7. Your best friend has been moody. You:

    A. Ask him what is going on.

B. Ignore him; he'll snap out of it at some point.

C. Tell him you'd love to hang out with him, but that he needs to lighten up.

8. You get back a calculus test from last week and discover that you did not do as well as you thought. You:

A. Try to figure out why you did not do as well.

B. Feel as if no amount of studying ever makes you prepared for this professor's exams.

C. Feel angry because this professor always makes impossibly hard exams.

9. Your older sister seems to be drinking a lot lately. She seems less interested in her work and is not taking adequate care of her apartment. You:

A. Tell her you notice things aren't going well for her right now and remind her that you are available if she wants to talk.

B. Hesitate – it is hard to know what to do in a situation like this.

C. Tell her she needs to get it together, or else you will alert your parents to the problem.

10. You've gotten into a prestigious graduate program at your first-choice school. You will be moving to a state you've never even visited. When you think about the move, you:

A. Are nervous, but also excited about this new phase in your life.

B. Feel stressed and anxious about moving and starting a new program.

C. Feel excited about the prestige of attending the number one program in your field.

. . . .

Scoring:

• If you chose mostly As, your motivation comes from inside you. You tend to choose opportunities that will challenge you to grow as a person. You take responsibility for your own actions. Others may not understand some of your choices.

• If you chose mostly Bs, you tend to believe that success and achievement are matters of luck. If you are often feeling anxious, it may be because you don't realize your own power to change a situation or improve your skills. You are waiting for motivation to come from another source, but you need to find it within yourself.

• If you chose mostly Cs, you are stimulated into action from extrinsic sources. Rewards, deadlines, and directions from others make you feel secure and motivate your taking the next step. You tend to choose wealth, fame, or rewards that make you stand out in the crowd. Extrinsic motivation works to a certain extent, but you might get caught up in doing what others want while ignoring your own desires.

- Adapted from Desi and Ryan, 1985

References

Covey, R., Merrill, R. & Merrill, R. (1994). *First things first: To live, to love, to learn, to leave a legacy.* New York: Simon and Schuster.

Desi, E. L., & Ryan, R. M. (1985). The general causality orientations scale: Self-determination in personality. *Journal of Research In Personality, 19,* 109-134.

Hopper, C. H. (2004). *Practicing college learning strategies,* 3rd ed. Boston: Houghton Mifflin Co.

Hyman, J. S. & Jacobs, L. F. (2010). *18 etiquette tips for e-mailing your professor. U.S. News & World Report.* Retrieved from http://www.usnews.com/education/blogs/professors-guide/2010/09/30/18-etiquette-tipsfor-e-mailing-your-professor.

Jacobs, L.F. & Hyman, J.S. (2010, September 1). The 5 biggest mistakes college students make. *U.S. News and World Report.*

Kiewra, K. A. (1985). Investigating notetaking and review: A depth of processing alternative. *Educational Psychologist, 20*(1), 73-77.

Meyer, P.J. (2006). *Attitude is everything!* Merced, CA: Leading Edge Publishing Co.

Robinson, D. (1998). How dreams become goals. Retrieved from http://topachievement.com/dianarobinson.html.

Seidman, A. (2005). Minority student retention: Resources for practitioners. Retrieved from http://www.cscsr.org/docs/MinorityStudentRetentionResourcesforPractitioners2006.pdf. Seidman, 2005, p.14

Waitley, D. (2010). *Psychology of success: Finding meaning in work and life.* New York: McGraw-Hill Co.

Chapter 2 REI
Mastering Executive Functions

R Reflect

Many students struggle with issues of procrastination or lack of motivation. What are some of the causes of procrastination for you? Has it ever prevented you from achieving your goals? Do you believe this is an ongoing problem for you? Why or why not?

· ·

E Engage

Take the "What Motivates You? Motivation Quiz" Activity 2.1 on pages 35 and 36.

· ·

I Impact

What was your Motivation Style? How can you use motivation to decrease procrastination? How can you use the information you have learned about your motivation style to achieve your S.M.A.R.T. goals in both the short term and the long term?

· ·

Chapter 3

Establishing Effective Academic Skills: *Reading, Writing, Note-Taking, and Test-Taking Skills*

Lillian Miller, M.Ed., Director, Freshman Programs and various contributing authors

In this chapter, you will:

- Understand effective reading strategies needed in college.
- Learn effective note-taking systems.
- Learn college-level writing expectations.
- Describe academic integrity at OU.
- Understand effective test-taking strategies.
- Learn how to address test anxiety.

"Making good decisions is crucial at every level."

- Peter Drucker, Writer and Management Expert

One of the most difficult challenges of transferring your academic skills from high school to college is figuring out what is expected at the college level. Unfortunately, there is no "easy" way to answer that question, as there are different expectations in different majors and classes. This chapter will highlight some general expectations in regards to academic reading, writing, notetaking, and test-taking. It will also provide techniques that can help you become an active learner and study more effectively in college.

Academic Reading

Jennifer Dorsey, Writing Center Consultant, OU Writing Center
Gul Nahar, Writing Center Consultant, OU Writing Center

Reading in college is different than in high school because college texts are written at a higher level that requires readers to understand more complex and in-depth ideas within much less time. In college, you will encounter multiple genres of writing ranging from American history to world literature and from journal articles to scientific studies. However, it is possible for college students to overcome reading challenges by applying specific strategies. Effective reading strategies are key to success in many classes. Remember, reading informational texts differs from reading literary texts. Knowing how to use the elements of an informational text can help you better comprehend the material and study more efficiently.

PQ4R

The six-step reading strategy, PQ4R, has proved effective for analyzing texts because it allows you to break the information into chunks before you plunge into the entire written piece.

PQ4R is an acronym for Preview, Question, Read, Reflect, Recite, and Review. This strategy will help you to think consciously about a text's purpose and meaning and to achieve a greater depth of understanding.

Preview

A Textbook

Before you begin reading your textbook for the first time, you should familiarize yourself with the book's organization. This process should include:

- Reading the table of contents to help you figure out what is important.
- Looking at the preface/forward so you understand the text's purpose.
- Examining the back materials, such as the index and glossary, so you can determine the text's difficulty and know where to find concepts.

A Chapter or Article

Each time you read a chapter or informational article, it can help your reading retention if you get the big picture before you read the actual text. To do this:

1. Divide the text into manageable chunks. Ten pages or so tends to be reasonable.
2. Then, use the chunks to determine how long the reading will take, and plan "chunks" of time to read each piece.
3. Read the title, headings, and subheadings. If there are no headings, read the first sentences for each paragraph.
4. Look at each chart, figure, and picture.
5. Glance at the bold and/or italicized words. These represent key vocabulary words and concepts.
6. Read any summaries or questions at the end of sections.

Question

Through previewing, you have already gained a fair number of ideas about the written materials. Ask yourself questions, and write them down, as they will keep you interested in searching for the answers while reading. Raise questions that will drive you to find the main points or that will address what you anticipate to learn at the end of the reading.

Read

Begin active reading with a highlighter nearby. As you read, write down the questions you have. After you read a chunk of information, go back and annotate by adding notes to the text. (Note: See annotation tips on page 43 for guidelines on annotating a text.) Write down answers to the questions you generated in a notebook or in the margins. You will be reviewing those answers in the process of reflecting and revising later. While you read, it is likely that you will generate more questions. Write down those questions in either the margins or your notebook, as well.

Reflect

Now, it is time to reflect on what you have learned in order to gain a broader understanding. Engage yourself in deep thinking to find connections between your previous understandings and the text. Focus on information that has either surprised or shocked you, and write those points in your notebooks, as well.

Recite

Next, discuss the text with your instructor or classmates. Write down the main points or any new revelations drawn from this conversation. Share your responses with different people to get feedback from different perspectives. You can also develop a graphic organizer as a way to better grasp the information and to show relationships among the concepts presented in the readings.

Review

Finally, it is time to assess your learning. To do this, go back to the questions you wrote. Re-answer the questions and compare the responses. Ask yourself: Do you see differences? If so, how do they differ? Do you think that you have understood the bigger picture the writer intended for the readers?

Reading Tips

When reading academic texts, remember that you are not reading a novel. You do not have to read the whole thing from beginning to end. It is best not to try to read an entire chapter or reading assignment in one sitting. It is harder to comprehend that way. Do not worry about making notes as you are reading the first time. Doing so breaks up the flow of your reading. Instead, read the section once, and then, go back and annotate.

Reading Tips: Student to Student

- Identify all bold/vocabulary words, and define them.
- Become familiar with chapter titles, headings, and sub-headings.
- Re-read content at a normal pace for a better understanding.

  - Gerald Green, Senior, MIS

- You might think your friend and/or that new Will Ferrell movie are great accessories to your reading, they're not.
- Read somewhere without a bed or puffy leather couch. Sleep is usually on the horizon once you get super relaxed.
- Read it once, think about it, write it, then read it again.
- If I don't understand what I'm reading, I ask a friend, classmate, or professor to help interpret.

  - Shelby Simpson, OU Graduate Writing Consultant

Effective Note-Taking

Jennifer Dorsey, Writing Center Consultant, OU Writing Center

Johnnie-Margaret McConnell, Director, Center for Student Advancement

Gul Nahar, Writing Center Consultant, OU Writing Center

Annotating What You Have Read

One effective way to study is to annotate. Annotating works best if you read an entire section of text first. For example, you could read all of the text under a heading and, then, annotate that information. When you start annotating, begin by highlighting or underlining key terms, dates, or phrases. The idea is that you could re-read just what you highlight to study later. After you highlight the main ideas, look over what you highlighted, and write notes or questions in the margins that will engage your thinking about the information and will help you comprehend what you read.

Tips & Hints

Annotation can be more useful if you develop a thoughtful system to annotate all of your texts. The following hints may help you create your own:

- Use different colors and/or symbols to indicate different kinds of information in a text.
  - » Color Example: green = key ideas, yellow = points to ponder, pink = references to other sources, orange = definitions.
  - » Symbol example: * =key ideas, ? = points to ponder,

Global English

Most Common Language?
Although English is used around the world, it is not the most common native language (language spoken at home). There are about 372 million native English speakers in the world. About 5700 million people speak a native language other than English. The native language spoken by the most people in the world is Chinese. After Chinese, Hindi and Urdu have the second most speakers, followed by English. Spanish and Arabic have almost as many native speakers as English. Even in the United States, Spanish and Chinese are the native languages for many people.

Ways English Is Used
In many countries, English is spoken as a second language. It is used for business and in government. English is the official language of government in more than 75 countries. Even the European Central Bank has English as its official language. In India, English is very widely used. Indian English has many special words, though, and there are dictionaries of Indian English. Some countries have even developed a special kind of English that is hard for other speakers of English to understand. For example, there is Spanglish (English and Spanish), Singlish (Singaporean English) and Taglish (spoken in the Philippines).

English & the Internet
English is the most common language used on the Internet, but this is changing. Currently, about 80% of what is on the Internet is in English. In 1999, about 54% of Internet users were native English speakers. However, non-native English speakers are the fastest growing group of new Internet users. As the use of the Internet grows around the world, other languages will be used more and more. But English will still be the language most often used to communicate between speakers of other languages, especially in business.

Recall: Headings help identify key ideas and help you choose what to annotate.

Notice how only key words and phrases are highlighted? This makes the important information stand out. Be careful not to annotate too much. You want key concepts to really pop!

After highlighting, add questions or notes to provoke thinking. In this section, you might ask, "How will English still be used?" Later, when you study, you can try to answer the questions without reading.

Figure 3.1

+ = references to other sources, box = definitions (define the word in the margins.)

- Arrows can be used to show connections between ideas.
- Write summaries of key information at the end of sections, if that is useful to you. This can be done on the text or on sticky notes.
- Make information easier to locate, by either:
  » Marking pages using tabs or sticky notes. You can color code tabs by topic.
  » Making a list of important pages, linked by topic. Keep this list at the beginning of the text.

Note-Taking Formats

Over the years, I have heard many students say that they do not need to take notes because they can remember what is important. However, studies suggest that many people only absorb twenty percent of what they hear (Metcalf, 1997).

By now, you have learned that professors speak very fast, faster than you can write. So, what is the most efficient way to retain what a professor is saying, in order to prepare for the tests? While students who focus on listening have a good idea, simply listening is not practical. You need to record this content so that later, when memory fails, you have something to recall. And, remember, you are taking in a great deal of information! How in the world can you keep it straight? And how do you have the best chance of remembering what is important? Taking notes is the traditional method of recording class information.

In fact, when you take notes, you often pay more attention and are consequently more interested in the class.

Always ask for permission before audio recording a professor. It is the professor's choice if his/her lectures can be audio-recorded.

The Cornell System

Walter Pauk at Cornell University created this two-column note-taking system in the 1950s. After becoming acquainted with this method of note-taking, you will find that it is efficient and saves time. Like all skills, the more you use it, the better you become.

You will need loose-leaf notebook paper with wide-ruled lines. While some students prefer spiral-bound notebooks, a loose-leaf or three-hole-punch notebook allows more flexibility and saves time if corrections need to be made.

Figure 3.2

The Cornell System

Keywords	Notes	Class Lecture 10/25/13
AURAL/AUDITORY LEARNERS	*Aural/Auditory* -- *use listening and speaking as primary mode of learning* -- *remember what they hear or say*	
VISUAL LEARNERS	*Visual* -- *like to see pictures, charts, graphs, and colors* -- *are attuned to physical environments* -- *like things orderly*	
KINESTHETIC LEARNERS	*Kinesthetic* -- *like to act out a situation* -- *like to move and be physically busy or involved* -- *like to see something in action, like a lab experiment*	

Summary
Different learners favor different kinds of sensory input.
Aural/Auditory = listening and speaking
Visual = seeing and ordering
Kinesthetic = moving and seeing action

TO ASK IN CLASS:
Can a learner change his/her learning preferences? How?

Before class, prepare your paper by drawing a vertical line about 2.5" from the left side and two horizontal lines – one about 1" from the top and another about 2.5" from the bottom. You will write your notes in the large space on the right side. Then, after class, while reviewing your notes, place labels, keywords, and/or questions in the left margin. Summarize any main points in the box on the bottom of the page. Also, place any questions to ask in class or to answer in future reading in the column on the left. If you want to ask it in class, highlight it or put a sticky-note on the page to remind yourself easily.

The Outline Format

The outline format is another common note-taking system. In a formal outline, you should note each main point with a Roman numeral. Ideas related to this point should be listed below and organized by upper-case letters, numbers, and lower-case letters. Depending on how your professor organizes his/her lecture, it can sometimes be difficult to capture information in this format. In those cases, it may be more appropriate to use an informal outline or an outline that identifies each major point with a Roman numeral and then organizes related information with indention and bullets.

Personalizing Your Notes

Give the Cornell System or one of the outline formats a try. Amend them if something works better for you. The key to being a good note-taker is figuring out what works for you. Here are some ideas for personalization:

- Develop your own note-taking language, including abbreviations for common words ("govt" for government, "b/c" for because, "w/" for with). Imagine that you are texting and that you are limited in space or characters. This will help you to develop an individualized shorthand that will allow you to capture more of what the professor is saying.

- It is tempting to want to write down every word you hear during a lecture. This is nearly impossible. As you listen to the professor, keep a running commentary in your head of a way to put the same point into your own words. Your interior commentator can also make connections

Formal Outline

I. Point One

II. Point Two

III. Point Three
    A. Sub-Point
        1. example
        2. example
    B. Sub-Point
    C. Sub-Point

IV. Point Four
    A. Sub-Point
        1. example
        2. example
    B. Sub-Point
    C. Sub-Point

Figure 3.3

Informal Outline

I. Point One

II. Point Two

III. Point Three
    • Sub-Point
        *example
        *example
    • Sub-Point

IV. Point Four
    • Sub-Point
        *example
        *example
    • Sub-Point
        *example

with earlier material, ask questions that need answering, and make notes about the relevance of the information. This skill takes practice and time before it feels natural, so be patient with yourself.

- Look online for Cornell-style templates and other note-taking systems. (Another method of both note-taking and review is called mind-mapping or concept-mapping.)
- Register to have studying and organization hints sent to you via list-servs.
- Many students choose to take notes on their laptop or tablet. Students should first make sure electronic devices are permissible during class. Consider a note-taking computer program or application. EverNote and similar programs are handy, in that your notes are stored "in the cloud." Some programs can even convert your handwritten notes into typed form.

Constance Staley (2013) suggests six steps to help you take and organize your notes.

1. Listen for an organizing pattern. Has the professor been covering the information in chronological order? Has the professor been listing theories by specific topics?
2. Note whether a handout accompanies lecture materials. If the professor refers to the handout during the lecture, this is a cue that it contains important information.
3. Recognize verbal cues. Listen for signals such as, "There are three stages to…" "For example…" and "In summary…."
4. When in doubt, write it down. If you are unsure whether information is important, use the motto, "Better safe than sorry." If you do not know a word, leave a blank in your notes or sound out, as you are writing it, so you can correct it later. Write down formulas, definitions, charts, and diagrams.
5. Consider your learning-style preferences. If you are a visual learner, your note taking system should contain pictures, charts, and symbols. Use whatever method is necessary to spark your memory.
6. Create a shorthand system that works for you. As stated earlier, the abbreviations for texting might come in handy at this time.

Distributed Practice

Once you have finished taking notes, it is important to review them in a consistent manner. Tony Buzan (1990) suggests *distributed practice,* a study method in which you spread out, or distribute, your review process over time - not just the night before the test.

Review class notes within 24 hours of taking them. Spend time correcting the spelling, elaborating on concepts, or filling in names and dates. This will help you recall information later.

- The second note review should take place within one day and should probably not take longer than three (3) or four (4) minutes. If you use the Cornell Method, you should review keywords and their definitions, and you should think of questions to test your understanding of all concepts.
- The third review should occur before the week's end. It should require only a few minutes, since you are reviewing, not relearning, the information.
- A fourth review will probably be required if you have not used the material within a month. This review should firmly place the information into your long-term memory.
- At least once during this distributed review, you should recite summaries of your notes aloud. Doing so will activate not just your visual memories of the materials (what you read and wrote), but also your auditory memories (what you heard yourself saying about the materials). Using your senses to their full extent in studying increases the likelihood of your remembering the information.

Remember that note-taking requires practice and discovery of what works best for you. Over time, you will find a routine and pattern that help you to recall the information.

The Writing Process
Katie Bramlett, First Year Composition Instructor, OU Writing Center Consultant

Do you love to write or do you avoid writing at all costs? While few people willingly sit down to write a 10 page research paper, students around the world use online communication on a daily basis and are finding it more and more important to learn to write. Unfortunately (or fortunately), there is no right or wrong way to write. Therefore, no easy formula on "how to write" exists. So, whether you are writing an English Composition paper, writing a lab report, or texting a friend, one of the best ways you can become a better writer is to figure out what type of writer you are and what works best for you.

Writing Style Quiz

Want to make your college career easier? Take this writing profile quiz to see what type of writer you are.

1. What time of day do you do your best writing?
	a. Mornings
	b. Afternoons or Evenings
	c. Late at Night/Early Mornings
	d. Not Sure

2. What time of day do you actually end up writing?
	a. Mornings
	b. Afternoons or Evenings
	c. Late at Night/Early Mornings
	d. Depends

3. How often do you work with others as you write?
	a. I work with others on occasion, mostly when I have a solid rough draft.
	b. Working with others as I write is a must for me. This might mean having a friend read my essay, making an appointment at the OU Writing Center, or just being with or around others as I write.
	c. I usually like to write in a quiet place where I can be alone.
	d. I sometimes like working with others during my writing process.

4. What do you do to help you get started writing?
	a. I like to do an organized, numbered outline, based on research.
	b. I like to talk to my friends or professors.
	c. I like to do hands-on brainstorming – like jotting down ideas or creating a mental map.
	d. I like to do different things depending on the assignment.

5. How organized are you as you write?
	a. Very organized – I often use my outline and will write paragraph-by-paragraph, starting with my introduction.
	b. Generally organized - I don't have a specific order that I write in, but find myself writing a rough draft and then going back to fill in evidence or adding paragraphs.
	c. Not very organized – I like to write my thoughts down as I think them and then go back and edit, research, or change things creatively.
	d. Sporadic organization – Sometimes I am very organized, and sometimes I'm not.

6. Do you keep a writing calendar? (Do you have a plan for when you will write?)
	a. I plan out by the hour/day when I will write.
	b. I set aside small chunks of time throughout several days to write.
	c. I usually don't plan when I will write.
	d. I make a plan, but sometimes don't follow it.

7. Do you find yourself procrastinating as you write?
	a. No, I get things done according to my schedule.
	b. Always, I often get distracted or something will come up.

c. I procrastinate on writing assignments I am not interested in.

d. Sometimes.

8. What do you do when you take a break from writing?

    a. I like to exercise or do something productive.

    b. I like to hang out with friends or watch TV.

    c. I like to sleep or eat a snack.

    d. I like to do different things.

9. What do you listen to as you write?

    a. I prefer silence when I write.

    b. I like to listen to my favorite bands and singers.

    c. I like classical, jazz, or music without words.

    d. I have no preference.

Count up the amount of letters from your responses.

Mostly A's – The Tetris Ninja

Just like the game, you are the type of writer that likes to plan things out. You pay particular attention to making time for writing what needs to be written and finish in a timely manner. As a result, you tend to think through your argument/assignment thoroughly. You are a little slower in actually writing, but this is because you take your time and have a solid product that needs little editing. As a writer, you should schedule writing and research time and find a quiet place to help you organize your thoughts. Don't be afraid to take advantage of sharing your ideas, because this might help you further develop your analysis. Seek out a Picasso writer to add variation to your writing process.

Mostly B's – The Wolf Pack

Like a pack of wolves, you like to be around people. You do your best work and find inspiration when you collaborate or are with people. This means that you often find yourself seeking out social environments to work in (like a coffee shop) or even talk to friends or have them read your writing. You often think through your arguments and critically engage with your topic. However, as a writer, you might be tempted to do more socializing than writing. Try finding a quiet place and people who will encourage you to write in order to keep you on track. Seek out Creative Cave writers who will give you space to write but still keep you company.

Mostly C's – The Creative Cave

As a writer, you may find the image of the cave comforting. This is because you do your best writing in the comfort of your "cave." Whether this is at your desk, in your room, or an in isolated place in the library, you like to find someplace quiet to explore your thoughts. You often write for long periods of time and produce creative and original work. However, because you like to work alone, you also must be wary about asserting ideas that might not be "truth" and need more explanation or support. Seek out Wolf Pack writers to help you escape your cave and critically analyze your position.

Mostly D's – The Picasso

Picasso would be proud. Just like the artist, you like to put your own spin on your writing. This often means you will change the way you write or how you write to fit the situation. You like to try new ways to brainstorm, draft, and edit, and you have no "set" way that you have to write. This means you are often spontaneous and work well in varied environments. As a writer, you should try keeping a writing journal to keep track of what you do that works well and other approaches that do not. Use this journal to help you find what works well for you, but also as a source of creativity to inspire you if you get stuck. Seek out Tetris Ninja writers as a resource for getting organized and staying on task.

College Level Writing Expectations

Key aspects of college-level writing often include strong critical thinking skills and organization. Critical thinking involves asking yourself questions about your topic to make sure you have thought out your position in a way that considers a wider audience and that challenges assumptions that you feel are "truth." By putting yourself in another's shoes, you can make sure you do not make grand statements without support or forget a key element that makes your argument more convincing. Unfortunately, there is also no easy formula for organization, and instructors expect essays to be logically structured. A good way to think about organization is to think about what someone who is unfamiliar with your topic needs to know first, second, third, etc. in order to understand your position. As you move from point to point, you should try to show your reasoning behind each topic switch to make the connection clear. Using transition words (*although, in addition, in contrast,* etc.) to show how the two thoughts relate often helps with the "flow" of the writing.

Specific expectations for writing from instructors are often expressed in terms of being "clear, concise, well-thought-out and organized," but unless it is a writing class, instructors may give little guidance about how to meet their expectations. By taking initiative and being proactive in the class, you can make sure you avoid misunderstandings about coursework expectations. Leaving time to edit your work and using your available resources can help you figure out what needs to be done to produce a quality document.

Brainstorming

What do you do before you start writing? Brainstorming is one of the most important steps in the writing process. It can help you think through your topic for inspiration and direction.

Free Writing

One method that some writers find effective is simply writing any thoughts they have about a topic without stopping. This means you have to turn off the editor, forget about "correct" grammar, and just put your thoughts on paper.

Mind Maps

This is a process that focuses on a specific topic. The writer begins with the topic and incorporates ideas that "branch" off it or connect to it in some way.

Research/Note Taking

Some writers prefer a more hands-on process and start researching their topic and while taking notes on what others are saying. They find that this method inspires their own thought processes.

"My brainstorming process is pretty easy. When I get the prompt of what I'm supposed to write, I write down all of the ideas that pop into my head, no matter how obscure they sound. I then go through the list I have and narrow it down to the things that are most interesting to me. From that smaller list, I then decide which to actually write about, based on what I think I will be able to write the best paper on. This is important to me because, if I don't write down all of the weird ideas I have, I might miss out on writing about something that turns out to be really fun."

-Beverly, Biology and Pre-Med Sophomore

Writing a Thesis

A *thesis* is the main point of every essay and is often argumentative. A good thesis should also guide and structure the rest of the essay. For many undergraduate courses, the thesis is expected to be the last sentence of the first paragraph. In high school, theses often followed the pattern:

X is or is not Y because of A, B, and C.

Example: Oklahoma history is something all students should study because of the Native Americans, the Land Runs and settlers, and the culture.

The natural response to this type of thesis is to provide three support paragraphs, each in support of A, B, and C, respectively. While there is technically nothing wrong with this formula, many instructors find such theses too simplistic. Additionally, the structure of the five-paragraph essay is often inadequate for longer assignments.

As you write a thesis/introduction, use the following to help you think through your argument:

Present a wider scope – Before you jump into a topic, research and explain what others are saying about what you want to argue. This might be general information about your topic or even an opposing opinion.

Thesis Building - Find a place where you disagree or agree, and insert your own position. Here is a basic formula to get started:

"I argue _____, because_____".

Example: I argue that Oklahoma history is a relevant topic to study because of the unique history and culture created by the complicated relationship between Native Americans and white settlers.

In this formula, the "because" clause is similar to the "A, B, C" reasons from the five-paragraph essay formula. Potentially, you could write the same three support paragraphs, or you could rearrange your argument and add background information, address who specifically should be studying Oklahoma history, analyze the relationship between the two groups and Oklahoma culture, etc.

Popular vs. Scholarly Information

Many types of information are freely available to us. We use Google and other search engines to find a wide variety of websites, online newspapers, magazines, blogs, etc. These "popular information" sources help us learn about things we are interested in and stay informed about what is going on in the world.

In college, professors often require students to find and use "scholarly information" (also known as academic, refereed, or peer-reviewed sources) to complete assignments and research papers. Scholarly literature is written by people who have subject expertise, and it goes through a quality control process before it is published. Thus, it is considered one of the most credible and authoritative types of information available.

Scholarly information can be accessed online, but it usually is not free. Here is the good news: the scholarly journal articles you need in order to be successful in college are right at your fingertips! The OU library pays for thousands of scholarly journals that can be searched and read online through library databases. So, always begin your search for scholarly information at libraries.ou.edu.

Want to know more about the differences between popular and scholarly information? Ask a librarian or just Google it!

Box 3.1

As some instructors do not like students to use the word "I" in their writing, theses can be rewritten around a thematic argument that will help structure the rest of the argument.

Example: Oklahoma history is a reflection of race relations in the United States and should be an area of study for scholars around the country.

In the final version of the thesis, the same ideas are in a thematic argument concerning the relationship between Native Americans, settlers, and U.S. race relations. The author of this thesis should then return to their brainstorming process and their original theses for inspiration to continue writing.

Figure 3.4

Citation Styles

You should have familiarity with the three most common citation styles for academic work: APA Style, MLA Style, and Chicago Style. Each style emphasizes different aspects of a source when referencing it. The citation examples are provided for a book (as opposed to a journal article, etc.). For other examples and for more information on citation styles, please visit:
http://www.ou.edu/writingcenter/guides/citation_guides.html

APA Style	MLA Style	Chicago Style: Notes and Bibliography system	Chicago Style: Author-Date system
APA Rules of Style The rules of APA Style are outlined by the American Psychological Association in the *Publication Manual of the American Psychological Association*. This style is used most often in the social sciences and business disciplines. This style emphasizes the date the work was created.	*MLA Rules of Style* The rules of this style are set by the Modern Language Association in the *MLA Handbook for Writers of Research Papers*. This style is used most often in the liberal arts and humanities. This style emphasizes authorship.	*Chicago Rules of Style* This style is also known as the Turabian system. It is outlined by the University of Chicago in the *Chicago Manual of Style*. This style is used most often in history and other humanities fields and places an emphasis on the origin of the sources being cited. There are two different systems of Chicago Manual of Style documentation. The first is the notes and bibliography system. This system provides footnotes, (which correlate to specific numbers assigned to information in the text and allow space for annotation about the sources at the end of the page), and a bibliography. The second, the author-date system, provides the author's last name and the date of publication in the text, as well as a corresponding reference list.	
In-Text Citation Schmidt and Cohen (2013) suggested that people will continue to have tension with states concerning the physical and virtual worlds. The tension between people and states will increase as the virtual world begins to "complicate almost every behavior" (Schmidt & Cohen, 2013).	*In-Text Citation* Schmidt and Cohen explore the tension people and states will continue to have concerning the physical and virtual worlds (255). The tension between people and states will increase as the virtual world will "complicate almost every behavior" (Schmidt and Cohen 255).	*In-Text Citation* The tension between people and states will increase as the virtual world will "complicate almost every behavior."[2] *Footnote* 1. Eric Schmidt and Jared Cohen, The New Digital Age, (New York: Knopf, 2013), 10-11. 2. Schmidt and Cohen, Digital, 255.	*In-Text Citation* The tension between people and states will increase as the virtual world will "complicate almost every behavior" (Schmidt and Cohen 2013, 255).

APA Style	MLA Style	Chicago Style: Notes and Bibliography system	Chicago Style: Author-Date system
References Page Schmidt, E., & Cohen, J. (2013). *The new digital age.* New York: NY: Knopf.	*Works Cited Page* Schmidt, Eric and Jared Cohen. The New Digital Age New York: Knopf, 2013. Print.	*Bibliograohy Page* Schmidt, Eric and Jared Cohen, The New Digital Age (New York: Knopf, 2013).	*Reference Page* Schmidt, Eric and Jared Cohen, The New Digital Age. New York: Knopf.
For more information, visit: www.apastyle.org	For more information, visit: www.mla.org/style	For more information: www.chicagomanualofstyle.org/home.html	

There are other citation styles used in the various disciplines. In writing academic papers, be sure to understand the formatting, citing, and referencing expectations of your professors. Also, be aware of citation builders available online. Although they may be helpful in getting you started, these do not all accurately cite. Therefore, you should review the rules for the style you are using.

Checklist for The Writing Process

☐ Read the syllabus/essay guidelines thoroughly.

☐ Analyze the assigned class texts.

☐ Ask your professor about basic formatting expectations:
  » Citation method (MLA, APA, Chicago, etc.)
  » Use of "I"
  » Verb tense (active voice, past tense, etc.)

☐ Think about your audience - Who are you writing for, and what do they need to know to understand your purpose?

☐ Drop by the OU Writing Center.

☐ Edit your paper.

☐ Try reading your essay aloud or printing off a hard copy. Here is a short list of a few weaknesses to watch for:
  » Repetition – look for moments where you use the same words again and again.
  » Using too many words – look for places where you say something in six words that could be said in three.
  » Undefined terms – make sure you do not leave any terms undefined.

Resources for OU Students

OU students have numerous resources available for assistance with brainstorming, research, and other aspects of the writing process.

The OU Writing Center

The OU Writing Center is not just a place to fix grammar or "correct" writing. It is a place where you can receive help with brainstorming processes, critical thinking, and other writing processes. Graduates and undergraduates from majors across the campus can help with any writing project, from composition essays to biology lab reports to graduate level work. Stop by to work with someone in the Wagner, Cate, or Bizzell Writing Centers, submit an essay online, or check out their other resources at *ou.edu/writingcenter.html*.

The OU Library

The OU library is not just a place to check out books or study, it is also a place to receive help in your research process. Stop by for research assistance from any of the reference librarians, or check out their resources at *libraries.ou.edu.*

"The hardest thing about writing I continue to overcome every day is simply the anxiety that comes with putting pencil to paper or fingers to keyboard. Just beginning to write, I think, is a common struggle. When I'm consulting with writers in the writing center, this is probably one of the most prevalent hindrances. The best way to just begin writing is to, first, know how you write best. I am more inclined to actually write words when I'm sitting in a rather busy cafe with a soda in a booth, not a table and listening to my classical piano Pandora station. Doing a little self-inventory is the best way, in my opinion, to overcome 'blank page' writer's block, which is really nothing more then an illusion!"

- Lindsey, OU Writing Center Consultant

Tips for Presentations

Know Your Rubric – When you are presenting in class, make sure that you have read and fully understand the rubric by which you are being graded. Pay attention to the guidelines your instructor has provided for the assignment required including duration, subject, number of sources, etc. Take time to consider the purpose and intended outcome of your presentation.

Rehearse Your Presentation – Not only will rehearsing your presentation give you an idea of the duration, but also, it will help you clarify your ideas and memorize the content. Instead of worrying about presenting your information word-for-word each time, try to understand and know the content well enough to present freely.

Look and Feel Your Best – During the delivery of a presentation, it is alright to have notes as cue cards, but you should strive to look up at your audience. You do not need to worry about remaining perfectly still, but make sure your movements or motions are not distracting to the audience. Try your best to stay relaxed and to smile!

Using Visual Aids – Using visual aids can be a great way to demonstrate the points you are trying to make during a presentation. You can use images, charts, graphs, or quotes to help you convey your message. You should not be reading directly from your visual aid. Instead, visual resources should serve to support or supplement your presentation.

Academic Integrity

Breea Clark, J.D., Associate Director of Academic Integrity

Academic integrity means honesty and responsibility in scholarship. Academic assignments exist to help students learn and grades exist to show how fully this goal is attained. Therefore, all work and all grades should result from the student's own understanding and effort. It is important for the university to promote fairness and civility between students, instructors and the campus community as a whole. Maintaining academic integrity is one of the most important ways the university can uphold these virtues.

OU students have the major responsibility of upholding the OU community's academic integrity system. The responsible student organization for monitoring academic honesty is the Integrity Council. Its official duties include chairing academic misconduct hearings, conducting investigations for reported acts of academic misconduct, reviewing actual academic misconduct cases and recommending sanctions, and serving as peer educators in integrity training for students who have violated the Academic Integrity Code. The Integrity Council website is *integrity.ou.edu*

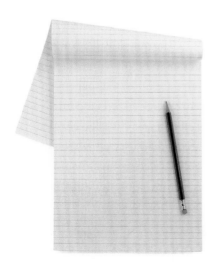

The Top Five Ways to Save Time at the Library

It's no surprise that students who learn to use the library get better grades and are more likely to graduate. But the library can seem overwhelming at first. Bizzell Memorial Library is huge, and there are so many books and databases! If you are intimidated by the thought of using the library, start here. These five tips offer you quick ways to reap the library's benefits.

1. Talk with a librarian. Visit the Research Help Desk in Bizzell Memorial Library, call on the phone, or use live chat (libraries.ou.edu/help/askus). Students report that spending 15 minutes with a librarian saves them hours of wasted time looking for information. Talking with a librarian will help you find the most useful books and articles. Often, it will also help you focus your ideas and figure out how to approach your assignment.

2. Talk with your specific librarian. Many students are unaware that every OU subject has a specialist librarian. So, for instance, when you're writing a paper for your history class, talk with the history librarian. Find your librarian at libraries.ou.edu/liaisons.

3. Get to know Academic Search Elite. The library provides access to hundreds of databases, but Academic Search Elite is a great (and easy!) one to start with. It's available on the library website – click on "Databases" and then click the letter "A" for Academic Search Elite. Academic Search Elite will retrieve articles from newspapers, magazines, and scholarly journals.

4. Use Sooner Xpress, the library's book delivery service. Instead of wandering the stacks looking for the book you need, place a request using Sooner Xpress, and the book will be held for you to pick up at the front desk. Just look up the book in the catalog (libraries.ou.edu/catalog), and click "Get It" and then "Request via Sooner Xpress." You'll receive an email when the book has been retrieved for you – usually within 24 hours.

5. Explore the library's research guides at guides.ou.edu. OU librarians have developed dozens of research guides for topics ranging from English composition to microbiology to financial literacy. Here, you'll find links to the resources you need, all in one convenient place to save you time and hassle.

Box 3.2

Academic Misconduct

Academic misconduct is any act which improperly affects the evaluation of a student's academic performance or achievement. Misconduct occurs when the student either knows or reasonably should know that the act constitutes misconduct. "I didn't mean to" is never an excuse for academic misconduct. Types of academic misconduct include: cheating or using unauthorized materials on exams and other assignments, working together inappropriately with other students on assignments, cheating in online courses, assisting others in academic misconduct, submitting the same assignment for different classes, lying on attendance sheets, using someone else's clicker, plagiarism, or even attempting to commit academic misconduct.

Plagiarism

Plagiarism occurs when a student represent someone else's words or ideas as his or her own. There is basically no college-level assignment that can be satisfactorily completed by copying. OU's basic assumption about writing is that all written assignments show the student's own understanding in the student's own words. That means all writing assignments, in class or out, are assumed to be composed entirely of words generated (not simply found) by the student, except where words written by someone else are specifically marked as such with proper quotation marks and citation. Including other people's words in your paper is helpful when you do it honestly and correctly. When you do not, it is plagiarism.

There is a form of plagiarism known as **self-plagiarism** that involves submitting the same assignment for a second class. This is wrong because it violates the assumption that every assignment advances a student's learning and growth. Unless the second instructor expressly allows it, submitting an assignment already submitted for another class is a form of academic misconduct.

Think – don't just recite facts. Think about your paper topic and what the point of the paper is. Make sure you have actually thought about the points in your paper well enough to explain them in your own words. Make sure you start the assignment soon enough to think and understand, not just research and type.

Write – don't just copy. Generate your own words to express your own understanding. If you cannot get started, or if you think your words are just too clumsy or inadequate, get help from your professor or the Writing Center. Other people's words should always be a supplement, not a substitute, for your own writing.

Signal – say why the quoted words are in your paper. Clearly signal whenever you are using someone else's words, whether you are using them by direct quotation or paraphrase. Any direct quotation must be indicated by two things: "quotation marks" (or else "block quotation") plus a "reference" (also called a "citation") to the source. A reference, alone, is not sufficient to signal a direct quotation. In addition, when you are writing, you should signal a quotation with an indication, in your own words, about where the quotation comes from and why you included it – perhaps because it is well-known, was written by an expert, or expresses an idea that is particularly mistaken or silly.

Quotation Marks, References, and Paraphrasing

Quotation marks are a form of punctuation used to indicate that words were said or written by someone else.
Put one quotation mark at the beginning of the quote and another one at the end. Quotation marks are usually used around no more than 20 or 25 words. Quotations longer than that should be in block quote format, indented on both sides.

A **reference or citation** tells the reader where quoted material comes from. The most common reference forms are text references, footnotes, and endnotes. Which form you should use depends on what class your paper is for. Text references provide source information within the body of the text, usually in parentheses. Footnotes and endnotes consist of a signal in the text, usually a numeral, that is inserted right after the quotation or paraphrase. Information about the source may be placed at the bottom of the page (footnote) or at the end of the paper (endnote). All three kinds of references may be accompanied by an extra page at the end of the paper, usually entitled "Bibliography" or "Works Cited" that lists all of the paper's sources in alphabetical order. Merely including the source in your bibliography is insufficient to indicate that a passage quoted from that source is not your own writing.

Paraphrasing is repeating in your own words the thought expressed in someone else's words. A paraphrase ranges from a loose rewording of the text's basic idea (acceptable) to a nearly identical version of the words or sentence structure of the original text (unacceptable). Basically, a paraphrase is inappropriate where a reasonable person would say that you have stopped thinking and writing in your own words and are simply restating someone else's thoughts. Most commonly, students get in trouble by writing words that stay too close to the original source for too long with no signal but a reference to indicate the source.

Test-Taking

Johnnie-Margaret McConnell, Director, Center for Student Advancement

Lisa Portwood, Assistant Dean, University College

Preparing for Tests – the Study Cycle

For each of your classes, you should follow a basic pattern of test preparation (University of Texas, 2013).

Step One: Prepare for Success

Create a study schedule, during the first week of classes, and stick to it. Treat college like a full-time job that requires 40 hours per week of your time. Even if you are in class for only 15 hours per week, you should use the remaining 25 hours to study. Determine the best study environment for you. Eliminate distractions! Log off your social networking sites, while studying. Resist temptations to surf the Internet or to play episode of your favorite sitcom. Silence your cell phone. Effective studying takes full concentration.

Step Two: Preview, Read, Recall

Spend time familiarizing yourself with how your textbooks are organized, in order to guide your studying. Most beginning college classes use survey textbooks that are written in chapter form. Each chapter represents a main topic that is defined, explained, and often applied through various examples. You can get an overall idea of the chapter topic by reading the chapter headings, along with the introduction and the conclusion. Many chapters will also include opening highlights, graphs, pictures, and a glossary of terms. Be sure to review all before you begin reading the chapter's text.

Reading your course materials should not be a passive activity. Instead, you should engage in active reading, by highlighting, taking notes, and posing questions. Read in chunks. Do not try to read an entire biology chapter all at once, but instead,

Buchanan Hall

This building was named for historian and administrator James S. Buchanan when it was erected in 1926. He was OU's fourth president, serving from 1924-1925, and was known as "Uncle Buck" by students and faculty alike. It first housed Liberal Arts, but now it contains administrative offices. The Bursar's Office is on the first floor – this is where you go to pay university tuition and fees. The Records Office is on the second floor – this is where you may get free copies of your transcripts when applying to jobs and graduate schools. (Check out the Bursar's Office during Howdy Week for free giveaways!)

break it into small 10-20 minute sessions, allowing yourself to review what you have just read and/or take a small break.

Recall material you have read to assess what you have learned. In your own words, either in written form or aloud, summarize what you have just read. Next, form questions to pose to yourself or others about the material you have read. Actively reviewing the material through your own words will help you internalize the information and commit it to long-term memory.

Step Three: Self-Test

There is no better way to prepare for a test than to test yourself. Self-testing means asking yourself questions to see where your strengths and weaknesses lie regarding a topic. Many OU professors offer old tests online for students to review in preparation for tests. You can also create your own test questions by turning chapter headings and subheadings into questions to be answered. Sometimes, self-testing is best done in conjunction with classmates. Depending on how well you performed on your self-test, you may need to return to Step Two. Give yourself time to discover and focus on identified areas of weakness.

Step Four: Test

Students sometimes become so focused on studying the material that they forget to prepare for the actual test day.

- The night before, make sure you have all the materials you need for the test packed and ready.
- Get plenty of rest.
- The day of the test, be sure to eat and to drink plenty of fluids. Make sure to arrive early to class to ensure that you have time to situate yourself and to relax.
- Before you begin the test, take a minute to take in a few deep breaths to calm yourself or to "brain dump" (if space allows on your test papers) any material you are afraid you might forget.
- Do not worry if you cannot remember the answers to the first few questions. Keep reading questions until you find one you are certain about, and get started. You will have time to come back and answer the first few questions.
- Finally, use the allotted time to complete the test. Always take time to review your work before you turn it in. Students who use the entire time provided to complete their exams are more likely to perform well.

Dealing with Test Anxiety

Some students become so anxious, when taking tests, that they "freeze," experiencing a sensation of being unable to think or to act. Known as "test anxiety," this form of anxiety is usually accompanied by negative thoughts about ability, and it often causes physical symptoms, such as sweating, shortness of breath, and nausea. This feeling usually passes after a few minutes. For some students, however, test anxiety may cause academic difficulties.

There are two main types of test anxiety: anticipatory and situational. ***Anticipatory anxiety*** is the type of test anxiety that occurs before the test, when you are thinking and worrying over what might happen. ***Situational anxiety*** is the type of test anxiety that occurs during the test. The good news is that, with effort and support, students can use strategies to assist with lowering their anxiety. Below are just a few tactics to get started:

- Beware of negative self-talk, e.g. "I'm just not smart in math."
- Follow an established study plan that begins at least a week in advance of the test.
- Remember that proper rest and nutrition will help your mind and body stay balanced.
- Rid your body of tension through progressive muscle relaxation and/or deep-breathing techniques.

Most students find that their test anxiety weakens as they take more college classes and gain more study experience. Adequately preparing for tests and avoiding cramming also lessens the symptoms.

If you experience testing anxiety, determine if it stems from lack of preparation or from some other component. If you believe that you have testing anxiety, you may have it assessed by trained counselors at the University Counseling Center, located in Goddard Health Services.

The Test-Taking Cycle

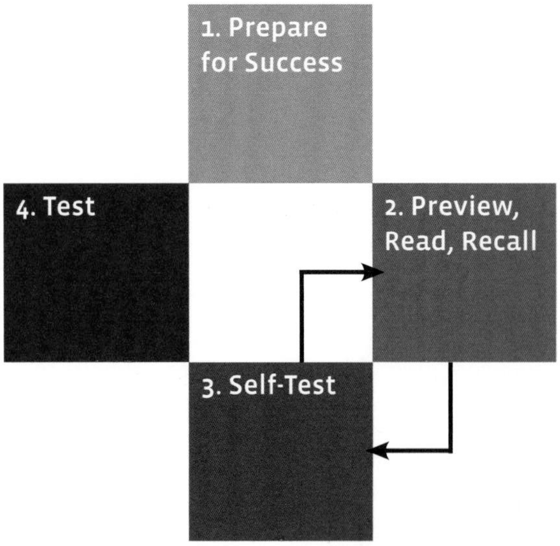

1. Prepare for Success
2. Preview, Read, Recall
3. Self-Test
4. Test

Figure 3.5

Test Anxiety Self-Assessment

- Do you have a difficult time studying?

- Do you become easily distracted while studying?

- Do you expect to do poorly on tests?

- Do you experience physical discomfort during tests?

- Is it difficult for you to understand instructions or questions?

- Is it difficult for you to organize your thoughts?

- Do you often "draw a blank" during tests?

- Do you find your mind wandering to other things?

- Are your test scores lower than the scores on your assignments?

- Do you remember more information after the test than you did during the test?

You may be experiencing some level of test anxiety if you answered YES to at least 4 of these questions.

References

Buzan, T. (1990). *Use both sides of your brain* (Rev. and updated ed., 1st ed.). New York: E.P. Dutton.

Metcalf, T. (1997). Listening to your clients. *Life Association News, 92*(7), 16-18.

Pauk, W. & Owens, R. J. Q. (2010 [1962]). *How to study in college* (10 ed.). New York: Cengage Learning.

School of Undergraduate Studies, University of Texas at Austin (2013). Study smart, not hard. Retrieved from http://www.salisbury.edu/counseling/new/7_critical_reading_strategies.html

Staley, C. (2013). *Focus on college success.* Boston, MA: Wadsworth Cengage Learning.

Chapter 3 REI
Establishing Effective Academic Skills

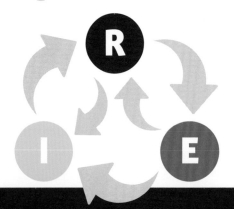

R Reflect

Writing in college can be a difficult adjustment for many students. In what ways have you noticed that writing in college is different from writing in high school? What are some of the things you struggle with while writing?

....

E Engage

Take the "Writing Style Quiz" on page 47 and 48.

....

I Impact

Now that you have taken the Writing Style Quiz (on page 47-48), consider your writing style, and create a plan of action.

The next time you have to write a paper, what specific steps will you take to ensure your success? Do you anticipate challenges in writing at the college level? What will you do to overcome these challenges?

....

Chapter 4

Enhancing Your Learning: *Critical Thinking, Learning Styles, and Cognitive Development*

Cornelia Lambert, Ph.D., former Adjunct Lecturer, Freshman Programs

In this chapter, you will:

- Become aware of how college is different from high school.
- Understand critical thinking and how college professors challenge your cognitive skills.
- Determine your learning style preferences and identify how to maximize your learning success.
- Learn how memory works, in order to improve your long-term memory skills.
- Understand how you can effectively engage in independent and collaborative learning.

"The only person who is educated is the one who has learned how to learn and change."

- Carl Rogers, American Psychologist

This chapter begins with a description of the key differences between the way most students learn in high school and the way they are asked to learn in college. Then, it explores the notion of multiple intelligences and learning styles. Since understanding how your brain stores and retrieves information can help you to better use your mental resources, the chapter ends with a description of how humans learn.

October Realizations - When Ashley arrived at OU, she hardly considered what her classes were going to be like. Getting along with her roommate, rushing for a sorority, and getting involved in campus activities took up most of her energy for the first few weeks of school. Plus, she had maintained a 4.0 in high school without ever having to study. Clearly, she was smart and would do well in college.

By mid-October, however, Ashley began to doubt her intelligence. She failed her first Zoology exam and earned C's on her papers in American Government and English. When her friends started forming study groups, she joined in, but she was not quite sure what she was supposed to be learning from each session. She struggled to keep up with the massive amounts of assigned reading. Suddenly, Ashley was not sure if she was as smart as she had previously thought. What Ashley began to realize was that there are vast differences between

high school and college and that life at The University of Oklahoma was going to be a challenge.

Ashley's experience is quite common for college freshmen. While Ashley feels like an "A" student, she probably does not know that in the past decades, high school students' grades have become inflated, as schools struggle to "teach to the test" and cram more students into Advanced Placement (AP) courses (Howe & Strauss, 2000). As a result of these and other trends, Millennial students are likely to favor rote learning (learning acquired through repetition) over creative pursuits, and they also tend to feel a great deal of pressure to please their parents, teachers, and employers. What Ashley will learn in college is that there is much more to academic work than memorizing.

This chapter is about Ashley's predicament and what she

"Tell me and I forget. Teach me and I remember. Involve me and I learn."

-Benjamin Franklin

can do to improve her grades and to reclaim her intellectual self-esteem. The truth is that Ashley is intelligent. However, she needs to learn how to locate that intelligence and how to use it to her benefit in college.

High School vs. University Level Learning

Teachers versus Professors

One of the key differences between high school and college is the way information is shared. In high school, teachers who have completed college degrees in education teach students material. Teachers are skilled in presenting information to learners at specific moments in their development. They help students keep track of when assignments are due and remind them of upcoming tests. Teachers also keep a close eye on the performance of each student, helping those who have missed class or those who are struggling with information to "catch up."

Professors, on the other hand, are trained in their specific subject areas, and they typically hold graduate degrees in those fields. Professors frequently engage in scholarly pursuits outside of the classroom, including conducting research, authoring scholarly articles and/or books, providing consultation services, etc. Therefore, the expectation in college is that professors will provide the students with highly specialized information and that the students will proactively pursue, through their own motivation, the additional understanding or clarification they need. Rather than closely monitoring their students' individual class attendance, performance, etc., professors are more likely to trust that, since their students are adults, the students will take responsibility for their own performance in the course.

University teaching is not only defined by *how* information is shared, but also by *what* information is shared. Professors, at times, "profess," as their titles imply. As experts in their fields, your college professors have developed opinions, with which you may or may not agree. Whereas high school teachers limit what they share with students, based on societal conventions (and limitations set by school boards), college professors often will not limit topics of discussion to "acceptable" topics. They may talk openly about controversial issues including politics, sex, and other topics with which you may feel uncomfortable.

If you find yourself ill-at-ease with a class discussion or lecture, remember that college is a place where you will encounter many new ideas. You do not have to agree with alternate ideas, but you should allow yourself to listen openly and think critically.

How do you feel about learning?

How do feelings about your own intelligence contribute to your learning?

Are there certain feelings that impact your learning more positively than others?

Basic Thinking versus Critical Thinking

The second difference between learning in high school and in college concerns the type of work you are asked to complete. A helpful way to understand the distinction is to apply *Bloom's Taxonomy*, a hierarchical list of six common cognitive tasks in order of their difficulty. (See figure 4.1 on page 63.) This theory is often used by professors to craft your exams and projects. When you are asked to complete an assignment, you are challenging your mind to engage in a cognitive task. In other words, your brain will have to work in a certain way to help you retrieve the information you need or to formulate new material. Benjamin Bloom first proposed his taxonomy, or hierarchical list, of thinking skills in his 1956 book, *Taxonomy of Educational Objectives: The Classification of Educational Goals.* Reviewing Bloom's Taxonomy can help us understand why Ashley earned a poor grade on her first Zoology test.

At the bottom of the list are the basic skills of *Remembering*, *Understanding*, and *Applying*. Much of high school work centers around these tasks: remembering, for example, the formula for a right triangle's hypotenuse; understanding how and why the formula gives you the hypotenuse; and, applying the formula to various situations, such as a word problem.

At the upper end of the taxonomy, are critical skills: *Analyzing*, *Evaluating*, and *Creating*. Although you've probably engaged in some critical and creative tasks in high school, the ways in which you will be evaluated in college – through exams, research papers, and large projects – are specifically designed to challenge your critical thinking skills.

Critical thinking means engagement in cognitive tasks that go beyond memory and understanding to involve more complex manipulation of information. True, much of your studying will be concerned with the basic tasks of remembering and understanding, but in order to fully prepare for tests and other evaluations, you need to understand how to take that information farther.

Cognitive Maturity - The "Right" Answers

A final big difference between high school and college learning

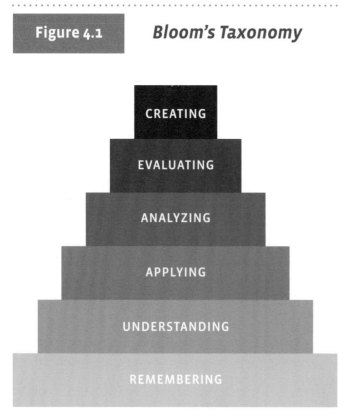

Figure 4.1   **Bloom's Taxonomy**

CREATING

EVALUATING

ANALYZING

APPLYING

UNDERSTANDING

REMEMBERING

is the most philosophical: it concerns your attitude towards questions and answers. When we were children, we were taught about the world in very concrete terms: apples are red, 2 + 2 = 4, and talking back to authority is WRONG. These "facts" allow children to begin to communicate in and to navigate a very detailed world. As we mature, however, we realize that life is more complicated: not all apples are red, and the ones that are red are not the solid red of a crayon. *Cognitive maturity* is the ability to understand that many questions have a variety of answers and that some questions have no verifiable answers.

The belief that every question has a concrete answer is called "Fact/Opinion Dualism," and it drives primary and secondary education. Students are taught to look for, and to memorize, "right answers." Indeed, just as when you were a small child, facts do still help you to navigate your world. However, the higher your level of learning, the more complex the problems you encounter. Thus, in college courses you will come across problems so complex that they do not have simple answers. Whether or not the Roman Empire fell apart because of governmental weakness, because of disease and poisoning from lead pipes, or due to the growing strength of the Sassanid Empire is an ongoing debate among historians of the period. Your history professor will not reveal one answer to this question, but will share with you the educated opinions of a variety of scholars on this topic. Therefore, on an exam, you may not be asked for THE answer to the question, but to explore the question itself. The same is true for questions of ethics. Whether the use of UAV's (Unmanned Aerial Vehicles, or "drones") in warfare is ethical or not, is up for debate – and professors are usually more interested in the debate, itself, than in actually answering the question.

Many students, like Ashley in our earlier example, are surprised when their "right answer" study methods fail to prepare them for university-level exams. Keep in mind that, when crafting your exam, your professor will think of ways to prompt you to use facts that you have learned and understand (the bottom tiers of Bloom's Taxonomy), in order to perform other higher-order cognitive functions (the top tiers of Bloom's Taxonomy). So, the history professor might not care whether you argue that it was weak governance or declining health that spelled the end of Roman expansion. She or he will likely be most concerned that you create a convincing argument or evaluate several arguments provided by historians.

Why do professors design their assignments and exams in this way? No matter your career goal, the world beyond college is one of complex problems. Life's biggest questions often do not have single, certain answers ("Is war ever justified?" "What causes cancer?"). In some cases, the unresolved questions are what create a career. The frontiers of science, law, medicine, and many other professions are based upon a search for answers through the application of critical thinking skills. Therefore, while it may seem like an extended exercise in torture, a professor's insistence that there is no one right answer to a question is the best preparation for the professional world of complicated questions and hard-to-find answers.

Multiple Intelligences and Learning Styles

Multiple Intelligences

Howard Gardner (1983) proposed a theory of multiple intelligences in his book, *Frames of Mind: The Theory of Multiple Intelligences*. In his theory, Gardner proposed that people have various cognitive "modalities" which help to explain their abilities and interests. The theory of *multiple intelligences* is the proposal that people possess various cognitive domains in which they may demonstrate ability and competency. As defined by Gardner, the eight common intelligences are *logical-mathematical, visual-spatial, verbal-linguistic, bodily-kinesthetic, musical, interpersonal, intrapersonal, and naturalistic*.

The American educational system has evolved to highly reward students who excel in the logical-mathematical, spatial, and linguistic domains. Standardized tests, such as the ACT and the SAT, emphasize mastery of such skills (e.g. in the form of algebra, geometry, and literature questions), while often neglecting other domains. The reality, however, is that only some people are going to excel in traditional academic subjects. Others may not flourish in these areas, but that does not mean they are unintelligent. Instead, it means that their skills lie in different, though equally important, areas. Fortunately, many universities take into account the limited meaning of standardized test scores when designing their admissions policies. Ultimately, university communities are stronger and more interesting when they contain a diverse population of thinkers and learners.

As you begin your journey at OU, do not be surprised if you discover that you suddenly excel in some academic area which you previously found uninteresting. University curriculum has much more variety than that of high school, and courses

Figure 4.2

BODILY-KINESTHETIC INTELLIGENCE
- Feeling and expressing things physically; doing hands on work

INTERPERSONAL INTELLIGENCE
- Understanding the feelings, needs and purposes of others

VERBAL-LINGUISTIC INTELLIGENCE
- Using language to present your ideas, to express your feelings or to persuade others

LOGICAL-MATHEMATICAL INTELLIGENCE
- Reasoning, logical, thinking; handling mathematical problems

NATURALISTIC INTELLIGENCE
- Understanding nature, seeing patters in the way nature works; classifying things

INTRAPERSONAL INTELLIGENCE
- Understanding your own interior thoughts and feelings in a very clear way

VISUAL-SPATIAL INTELLIGENCE
- Creating and interpreting visual images; thinking in three dimensions

MUSICAL INTELLIGENCE
- Creating and feeling a rhythm to express a mood; detecting and analyzing musical themes

and whole majors draw upon a wider assortment of types of intelligence. This is one reason that the university asks you to take a wide variety of liberal arts courses, and this is also why advisors and professors may urge you to take a variety of courses if you are undecided on your major. You never know what special career, using your unique talents, lies just over the horizon.

Fred Jones, Jr., Museum of Art

The university's first art museum was housed in Jacobson Hall, named for OU's first director of the School of Art, Oscar Jacobson. Over the years, the collection expanded enough to need a new facility, and one was made possible in 1971 by a donation from Mr. and Mrs. Fred Jones, Sr., in memory of their son, who died in an airplane crash when a senior at OU. The museum houses invaluable works by artists such as Georgia O'Keeffe, Degas, and Monet. Thanks to a generous donation from the OU Athletics Department, admission to the museum is free to all visitors.

Talents and Intelligence

Think about a unique talent or ability you have.

How many of Gardner's intelligences does your talent or ability exemplify? (eg. playing guitar exemplifies musical intelligence, etc.) Try to come up with at least 5.

Do you think it is possible that your talent or ability could be exemplified in all eight intelligences?

Learning Styles

Closely related to theories of multiple intelligences is the idea that people exhibit particular learning styles, or ways of learning, that feel most comfortable to them. *Learning styles* are the ways in which a learner prefers to take in new information. This makes sense for, if you are gifted in the spatial modality, it stands to reason that you might also like to learn from pictures and other visual representations.

Many educators and psychologists have proposed models to describe the typical ways that learners approach information. One that is currently favored by educators is the VARK model, which stands for Visual, Aural/Auditory, Read-Write, and Kinesthetic. This model and the learning strategies it suggests were first developed by Neil Fleming (2001), an educator in New Zealand. At its core, Fleming's system concerns information intake, learning, and output. Visual learners take in material best via pictures, graphs, and other symbolic representations of information, while Aural/Auditory learners are more likely to recall information which they have heard. Read-Write learners remember information they have read or written down, while Kinesthetic learners learn best when they have had an opportunity to experience the information (e.g. as one does in laboratory exercises).

To identify your own VARK style of learning, take the

VARK online questionnaire (*vark-learn.com*). In addition to identifying your learning style, this web site will also provide you with advice on how to maximize your learning success by adjusting how you take in, remember, and express new information.

Barbara A. Soloman and Richard M. Felder (1997) also formulated a model of learning styles. They theorized that an individual's learning style exists on the following spectra:

Active – Reflective
Sensing – Intuitive
Visual – Verbal
Sequential – Global

The first spectrum concerns a student's preference for activity (such as a laboratory experiment or a field trip) versus reflective activities (such as re-reading and organizing notes). A learner's ability to sense information is on one end of the second spectrum, while on the other end is the ability to intuit, or perceive, conclusions before gathering particular information.

Have you ever been in class, itching to ask a question, but hesitated because you were unsure if it was a "stupid" question? As far as course content goes, there are no stupid questions. If you do not understand something, raise your hand, and ask for an explanation! There are, however, cases in which a question can be a waste of time for both you and your professor. Why? Because you already have the answers!

1. "What is going to be on the test?"
You may safely assume that anything covered in class, in assigned readings, or in lab exercises is fair game for test material. Your syllabus is a ready-made list of all of the materials covered.

2. "I was absent on Thursday. Did I miss anything important?"
As you have no doubt noticed, you have very little class time in college. Every minute of class time is important. Whether you missed a lecture, a group activity, or even a film, the professor has made wise use of that time and has shared something "important" with the class. Always check with a classmate after an absence to get notes and to hear what took place in class.

3. "What grade do I have to make [on a test, on a project, etc.] to get an A?"
Professors provide all of the information you need to understand the mechanics of your course in the class syllabus. Asking a professor a question about your particular grade implies 1) that the professor knows your specific grades in the course, despite the reality that she or he has tens or even hundreds of students, and 2) that it is his or her responsibility to monitor your grades. Neither of these is true. Although professors are invested in your learning, it is your responsibility to monitor your grades and to gauge your understanding of the material.

The third spectrum looks at a student's preference for visual stimulation versus verbal input. And, finally, the fourth spectrum considers whether a student prefers to collect discrete pieces of data, before forming an overall impression of the material, or tends to seek the "big picture," before filling it in with details.

Soloman and Felders' online Learning Styles Inventory (*engr.ncsu.edu/learningstyles/ilsweb*) gives you feedback on where your learning style exists on the spectra and offers advice on how to make the most of your particular learning approach.

There are several important points to learn from these models of learning. First, the existence of several models indicates that there is no "one right way" to think about your learning style. As Fleming (2001) suggests, a person's learning modality is influenced by many factors, including room temperature, amount of light, level of food intake, and whether or not someone prefers working alone or with others. In other words, you can take questionnaires to get a general idea of what

works for you, but you should also pay attention to your own experiences and think critically about what helps you to perform the best.

For example, when Althea took her qualifying exams to enter graduate school, she scheduled them for early in the morning because she noticed that her ability to concentrate eroded over the course of the day as she interacted with others. On the morning of the exam, she ate a small, protein-rich breakfast, drank a moderate amount of water, and took a sweater so she would not get cold, since she knew that feeling cold is distracting to her. She scored high on her exams, and she noted that she does not believe she would have performed as well, had she been required to take them in the afternoon.

Another point to note is that everyone exhibits aspects of all learning styles. For this reason, it is best to bear in mind that learning styles are preferences. If you were training at a gym, you might enjoy squats because your legs are strong. Any trainer, however, would tell you to concentrate on building your upper-body strength too, because you want your strengths

to be balanced. The same is true for learning and studying. If you tend to approach material globally and find it easy to grasp the big picture, it is a worthwhile exercise for you to go back through your texts and lecture notes in order to learn the details. Both global conceptualization and awareness of details are important, and professors need to observe that you understand both the specific characteristics and the larger themes of course material.

Finally, understanding your learning preferences can help you determine your success in a given class. If you are a highly visual and kinesthetic learner and find yourself in a history course with a professor who lectures without slides, pictures, or maps, you might find it difficult to concentrate and to learn the material. A useful strategy, then, would be to read the course material before class, taking note of maps, charts, and other visual representations. Then, keep your book open as your professor lectures, in order to follow along with the visual material and to remain engaged. Although it may be tempting to simply drop the course (and in some cases, this may be advisable), knowing what your particular challenge in a course will be is part of crafting a strategy for success.

Memory Process - Retaining What You Have Learned

Thinking About Thinking

As you may recall from high school biology classes, the brain is the seat of learning, and different areas of this organ have specialized memory functions. Learning is not as straightforward as bringing information into your brain, like you would stock a cabinet with supplies or write a word on a chalkboard. Rather, memory is a complex process, which involves several parts of the brain, your senses, and your emotions. It stands to reason that, if you can understand how these parts work together, you can harness their awesome powers to improve your memory.

The process of memory has three distinct stages: encoding, storage, and retrieval. (If this sounds familiar, it is because the process of memory resembles Fleming's description of a learner's preferences for intake, learning, and output, as described in the "Learning Styles" section above.) **Memory encoding** is the processing of information so that it can be stored in memory for later retrieval. Storage is exactly what it sounds like - holding the information until it is needed again. Retrieval is the act of recalling information.

In the late 1600s, the philosopher John Locke wrote that the mind was like a blank slate (he used the Latin term, *tabula rasa*). If you wrote upon the slate, the memory would be there when you returned. Locke's argument was radical in his day, but conceptualizing memory in this way seems primitive by today's standards. We now know that the brain is far more complex than a chalkboard.

At the anatomical level, learning occurs via the use of pathways between the cells of your brain. These cells, called neurons, communicate through electrical charges and via chemicals called neurotransmitters. When neurons communicate, they form a path that leads from a stimulus, like "Emancipation Proclamation," to a response, "1863."

If you did not know anything about American history, remembering that the Emancipation Proclamation was signed in 1863 might be difficult. However, if you are able to connect this chunk of information with something you already know, such as "Abraham Lincoln" and "the Civil War," you are more likely to remember it. This connection allows the brain to form a link between the new data you are supplying to it and previously constructed neural pathways. This is why learning material "from scratch" is so difficult, while learning information, after you have been introduced to a basic idea, is less demanding. For example, playing the guitar is a challenge, but if you already play the cello, it will be easier to grasp. Another way to look at encoding is that it is a lot like shelving a book in the library. The librarian does not put the book on just any shelf, on just any floor in the building, but stores it with other books with the same subject matter.

So what does this mean for college learning? Here are four tips to help you maximize your brain's natural capacities for encoding, storing, and retrieving memories:

1. Shift Gears!

Which is better: to devote five consecutive hours to studying for your upcoming history exam or to study one hour for each of four subjects, with fifteen-minute breaks every hour? The answer is actually the latter. Changing subject material can be useful because, when you ask your brain to "switch gears," it has to "reload" information, thereby reusing and strengthening the neural pathway. Challenging yourself to alternate between subject areas is also helpful in that it allows you to avoid or minimize mental fatigue or boredom, by keeping the materials fresh and interesting. It is easier for your brain to store information that you find interesting than information which you find boring or monotonous. For example, while studying for your history exam, stop for a minute to see if you can recall the twelve cranial nerves. The

first time, name them from front to back. The next time, list the nerves from back to front or alphabetically.

2. Whenever and Wherever!

Learning is context-dependent, which means that your learning is connected to where you are and to what you are doing at the moment. To develop long-term, durable memories, it is best to learn and re-learn information in as many different contexts as possible. Study in the lab, in your dorm room, and on the lawn of the South Oval. Study chemistry in the morning, one day, and then, in the evening, the next day. Once a memory is encoded, it needs to be activated, or tested and remembered, several times and in a variety of ways, in order to increase its strength.

3. Mix it Up!

It is important to move beyond the assumption that just listening to a lecture or reading a chapter will be enough exposure to the material to truly learn it. Taking in information in the same way every time (e.g. by listening to a recorded lecture, over and over again) does not promote new connections in your brain; in fact, it only reinforces one path for retrieving the information later. Therefore, for any set of material you would like to learn, see how many ways you can take it in. For example, listen to your T.A. explain the concepts; handwrite notes from your readings; and, draw concept maps and other visual representations of the ideas. Finally, after you gain competency with the material, teach it to a classmate or to a family member.

FUNKY FONTS?

Graphic designers work hard to make sure that the fonts used in books, on public signage, and on restaurant menus are easy to read. BUT RESEARCH SHOWS THAT YOU ARE MORE LIKELY TO REMEMBER INFORMATION WHEN YOU HAVE HAD TO WORK HARD TO READ IT. Try converting typewritten notes into a funky font on your computer before reading them through.

If you want to make your memories as durable and long-lasting as possible, it is best to challenge yourself, to study in as many different ways as possible, and to quiz yourself often.

4. Second that Emotion

It is common to consider cognitive tasks as separate from emotions, but psychologists are finding that emotions play an important role in learning and in memory (Houwer & Hermans, 2010). Although it may seem strange at first, working actively to engage your emotions while reading and studying will help your brain forge neural pathways into durable networks (Dolcos, Iordan, & Dolcos, 2011). In order to engage your emotions while learning, sympathize with a novel's characters; challenge yourself to see an argument from all sides; and imbue what you learn in your courses with its overall meaning for humankind. Emotions impact learning in another way: mental wellbeing provides a strong foundation for reliable memory. As you will learn in Chapter 5, part of your success in college will depend on your ability to handle your emotions. Studies show that negative emotions, like fear and self- doubt, literally slow down brain function (Öhman, 2001; Phelps, 2006). Therefore, your most fruitful studying will take place when you manage your stress level, avoid draining distractions, foster peaceful relationships with friends and family, and maintain a positive attitude. Maintaining emotional wellbeing will not only serve you in your social life, but in your intellectual development, as well.

Independent and Collaborative Learning

Another important part of learning is being flexible and adaptable in the ways you work with other people to acquire new material. In high school, you may have studied alone, and you may have found that the majority of your work could be completed with little or no guidance or input from others. We refer to this type of learning as independent learning. While elements of this learning will continue to work well for you in college, there will be many times when you will need to work in collaboration with others. Two types of learning incorporate assistance from others: interdependent learning and dependent learning. It is important to be aware of the most and least desirable times to utilize independent, interdependent, and dependent learning styles. This section will help you to identify which learning approach you should use for each particular academic situation.

When is independent learning preferable?

Independent learning is learning that is achieved through independent effort (e.g. studying alone, brainstorming alone, etc.). Independent learning should be your choice when deep thinking and reflection are necessary for performing well on an assignment, when noise and distraction would detract from the quality of your work, when you are completing reading assignments, and when your professor has instructed that you work alone. Independent learning is also preferred when your study needs are markedly different from your study partners' study needs.

For example, if your assignments are to read a chapter of your Native American Studies textbook and write a reflection essay on your opinions of the impact of positive stereotypes on Native American individuals, independent learning may be preferable. In this instance, independent learning would give you a quiet space to read your assignment, to reflect on your own thoughts and attitudes, and to keep your work unique to your own perspective.

When is interdependent work preferable?

Interdependent learning is learning that is achieved through working with others, sharing ideas, and helping each other (within the guidelines of Academic Integrity – see integrity.ou.edu to review the guidelines). Interdependent learning can be valuable to your college success, and engaging with others to achieve your academic goals can be a rewarding experience for everyone involved. Interdependent learning is helpful for brainstorming ideas, for proofreading each other's work, for gaining feedback, and for gauging the quality of your sources, writing level, presenting skills, etc. Interdependent learning often requires an element of intellectual humility because you must be able to admit that you have something to learn from your peers.

Interdependent learning can also make study sessions more effective. For example, if you have a very lengthy study guide for an exam, you might want to connect with other students who you believe will be as committed to excellence as you are and divide the study guide into sections, with each person assigned a specific area. With each student compiling notes, page numbers from the textbook, etc. for their section of the study guide, a study guide that might have been overwhelming for one student has now become more manageable. Interdependent learning might also include quizzing each other for exams, practicing presentations in front of each other, and sharing class notes/ diagrams. Additionally, interdependent learning can be incredibly helpful for gaining information about study strategies that have been effective for others in the course. For example, you might want to swap ideas as to what mnemonics (memory strategies) have been working well to remember the materials, as to what order of importance you are each giving to the different study materials, and as to steps you have taken to stay focused, motivated, etc. Keep in mind that working with others should not turn into you relying on others to earn the grade, but to learn material that will shape the rest of your life! Interdependent learning should enhance your ability to learn – not to replace your own efforts.

When is dependent learning preferable?

Dependent learning is learning that primarily relies on the guidance and mentorship of others. Dependent learning can be an asset when you are confused about class materials, but your reading and study efforts have not made the material clearer. For example, if you have listened to your professor's lecture in Business Calculus, have read the textbook

explanation of how to work your assigned problems, have reviewed your class notes, but still cannot understand how to work the problems, this would be an ideal time to engage in dependent learning. Dependent learning might take the form of visiting your professor during office hours, going to the Math Lab, signing up for a one-on-one tutor, or meeting with a classmate who is willing to explain the steps of solving the problem.

While dependent learning is necessary and desirable in some cases, your goal should be to only stay in the dependent learning situation long enough to transition to interdependent and/or independent learning. If you find yourself becoming dependent on others in an academic area that is challenging for you, make it your goal to learn to master the tools, yourself, so that you can grow out of the dependency.

Keep in mind that dependency on other students lowers your own view of yourself as being capable to achieve academic success and may eventually lead to resentment from the student on whom you are dependent. Also, bear in mind that, if you wait until the last minute to learn your materials, complete an assignment, etc. and become dependent, as a result, you are not being fair to yourself or the person who is helping you. Many students are willing to help another student who is temporarily struggling, but if the relationship becomes one of habitual dependency, the student who is helping may begin to feel leeched of energy and valuable time. Overall, temporary dependency is okay, as you are learning the ropes, but the goal should be to increase your skills to that of an interdependent or independent learner.

Warning about Academic Dishonesty When Working with Others

It is important to keep academic honesty in mind when engaging in collaborative learning. While it may be useful to work with other students by studying together, sharing/receiving feedback, bouncing ideas off each other, etc., it is important to keep in mind that work you should submit for your courses must be your own original work and use of anyone else's ideas and/or work should be acknowledged with citations. Examples of academic dishonesty include having others write all or portions of your papers, copying each other's answers on take-home exams, or sharing homework answers when permission has not been granted by your professor. If you are ever in doubt as to whether your collaborative learning efforts are violating OU's Academic Integrity Policy, you may review the policy at integrity. ou.edu.

Box 4.2

Choosing Study Partners

If you have not already discovered, not all study partners are created equal. Just because someone is in class or is your friend does not mean that you will be an asset to each other's learning process. When choosing a study partner, ask yourself, "Will this person share my commitment to making study time count?" Socializing, hanging out, and having fun are important parts of maintaining relationships, but if productive work is not being accomplished in your study sessions, you may not be using your time wisely by studying with this particular partner. You might want to continue hanging out with this person socially, but find someone else who is more focused for a study partner.

Another question to ask is, "Will this person and I be able to contribute to each other's success?" It is important that you do not continually devote your valuable study time primarily to helping others master areas that you have already mastered. On the flip side, your own efforts should not be dependent on a study partner in a way that impedes their success. Ideally, study sessions should reflect a balance between them helping you and you helping them. That said, bear in mind that some study partners will be able to help you in your areas of weakness (e.g. calculus), while you can help them in your areas of strength (e.g. writing). Overall, it is important that you and your study partner(s) find a healthy balance of interdependent learning that benefits you both.

Group Projects

During your time at OU, you will, no doubt, be assigned numerous group projects. Often, you will not have a say as to what group you belong to, so you will be working alongside students with varying personalities, communication styles, degrees of motivation, attitudes about responsibility, and abilities. This section will offer ideas on ways to make group projects successful. When you first receive a group project assignment, it is best to clearly agree on each member's specific contribution. As you are working together to divide up responsibilities, try to balance the amount of work each member must contribute. Frustrations often develop when one or two students feel overburdened and see other members contributing less. Additionally, in deciding on designated responsibilities, strive to have each member contribute in an area of personal strength, so that the overall project quality is its best. If each member is contributing in an area where they excel, the chances are greater that the overall project will be excellent. Further, it is a good plan to have each member do something that they are enthusiastic about doing. People who are enthusiastic about their share of an assignment are more likely to stay focused and motivated to complete the assignment. After group members have decided on individual responsibilities, it is a good idea to plan out a timeline of when the group will check in to monitor progress and of when each person's contribution will be due. (It is best to have group members submit work to the group several days prior to the due date, in case adjustments need to be made.) During the time period between the assignment of a group project and its due date, plan to meet at regular intervals to monitor progress, provide each other feedback, work through unexpected kinks, etc. Several days prior to the project's due date, students should plan to meet as a group to compile the materials, review the work, and polish the final product.

Now that you have an improved understanding of the ways you are intelligent and the ways that your feelings and emotions impact your learning, how does this fit with your choice of degree?

When choosing a major, which considerations are most important to you? Your feelings about your own talents or your feelings about the careers this degree can lead you to?

| Box 4.3 | **Group Projects - Things to Keep in Mind** |

Don't be a social loafer!

Have you ever worked on a team project and found that you took the assignment a little less seriously because you knew that other people were there to take up the slack if you did not quite pull off a stellar performance? If so, you were engaging in what social psychologists call social loafing. Social loafing occurs when individual effort decreases in the context of group responsibility.

Alan Ingham (1974) conducted an experiment in which people were blindfolded to play a game of tug-of-war. Some participants were told that someone else was helping them pull (although they were, in fact, pulling alone), while other participants were told that they were pulling alone. Those who believed they were pulling alone pulled 18 percent harder than those who believed someone else was helping them pull. Bibb Latané, Kipling Williams, and Stephen Karkins (1979; Karkins & others, 1980) conducted research in which they found that people who were told to clap and shout "as loud as you can" were three times louder when they were alone than when they were in a group of six people. This phenomenon of social loafing has been found in numerous other experiments (e.g. Sweeney, 1973; Hardy & Latané, 1986).

So, when you are working on a group project, be aware of your tendencies to slacken your efforts or to believe that others will fill in the gaps in your work. Keep in mind that your grade is riding upon the group's success, and focus on contributing your best efforts.

Turn in your work as early as possible.

Keep in mind that other group members are sharing in the responsibility and that their grades are also riding on your effort. Given that group success is tied to your contribution to the project, other group members might want to review the work you contributed, prior to submission. Also, other group members who have completed their work may become anxious and resentful if you wait until the last moment to submit your work to the rest of the group. Be careful that you do not put the group success in jeopardy.

Communicate with the group.

If you are running into obstacles in completing your portion of the group project, communicate with your group members and let them know the steps you are taking to make sure you complete your portion. Group members would often rather know about a problem and suggest solutions or provide encouragement than to arrive at the due date with an incomplete assignment.

Go above and beyond.

Each group will typically have students with varying levels of motivation and standards of performance. Some students might be content with simply passing the course, while others are shooting for an "A." Always give your best work to group projects so that no one's grade suffers as a result of your portion of the project. Go above and beyond in your contributions.

Be respectful of others' ideas.

Sometimes the most creative ideas arise from a mix of very different opinions. Sometimes even outlandish ideas can inspire others to come up with creative ideas that are perfect for the project. So, even if some of your group members are formulating pie-in-the-sky ideas, be respectful and thoughtfully evaluate whether there might be legitimacy to all or some part of their ideas. Sometimes, we can limit our creativity by thinking in a limited fashion. And, even if the ideas that are generated truly are outlandish, maintaining an attitude of respect, despite differences, will help to maintain group morale and will help to foster healthy relationships.

References

Bloom, B. (1956). *Taxonomy of educational objectives: The classification of educational goals.* New York: Longmans Green.

Dolcos, F., Iordan, A. D., & Dolcos, S. (2011). Neural correlates of emotion-cognition interactions: A review of evidence from brain imaging investigations. *Journal of Cognitive Psychology, 23* (6), 669-694.

Fleming, N. D., & Bonwell, C. C. (2001). *How do I learn best? A student's guide to improved learning. VARK: Visual, aural, read/write, kinesthetic.* Christchurch, N.Z.

Gardner, H. (1983). *Frames of mind: The theory of multiple intelligences.* New York: Basic Books.

Houwer, J., & Hermans, D. (2010). *Cognition and emotion: Reviews of current research and theories.* New York: Psychology Press.

Howe, N., & Strauss, W. (2000). *Millennials rising: The next great generation.* New York: Vintage.

Ingham, A.G., Levinger, G., Graves, J., & Peckham, V. (1974). The Ringelmann effect: Studies of group size and group performance. *Journal of Experimental Social Psychology, 10,* 371-384.

Latané, B., Williams, K., & Karkins, S. (1979). Many hands make light the work: The causes and consequences of social loafing. *Journal of Personality and Social Psychology, 37,* 822-832.

Öhman, A., Flykt, A., & Esteves, F. (2001). Emotion drives attention: Detecting the snake in the grass. *Journal of Experimental Psychology, 130,* 466-478.

Phelps, E. A. (2006). Emotion and cognition: Insights from studies of the human amygdala. *Annual Review of Psychology, 57,* 27-53.

Chapter 4 REI

Enhancing Your Learning

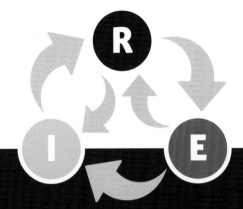

R Reflect

What does the word "intelligence" mean to you? Has your personal definition of this word changed?

List 1-2 forms of intelligence that you identify as your areas of relative weakness and as your areas of strength.

....

E Engage

Just as there are different forms of intelligence, there are different preferred styles of learning. Discover your learning style by completing the VARK online survey at: *vark-learn.com*

Click on the available link on your results page in order to access the study strategies based on your VARK style.

....

I Impact

Discuss your two (2) highest VARK scores, and based on your readings of Chapter 4 and the VARK website, explain what they mean. What strategies related to these preferences will you use to enhance your learning?

....

Chapter 5

Investigating Your Options: *Courses, Majors, Degrees, and Careers*

Anne Hedrick, M.S., Senior Academic Counselor, OU Scholars
Lillian Miller, M.Ed., Director, Freshman Programs

In this chapter, you will:

- Understand courses, majors, and minors at OU.

- Learn about the advising process at OU.

- Understand degree attainment in the United States.

- Identify ways to explore, prepare for, and execute your career goals.

- Become aware of campus resources available to help you investigate your course, major, and career options.

"Think not of yourself as the architect of your career but as the sculptor. Expect to have to do a lot of hard hammering and chiseling and scraping and polishing."

- B.C. Forbes, Journalist and founder of Forbes Magazine

As a first-semester freshman, it can be overwhelming to think about the courses you need to take next semester, not to mention your major, or even your future career. Although most college students take comfort in knowing that they can expect more career flexibility and achievement over their lifespan than non-college graduates, figuring out where to begin can be daunting. If you are unsure of what you want to do or of the proper steps to get there, you are not alone. By gaining an understanding of courses, majors, degrees, and the career development process, however, you will learn how to start your educational and professional journey on the right foot.

Understanding Courses at OU

Let's start the discussion of courses at OU by explaining what information the course number contains. The first digit of the four-digit course number designates the level of the course: 1000 and 2000 level courses are considered lower-division classes; 3000 and 4000 level courses are referred to as upper-division courses. You will take a wide range of courses during your undergraduate career at the University of Oklahoma. These courses will be comprised of a combination of both lower- and upper-division courses.

A closer look at your degree plan will reveal that each major requires you to complete a certain number of upper-division credit hours. Upper-division courses are not necessarily more difficult. These courses may just be more specific and, therefore, require a certain knowledge base that must be gained through other courses. These other courses, which can be either lower- or upper-division, are referred to as prerequisites. A **prerequisite** is a requirement that must be met prior to taking a particular course. Other upper-division

courses simply require you to attain a certain class standing, most commonly junior standing.

In addition to prerequisites, a course may also have a corequisite. A **corequisite** is a course that must be taken at the same time as another course. Sometimes, you will have the option to take the corequisite course prior to, or at the same time as, the other course.

Choosing Courses

You will hear a lot of advice from upperclassmen about how to pick courses and about which courses you should and should not take. While hearing their experiences can be useful, be careful that you are not making your course decisions solely based on the advice of others.

Along this same line, you also want to be cautious of class and professor rating websites. These websites often only give you a sampling of the best and the worst reviews as students with a neutral review of the course and/or professor may not be motivated to take the time to write a review.

Students who did not receive the grade that they desired may also write bad reviews.

In addition, be careful that you are not letting your desire for sleep dictate your choice of courses. A topic that you are interested in or that is required for you to progress in your degree will definitely be worth getting out of bed early a few days each week. Creating the ideal schedule should never be the sole reason for choosing a course. There may come a semester where you somehow find yourself in the lucky position of not having any classes on Fridays; however, make sure you are not cheating yourself out of a potentially rewarding experience to make it happen.

You have probably heard the phrase "Easy is not always best." As cliché as this may sound, keep this quote in mind when selecting courses. Try not to choose a course simply because it has a reputation for being easy. One course may be more challenging than another, but if your interest in the subject is strong, the challenge will be worth it. Almost everyone you meet will have a story about a course they took in college that they describe as one of the hardest of their college career, but also one of the best.

Each semester, strive to achieve a balance in your courses. If you have to take two lab sciences next semester, consider rounding out your semester with humanities courses that will add variety and will challenge you in different ways. Your advisor can help you achieve this balance. Seek your advisor's advice regarding which courses pair well together and which courses might be better to spread out over a few semesters.

Repeat Policy

The OU Norman campus does have a Repeat Policy. You may apply the Repeat Policy to any course in which you received a "D" or "F." It is important to understand that both your original grade in the course and the second grade will always appear on your permanent academic record and that both grades will be used to calculate your cumulative grade point average. You may only repeat four courses, not to exceed 18 credit hours. The original "D" or "F" received in a course that you designate as a repeated course will not be used when calculating your Graduation/Retention GPA which is reflected on your official transcript. For more details about the Repeat Policy, consult with your advisor.

Your advisor can also help you determine the appropriate sequence in which to take your courses. As mentioned previously, there will be some courses that have to be taken before others. Oftentimes, certain courses will only be offered during the fall semester or the spring semester. So, if you delay one course, it may result in delaying your graduation, as you will have to wait a full academic year for the course to be taught again.

There will also be courses that you have little or no interest in, but that are necessary to attain your desired degree. While you may not necessarily enjoy these courses, look at them in terms of the ultimate goal. That one semester that seems incredibly painful will soon be a distant memory.

What does a "W" mean?

A "W" simply means that you withdrew from the course. A "W" does not affect your GPA, but it does appear on your transcript. At OU, you are only allowed a total of 5 "W"s during your undergraduate career. It is important that you consult an advisor to evaluate the pros and cons of dropping a course.

Majors and Minors

Major Considerations

When considering your major, the first thing to keep in mind is that your major does not necessarily have to "match" your intended career. However, there are some exceptions. If you are interested in pursuing a technical career, such as engineering, nursing, or other health-related careers, you will need to earn a degree in that field. Obviously, you cannot become a civil engineer with a degree in history. The more people you talk to, the more you will find individuals in almost all jobs who have college degrees in seemingly unrelated disciplines.

As you may have already sensed, a college degree is not only about career preparation. By completing a college education, you are demonstrating to future employers that you have the ability to set a goal and work to attain it, that you have developed essential critical thinking skills, and that you are teachable. Most employers will train you in what you need to know once you have started your new job. Try to keep this in mind when selecting a major. Despite the 40 hours of required General Education courses and major support courses that you will take, the majority of the courses you take during your undergraduate experience will be within your major. For that reason, make sure to choose a major that you find interesting and engaging.

Despite what you may have been told, there is no "Pre-med" major at the University of Oklahoma. "Pre-med" is more of a designation to let advisors on campus know that your ultimate goal is to attend medical school. Knowing this, they can help you work through the required prerequisite courses to apply to medical school. There is also a myth that, if you are planning to go to medical school, you must major in a science, such as biology, microbiology, or chemistry. This is absolutely not true! Medical schools do not care what field of study you pursue as an undergraduate. The admissions boards will be mainly focused on whether you have completed the prerequisite sciences, what your GPA is, and what your MCAT (Medical College Admission Test) scores are. If you happen to love chemistry, a chemistry or biochemistry major might be perfect for you. However, if you have a passion for the French language, consider declaring French/Pre-med as your intended major. There are several pieces to the puzzle when applying to medical school. Talk to your advisor for all the details. The University of Oklahoma also has Pre-Med Advising to help students navigate the complicated process of preparing for, and applying to, medical school.

Students who plan to attend law school after the completion of their bachelor's degree are in a similar situation. You can literally major in anything you choose and attend law school. However, depending on the type of law you want to practice, there might be certain majors that make more sense than others. While there are no specific courses required to attend law school, there may be certain recommended courses to help you prepare for the LSAT (Law School Admission Test) and for the format of law school. OU has a Pre-law advisor on campus to help ensure the best preparation for those applying to law school.

Reminder: You can find your undergraduate degree requirements at *checksheets.ou.edu*

Understanding Minors

In addition to the majors that OU offers, there are also a wide variety of minors. A minor is a secondary area of interest, in addition to your major, usually comprised of 15-18 hours of coursework in the discipline. Typically, nine of these credit hours should be upper-division. Some majors at the university require students to complete a minor. For example, all majors within the Gaylord College of Journalism require students to complete either a minor or second major. Pursuing a minor could allow you to become fluent in a second language or to gain a more in-depth understanding of an area of interest. In addition, a minor can be a nice addition to your resume and may help you stand out when you begin applying for jobs.

Unless your major requires you to complete a minor, it is really up to you to decide whether you want to pursue one. There are a few considerations to keep in mind when you are making the decision to pursue a minor. First, look at the degree checksheet for your particular major. Is there flexibility in the sequencing of courses? Do you have many free electives that could be used for minor requirements? Will adding the additional minor requirements mean that you must take 18 or 19 hours every semester? There are some majors at OU that require several electives, so it may

Degree Designation

A common way of designating earned degrees is by placing special letters and abbreviations after the degree holder's name. These designators help to standardize credentialing in the United States. Some common abbreviations include:

A.A.- Associate of Arts
A.S.- Associate of Science
B.A.- Bachelor of Arts
B.B.A.- Bachelor of Business Administration
B.F.A.- Bachelor of Fine Arts
B.S.- Bachelor of Science
M.Ed.- Master of Education

M.S.- Master of Science
Ph.D.- Doctor of Philosophy
M.D.- Doctor of Medicine
D.O.- Doctor of Osteopathic Medicine
Pharm.D.- Doctor of Pharmacy
Ed.D.- Doctor of Education
J.D.- Juris Doctorate

make sense to use those electives toward earning a minor, rather than taking a random selection of courses. On the other hand, majors within the College of Engineering have very rigid requirements that can make it difficult to find room to fit in minor requirements. It is not impossible, but it may require some additional time to complete both the major and minor requirements. Your advisor can help you weigh the pros and cons of adding a minor in your unique situation.

Advising at the University of Oklahoma

The mission of academic advising at the University of Oklahoma is to educate and empower students as they design, develop, and implement individual academic plans. The objective is that students will experience intellectual and personal growth for success as citizens of the global community.

Academic advisors can assist with a wide range of questions and problems. These individuals are excellent resources for questions regarding courses, degree requirements, University policies, and general information, as you navigate your first year on campus.

For this reason, all students in University College, and in most degree-granting colleges, are required to meet with an advisor prior to each enrollment. Even if your particular degree program does not require advising prior to each semester, it is worthwhile to check with an advisor to make

IMPORTANT ADVISING POINTS

1. Students can freely add open courses online through the end of the first week of classes.

2. Students can drop a course online without receiving a "W" for the course through the end of the second week of classes.

3. Students can drop a course with an automatic "W" through the end of the 10th week of the semester (usually around OU/TX weekend in the Fall and after Spring Break in the Spring).

4. Freshman enrollment usually falls around Thanksgiving Break (check your oZone account for your specific enrollment window).

5. You may also notice a disclaimer similar to this at the bottom of your advising worksheets:

"Although college and departmental advisors are available to help students plan their programs of study, the individual student has the three-fold responsibility in this regard: 1. to know his/her academic standing based on printed standards, 2. to know and satisfy the stated degree requirements and 3. to know and observe academic deadlines, as printed in the official Academic Calendar online."

Box 5.1

sure your understanding of your requirements is accurate. Academic advising is key to staying on track with your degree and with progress toward graduation.

When it is time to schedule an advising appointment, University College students and students advised in the OU Scholars Program can easily schedule an appointment using the online appointment scheduler called iAdvise. iAdvise may be accessed at *iadvise.ou.edu*.

Once your records transfer to your degree-granting college, you will still have an advisor to assist you as you move toward graduation. Advising varies from college to college and from department to department. OU has a main advising website, *ou.edu/advising*, which has information about advisement through the different degree-granting colleges. When it comes time for you to begin advising through your degree-granting college, the OU Advising website will be an

Advising through the OU Scholars Program

Students who receive certain scholarships are eligible for advising through the OU Scholars Program. These students also receive early enrollment privileges during their first year. Since OU Scholars enroll almost a full month before the rest of the freshman class, it is important that OU Scholars begin the advising process early in the semester. Advising through the OU Scholars Program begins during the fourth week of each semester. In addition to OU Scholars, students who are members of certain campus groups, such as President's Leadership Class (PLC) and President's Community Scholars (PCS), also receive early enrollment privileges.

excellent resource to familiarize you with the new advising experience. In addition, in your Graduation Planner, you will find concise information regarding academic advising at OU.

During your advising appointments, your advisor will review your degree checksheet with you in detail so that you know what requirements you still need to meet. Not only do degree checksheets outline courses required to complete a degree, the checksheets also provide suggested course sequencing to demonstrate how students can complete all requirements in the desired timeframe. Your advisor will help you select appropriate courses and record those courses on an advising worksheet for your future reference.

Your Role in the Advising Process

As an OU student, you are responsible for knowing several important dates. Since it can be extremely difficult to keep all of these deadlines straight, it is a good idea to check the university's academic calendar each year and mark these deadlines in your academic planner in order to keep them on your radar.

Remember, your advisor is available to assist you with a variety of situations, but your education is ultimately your responsibility. Make sure that you read and understand your degree checksheet, and know where you stand with regard to the requirements. If you have questions or need help interpreting your degree checksheet, it is your responsibility to ask questions. Never be afraid to ask for help, whether it be with advising or with classes. If your advisors and your instructors do not know that you have a concern, they cannot help you!

Degree Attainment in the United States

At the end of your four years at the University of Oklahoma, you will become a member of a growing, yet privileged, population. According to a 2012 *New York Times* article, for the first time in the history of the United States, more than one-third of adults have earned a bachelor's degree (Perez-Pena, 2012). A *bachelor's degree* is the academic degree earned for an undergraduate course of study or major. The Department of Education reported that, in 2012, 40,561 of 204,579 adults aged 25 years and older had completed bachelor's degrees (U.S. Census Bureau, 2012).

Box 5.2   # FERPA

As a student, you have rights. Among the most important are the rights granted to students under FERPA. FERPA is the *Family Educational Rights and Privacy Act*. FERPA applies to any school that receives funds under programs administered by the Department of Education, which includes almost all public and private colleges and universities. FERPA is a very long and complex document. However, there are a couple of aspects of FERPA that are important for all students to know.

Under the stipulations of FERPA, the University of Oklahoma can only release what is termed as "directory information" to someone other than you without your specific written consent (U.S. Department of Education, 2011). Directory information at the university includes the following: the student's name, local and home addresses, e-mail address, telephone number, college, major, classification, current enrollment status, participation in recognized student activities and sports, dates of attendance, degrees and awards received and dates of receipt, posting of individual student grades and interim class evaluations by code number, or ID number and anticipated date of graduation. If you do not want this information to be accessed, you can fill out a Directory Information Hold Form and submit it to the Office of Academic Records. Directory information does NOT include your grades, academic progress, class attendance, or any information specific to your academic record. Unless you sign a release and designate specific individuals who can have access to this information, only you, faculty, and staff at the university have access to your academic record. For example, if your mother or father called your advisor to find out what grade you received in your chemistry course last semester, your advisor would not be able to give your parent any information.

Knowing that your advisor and instructors cannot divulge information to your family or other outside parties hopefully helps you feel safe to confide in your advisors and instructors and to speak openly about any issues or concerns you may be having.

Additionally, while men have long outnumbered women in educational attainment, women are quickly narrowing the gap (Perez-Pena, 2012).

There are also advanced degree options for individuals who choose to continue their formal education after completing their bachelor's degree, sometimes after gaining other experience. An **advanced degree** is conferred for the completion of prescribed study, beyond the bachelor's degree, that provides specialized learning in a given field or professional practice. In the United States, this level of study is often completed in graduate school. These master's degrees, doctoral degrees, and other professional degrees may also serve as the terminal degrees for given specializations. A **terminal degree** is the highest academic degree in a given field of study.

Advanced degree programs often have specific requirements concerning previous courses, majors, and/or type of degrees needed to qualify for admission to the program of study. The specifics of these requirements vary from school to school and from program to program. The requirements for some programs, including medical and law school, are many times not what students initially assume. Therefore, doing preliminary research is an important part of considering an advanced education.

While one-third of the adult population in the United States has received a bachelor's degree, those who obtain more advanced degrees remain more exclusive. One reason for this is that many fields do not require an advanced degree for job placement and advancement. These industries typically value experience in the field over continued formal education. However, it should be noted that earning an advanced degree can often allow more career flexibility and is tied to overall wellness. In addition, advanced degrees also continue to serve as the traditional entry into the professional middle class in America. An advanced degree can also offer a lower risk of unemployment and greater earning potential. When considering an advanced degree, it is important to evaluate your personal levels of perseverence and grit. These degrees are much more rigorous in nature and require high levels of self-regulation in order to be successfully completed.

Look at Figure 5.1 and consider the highest degree you hope to obtain. Does the median earnings for this level of education meet your expectations? Remember, this is the average earnings for workers with this educational attainment at all stages in their career, including entry, mid-level, and senior-level phases.

Unemployment Rates and Earnings by Educational Attainment
Education Pays
Unemployment and earnings for workers 25 & older by educational attainment
(earnings for full-time wage and salary workers)

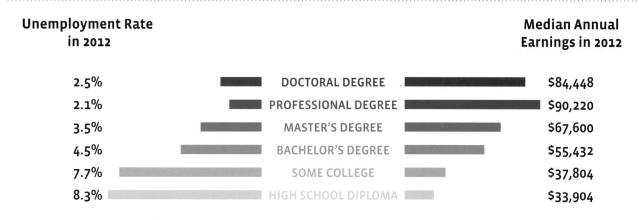

Unemployment Rate in 2012		Median Annual Earnings in 2012
2.5%	DOCTORAL DEGREE	$84,448
2.1%	PROFESSIONAL DEGREE	$90,220
3.5%	MASTER'S DEGREE	$67,600
4.5%	BACHELOR'S DEGREE	$55,432
7.7%	SOME COLLEGE	$37,804
8.3%	HIGH SCHOOL DIPLOMA	$33,904

Figure 5.1 *Source: U.S. Bureau of Labor Statistics, Current Population Survey, 2012*

Choosing a Career

As stated previously in this chapter, your major does not have to match your career. However, you should be intentional about using your time in college to gain both direction for your career and the experiences that will help you get started after you graduate. This is especially true since many students choose to attend college for the purposes of earning more money and landing a better job.

Unfortunately, many believe that a college degree, alone, will provide the knowledge, skills, and resources necessary for immediate job placement and professional achievement. In reality, proper career development involves four actions: assessment, exploration, preparation, and execution. You can expect to cycle through these stages several times over the course of your lifetime, and your college years will be the perfect time for you to become accustomed to them.

The University of Oklahoma provides many resources to serve students at each of these stages. To be most effective, you should begin utilizing these resources during your freshman year and should make intentional efforts to make progress during your time at OU.

Career Development Stages

Career development is the lifelong process of managing work experiences through a series of activities and events. There are four stages of career development:

Assessment – Taking stock of your personality, interests, values, and skills.

Exploration – Discovering your potential career options and narrowing your search.

Preparation – Preparing for your career(s) of interest through targeted learning objectives and deliberate developmental opportunities.

Execution – Taking intentional action that results in achieved career objectives.

1) Assessment

To identify your general career direction, you must first gain awareness of your personality, interests, values, and skills.

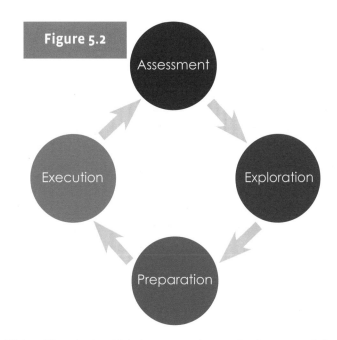

Figure 5.2

This self-analysis will help you understand what you might want from your career. Therefore, the Assessment Stage starts with what you already know about yourself, but requires you to dig deeper to discover additional aspects of yourself that might not be readily apparent to you.

Personality

An individual's personality is closely tied to their individual traits and behaviors. Therefore, it makes sense that there is a strong connection between personality types and career preferences. It is important for you to consider your personality when trying to figure out what careers might be most appropriate for you. Various personality assessments are available to help you explore and classify your preferences, styles, and strengths. The Meyers-Briggs Type Indicator, the Strengthsfinder assessment, and the True Colors personality assessment are a few nationally-recognized assessments now being used by college students.

Interests

Interests are areas toward which a person experiences feelings of attention, concern, and curiosity. Your interests will lead you to those activities that you are most passionate about doing. Just like your personality type, your patterns of interests can also be assessed and can describe your propensity towards certain activities. This knowledge can lead you to career fields to explore. Understanding your interests will also help you understand your potential desires within a career. Do you aspire to be an innovative leader, or are you more interested in execution and seeing plans through?

Within any field, there are likely to be positions for people with various interests and goals.

Values

Values are feelings about the usefulness, importance, or worth of something. It is important for you to consider how your personal values toward life, family, money, and ethics match the various aspects of particular careers. In order to identify your values, reflect on what you believe is most important in life, determine your desired lifestyle, and examine your needs. Most people find that they value much more than a paycheck. For example, many students look for careers in which they can help people or can "make the world a better place." In addition, many graduates today find they strongly desire a certain work-life balance.

Work-life balance is an individual's desired balance between his or her career and other aspects of life, and this idea impacts career selection for many graduates. Friedman (2008) proposed four domains of life: work, home, community, and self. He noted that balance is needed between the domains, in order for individuals to live rich and fulfilling lives. Once you have determined your personal values, seek the appropriate balance in each of these areas. You will find that the more your values are compatible with your work, the more you will value your work!

Skills

According to Metz (2005), skills are competencies that you can develop through learning and practice. You have come to college with a certain level of academic skill, and you also have a developed aptitude or capacity for learning new ones. Some majors will help you to develop career-specific skills. Graduates of petroleum engineering, accounting, and education programs will enter the workforce with the specific skills needed for careers in those fields. Other majors provide more general, transferable knowledge and skills which are easily adapted for, and useful in, many occupations. These include verbal and written abilities, computer and technical skills, as well as other basic competencies that employers desire. It is important for you to compare the skills you wish to acquire with an honest evaluation of your aptitude for gaining new ones.

University College Assessment Center

The University College Assessment Center provides services

Holland's Six Codes

There are a lot of tools you can use to reflect on your personality and interests: The Holland Codes consist of six domains and are used to determine how well a person with a particular personality will thrive in a particular career. Which two Holland Codes best describe your natural interests?

Realistic (R) – People with this code typically enjoy physical activity, working with their hands, and using tools and equipment. Individuals with this personality can be found working in fields that include lab work, field research, building projects, etc.

Investigative (I) – Individuals with this code typically enjoy observing, learning, and analyzing. Careers that include solving abstract problems, engaging in lab work, researching, and problem-solving emphasize the investigative aspect.

Artistic (A) – People with this code typically enjoy self-expression, creativity, and the arts. Individuals with this personality can be found in careers that involve a lot of creativity, independence, and imagination.

Social (S) – Individuals with this code typically enjoy helping, informing, training, and developing others. Careers that involve understanding people and society (past or present) have a strong social aspect to them.

Enterprising (E) – People with this code typically enjoy persuading, motivating, and influencing people and organizations. Careers that involve managing, selling, competing, leading others, setting goals, public speaking, and interacting with groups are a good fit for enterprising individuals.

Conventional (C) – Individuals with this code typically enjoy organization, data, numbers, and details. Good matches for the conventional code are careers that involve understanding processes, developing systems, analyzing numbers and data, and managing finances.

to help you select a major that fits your interests, skills, and career goals. OU's Major Exploration Coaches help you to discover your options and to decide on an academic major by administering interest assessment tests and by sharing their expert knowledge of OU majors and careers.

Finding and declaring a major should be a deliberate process, and the University College Assessment Center offers a variety of free resources to help, including:

- Online and in-office career assessments
- Worksheets for identifying interests, values, and skills
- Walk-in and by-appointment sessions to:
    » Interpret assessment outcomes
    » Identify academic and occupational relationships
- Seminars and presentations for student groups or organizations
- Annual Majors/Minors Fair each Spring

Now that you have had a chance to reflect on your Holland's Codes, use the online tool from OU Career Services to explore career options that may suit your personality.

ou.edu/career/students/choose-a-major/explore/holland-codes.html

Find 2-3 career matches that interest you, and discuss what you find appealing about them.

2) Exploration

If you are like most students, your parents have been the primary influence on the career knowledge you have at this point in your life. You have also possibly formulated ideas about careers by your exposure to television and other media. Unfortunately, many times, these sources do not provide a complete and accurate picture of any given profession. Therefore, you may have come to college without the breadth of knowledge needed to make accurate career decisions. The Exploration Stage involves purposefully learning what careers exist and what they entail. It is important to be open-minded when exploring careers because there are so many options to consider. There is a plethora of career information available, and you will need to learn how to locate, evaluate, and interpret accurate career information in order to be successful in this stage.

The internet can be an excellent source for accurate career information, but only if you find reliable sources. A couple of places to start include:

- *O*NET OnLine* (**onetonline.org**) - Provides accessible and detailed occupational descriptions that are useful to students, job seekers, employers, and researchers who are exploring and searching careers.

- *Occupational Outlook Handbook* (**bls.gov/ooh**) - Provides information on salaries, working conditions, required training, and projections for the availability of various occupations.

While exploring careers, you will find occupations grouped together into classifications. The *Standard Occupational Classification System* is the system used by the U.S. federal government that categorizes occupations with similar duties, education, training, and/or skills. This organization should help you find and understand how certain fields relate to one another.

In addition to conducting web-based research and taking classes, there are other ways for you to explore and investigate careers. Some of the most effective steps include:

Informational Interviews
In an *informational interview*, you interview professionals currently practicing in a career of interest, in order to learn more about the occupation. Questions you might ask a professional include:
-- *What are you primary responsibilities in your job?*
-- *What do you like most about your position?*
-- *What is your least favorite aspect of your job?*
-- *What advice would you give to a student preparing to enter this career?*

Shadowing
Shadowing is the process of observing an employee in her/his work environment, in order to learn more about a profession. Shadowing is a quick and easy way for you to see, firsthand, aspects of a career that may or may not interest you.

Narrowing the Search
In order to narrow your search, take time to evaluate how the information you gained during the exploration stage applies to what you learned about yourself in the assessment stage. There are many facets of a career that you should consider, during this process. For example: How do advancements in technology and/or global markets impact this career? How competitive is this particular field? Is it overcrowded? Is this a rapidly-growing career field?

After you have gathered the necessary information and made appropriate considerations, you should be ready to narrow your search to one or two career possibilities. Do not pressure yourself to believe that whatever career you choose now is the only career path you will ever have an opportunity to pursue. The number of career changes

Major Exploration Coaching

The coach of an athlete does not play the game. The athlete does. The coach helps the player understand the game and prepare for the game, but the athlete is who does the work and makes the decisions during the game. In the same way, our Major Exploration Coaches help you prepare for deciding on your major, but you are the one who will do the work and make the final decision. Major Exploration Coaches have three goals when meeting with students: to help students understand themselves, their options, and the decision-making process. Coaches help you to better understand yourself, through the use of interviews and interest inventory tests. They will discuss your options by reviewing the majors and your academic situation. Part of this process includes debunking myths about majors and careers in order for you to have a clearer understanding. Lastly, coaches will help you walk through the process of making a decision, which may include you gathering more information through research or interviews. Perhaps the biggest service our coaches provide to students is objectivity. Students can voice ideas and concerns to a neutral person who supports their decision making process.

Box 5.3

that individuals experience in a lifetime is increasing as individuals are working longer and as factors, such as promotions and resignations, are a part of every career. Many of you will experience what has been coined as a "boundary-less career" (Arthur & Rousseau, 1996). Unlike the former generations, when individuals joined companies as young adults and then retired from them several decades later, many of you will experience careers which include a variety of employers, specializations, and even industries. Consequently, you will likely change jobs multiple times throughout your lifespan, and your career decisions will continue to be shaped by your life stages.

3) Preparation
During the Preparation Stage, you will use the information you have learned about yourself and about available careers to plan what you hope to achieve professionally. You will also develop a strategy for how to gain the knowledge and skills that will properly prepare you to reach these goals. Even though "the working world" may seem far off, career

preparation should begin early. It is important for you to build your knowledge and skills, in order to establish a strong foundation for career success. According to Asher (2004), the number one predictor of your first job after college is the last job you held before graduating from college. Therefore, it is important for you to gain purposeful experiences now that will lead to the vocation you desire. In order to do so, you will want to engage in many of the following activities during this stage:

Networking

Networking is making contacts within your field in order to help you discover career possibilities and insights. Networking is about making connections that can enhance your awareness of trends in the field, your understanding of steps that have led to success for others, and your name-recognition among other professionals in your interest area. You can network either by contacting professionals outright or by contacting friends and acquaintances who might be able to introduce you to others. Traditionally, these connections have been made face-to-face or via telephone. However, today, many people are also using social networking websites, such as LinkedIn, to expand their professional network.

Volunteering

Volunteering at an organization can give you valuable insights into how it operates. Volunteer work can also help you make connections for networking, and can even familiarize staff members with your interests and your work ethic, should they suddenly need a new employee.

Summer Jobs/Part-time Jobs

Think ahead about what skills you should acquire for your anticipated field, and consider jobs that will help you to develop these skillsets before you graduate.

Internships

Career-related internships are a great way to gain the necessary work experience and qualifications that employers look for in recent graduates. You can take advantage of these temporary opportunities during the summer or the school year. You should consider full-time and part-time prospects, as well as internships that are paid or unpaid.

Preparation for International Students

Choosing a career and searching for a job can be overwhelming for any student. As an international student, you have the additional decision of whether to seek post-graduate employment in your home country, in the U.S., or within yet another country. If you choose to stay in the U.S., you will have to obtain authorization to become a legal employee.

There are extra complexities for international students who lack understanding of the U.S. employment regulations or who are unaware of the impact that career choice can have on a job search. Therefore, the first step in your job search process should be to seek employment information from the campus International Student Services Office and, perhaps, also from an experienced immigration attorney. It is also crucial to know if the degree you are pursuing is currently in demand in the U.S. job market. Hiring trends by region and by industry are available online at the Bureau of Labor Statistics website, *www.bls. gov.*

OU's Career Counselors can help you with your specific needs concerning your resume, your search for internship opportunities, and other tasks that might be more complex because of your foreign citizenship.

Attend campus career fairs and company information sessions to find out which employers are legally able to hire international employees, as not all companies can. Utilize Going Global and Passport Career, two online resources available at *hiresooner.ou.edu* to conduct research by company name or by the hiring trends for international students.

Box 5.4

4) Execution

After you have prepared for your next career move, it will be time to execute! The Execution Stage involves cover letter and resume writing, job searching, and interviewing. All of these processes are necessary for you to obtain the employment you desire. This stage will require you to maintain a positive outlook as you proactively and diligently utilize your resources to seek prospective opportunities. In order to be most effective, this will take commitment and persistence on your part. You can gain assistance with your search from OU Career Services or an employment agency. You can also get job leads and referrals from the people in your network. Additionally, you might consider joining and maintaining membership with a professional organization associated with your field of interest.

There are many factors that can impact the amount of time it takes you to find employment, including: economic conditions, the job market, or the location of your job search. It is important that you stay actively involved in the process in order to make appropriate progress. Employers will want to know that you have both a broad knowledge about many areas and specific skills necessary for your particular field of interest. Be ready to market yourself and to demonstrate why you should not only be called for an interview, but also should be offered the open position. For some professions, you might consider creating a personal website, a portfolio, and/or tailoring your résumé.

Post-Graduation Career Selection

Transitioning to your first job after college will be an adjustment similar to the one you are going through now, as a new student at OU. You will want to remind yourself of your personality traits, interests, values, and skills, so you can be sure that potential opportunities are a good match for you. If you are like most people, you will spend more waking hours on the job, during your working years, than anywhere else. As a result, finding a satisfying career can contribute greatly to your feelings of overall happiness and to your personal fulfillment post-graduation. Finding the right vocation can also create opportunities for you to contribute to society in a way that is meaningful to you. As a matter of fact, many people consider professional success to be achieving a career that provides opportunities to practice and develop preferred skills, to attain personal benefits and rewards, and to exercise their potential. You can conceptualize this idea as the 3 P's to Professional Success.

Preferred Skills Developed + Personal Benefits Received + Potential Exercised = Professional Success

When the time comes, you should also be sure not to overestimate the salary range for a given position or

What Employers Look for in New Graduates

What any employer in any industry wants in an employee can be summed up in one word: Fit. Companies and organizations want employees who match all aspects of a job, whether it is a required skill set or the personal traits and maturity typical for that organization's work culture. Let's examine each part of those needs.

Skills needed to be accountants, information technologists, or engineers are very specific, and the academic programs for these majors teach these skills. Your résumé for these types of positions should demonstrate these specific abilities prominently.

Other positions require less-specialized, but still definable, skills. Often referred to as "transferable skills," these assets are valued across many types of positions, including in specialized roles. Abilities such as writing, presentation or speaking skills, analytic ability, negotiation, and project management are assets in many job searches. This means that candidates with these "above and beyond" skill sets get asked back for more interviews. Be sure to include these assets in your skill listings.

Personality traits are equally important. You need to demonstrate that you can perform in team situations and can contribute to a collegial environment. Your work ethic, the discipline with which you approach your job, is vitally important. How you approach and solve problems, manage time, or lead a team will often make the difference between success and failure on the job. The techniques interviewers use and the questions they ask are designed to probe these areas of your personality. What employers want may vary from position to position, so think about what you do well and about how that will benefit the employer. Then, be able to express that.

Box 5.5

underestimate the intensity of work for that particular job. Once you are in your new position, be prepared to balance the need to learn the various aspects of your role over time with a readiness to make the contributions you can as quickly as possible. However tempting it may be, it is not sensible for you to base your job satisfaction on how easy it

Interview Tips

The interview is an opportunity for you to convince the employer that you have the skills, experiences, goals, and personal traits that make you the ideal person for the given position. You may think that all you have to do is be yourself, and if they like you, they will hire you. However, interviewing takes a lot more preparation.

First, it is important that you research the company. Showing enthusiasm about not only the position, but also the company as a whole, conveys commitment and passion, two important qualifications to employers.

You also need to prepare by anticipating questions that the interviewer might ask and by practicing answers that highlight your specific strengths. The content of your answers should be clear, logical, and relevant, and you should substantiate your answers by providing examples from past experiences.

Nonverbal communication is essential to your interview success. Greet the interviewer in a friendly, but professional, manner, and introduce yourself confidently with a firm handshake. Once in the interview room, wait to be offered a seat, and sit upright with confident posture. Maintain eye contact throughout the interview, and smile pleasantly.

Finally, always come prepared with 2-3 questions to ask the employer at the end of the interview. Asking questions shows interest and also allows you to evaluate whether this position or company is an appropriate fit for you.

Career Services offers mock interviews so that you may practice in a formal setting with a real interviewer who will give you feedback and answer any questions that you may have. Although interviewing can feel intimidating, remember that it is your time to shine!

---

is to perform your job responsibilities. Like college, some of the most exciting rewards can come out of tasks that require hard work and dedication.

Career Services

The University of Oklahoma's Career Services is a centralized office that helps OU students in the areas of career exploration, career development, internships and co-ops, and application to graduate school and professional employment upon graduation. The programs in this office assist students in exploring majors and careers, developing job search skills, implementing the job search, and connecting with hundreds of employers. The Career Services staff is committed to assisting students in making the transition from academic life to a chosen career.

The Career Services staff provides assistance in three ways. First, staff members can help you to identify career options and to develop a plan for exploring them. Second, they provide resources—both online and in Career Services— to help you develop your job search skills and to plan and

implement your individual job search strategy. Third, if you are seeking a job or internship, staff members will help you access employers through on-campus interview programs. Career Services also provides online access to *OptimalResume.com*, a comprehensive, web-based tool to create, present, and manage your résumés. The staff is available each week by appointment or during scheduled walk-in hours. Career advisors are familiar with careers related to your major and can assist you in choosing a major or career. For quick questions about topics such as résumés, cover letters, and job search strategies, a Career Consultant is available each week during scheduled walk-in hours.

Throughout this chapter, you have had some time to explore your interests and available careers.

Determine a few resources that could help you in pursuing the career path of your choice.

How can you start utilizing these resources?

HELPFUL WEB RESOURCES

Resource	Purpose	Location
Degree Check Sheet	Academic major requirements	checksheets.ou.edu
Academic Interests	Overview of undergraduate majors	ou.edu/content/go2/academics
Course Catalogue	Description of courses in each major	catalog.ou.edu/courses/
Student Life	List of student organizations	ou.edu/studentlife
Career Services	Career-related assistance (e.g. internships, resumes, etc.) Major and career exploration Videos about a variety of careers	ou.edu/career ou.edu/career/students/choose-a-major/explore/wcidwami ou.edu/career/students/choose-a-major/explore
Occupational Outlook Handbook	Job descriptions and outlook	bls.gov/oco
Explore Health Careers	Descriptions of all health professions	explorehealthcareers.org
OU Health Science Center	Academic requirements Job shadowing opportunities	ouhsc.edu/colleges.aspx ah.ouhsc.edu/main/observation/map.asp
Free! Major Exploration Coaching	Receive one-on-one assistance to find your major	ladvise.ou.edu/majors

Figure 5.3

Values in the Workplace Quiz
Adapted from quintcareers.com

Rate the degree of importance that you place on each of the following workplace values using a scale of 1-10 with 1 being not important at all and 10 being very important.

____ variety of work

____ mental challenge/problem solving

____ physical challenge/physically demanding

____ opportunity for balance between work life and family life

____ flexibility in work schedule

____ intellectual status i.e. an acknowledged "expert" in a given field

____ order and structure

____ high degree of competition

____ rewarding loyalty and dependability

____ having self-respect and pride in work

____ stability and job security

____ strong financial compensation

____ being recognized for quality of work in a visible/public way

____ having a positive impact on others and society

____ using creativity, imagination; being innovative

____ variety and a changing workplace

____ professional development and on-going learning and growth

____ teamwork and work groups

____ significance, prestige, respect, or a level of social status

____ routine, predictable work projects

____ deadlines and time demands

____ clear advancement tracks/opportunities for advancement

____ tranquility, comfort, and avoidance of pressure

____ dealing with the public/day-to-day contact with the public

____ using cutting edge or pioneering technologies or techniques

____ opportunities for supervision, power, leadership, influence

____ having the power to make the decisions

____ autonomy, independence, freedom

____ precision/attention to detail

____ adventure and excitement

____ location

____ opportunities for travel

Now, that you have completed the assessment, take time to identify the 10 most important values to you. Circle each of these from the list on the previous page.

Once you have the list of your top 10 core values in the workplace, the next step is to narrow down your list to the five core values that are most important to you. Think about these 5 values as the ones you can't live without in your job/workplace. List these below.

1. _____

2. _____

3. _____

4. _____

5. _____

Congratulations! You now have a list of core workplace values that represent the values that will help determine your level of satisfaction with your job and career.

Before deciding which career path you will go down, it is important to identify the nature of the work you will be doing and how well it aligns with your interests, values, skills, and personality. Here are some other items to consider when exploring careers:

☑ Identify the education or training that is required to enter and progress in the field and determine if you are willing to pursue that educational track.

☑ Research projected outlook and trends in the field using various tools (i.e. *onetonline.org*).

☑ Consider the monetary and nonmonetary rewards.

☑ Make a list of personal advantages and disadvantages of working in the field.

References

Arthur, M.B., & Rousseau, D.M. (1996). *The boundaryless career: A new employment principle for a new organizational era.* New York: Oxford University Press.

Asher, D. (2013). How to get any job with any major [Majors/Minors Fair speaker]. Norman, OK.

Asher, D. (2004). *How to get any job with any major: Career launch & re-launch for everyone under 30 or (how to avoid living in your parents' basement).* Berkeley, CA: Ten Speed Press.

Friedman, S. (2008). *Total leadership: Be a better leader, have a richer life.* Cambridge, MA: Harvard Business School Press.

Metz, A.J. (2005). Selecting instruments and exercises to facilitate the career development of students in transition. In P.A. Gore, Jr. (Ed.), *Facilitating the career development of students in transition* (Monograph No. 43, pp. 27-44). Columbia, SC: University of South Carolina, National Resource Center for the First-Year Experience and Students in Transition.

Perez-Pena, R. (2012). U.S. bachelor degree rate passes milestone. *The New York Times.* Retrieved from http://www.nytimes.com/2012/02/24/education/census-finds-bachelors-degrees-at-record-level.html?_r=0.

Reardon, R. C., & Lenz, J. J. (1998). *The self-directed search and related Holland career materials: A practitioner's guide.* Lutz: Psychological Assessment Recources, Inc.

U.S. Census Bureau (2012). Current population survey, 2012 annual social and economic supplement. Retrieved from http://www.census.gov/hhes/socdemo/education/data/cps/2012/tables.html.

U.S. Department of Education, Family Policy Compliance Office (2011). The family educational rights and privacy act guidance for eligible students. Retrieved from http://www2.ed.gov/policy/gen/guid/fpco/ferpa/for-eligible-students.pdf.

Chapter 5 REI

Investigating Your Options

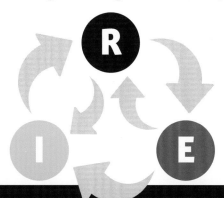

R ## Reflect

Think about a career you may be interested in pursuing after graduation. Who or what has influenced your career interests up until this point?

....

E ## Engage

Take the Values Quiz on pages 93-94 in Chapter 5.

....

I ## Impact

What were your top five most important work values? Do you see those values reflected in your career of choice? What desires would you be willing to give up, so that you stay true to things you value most?

....

Chapter 6

Understanding Self and Others: *Social, Emotional, and Cultural Competence*

Elizabeth Kendrick, Ph.D., Former Adjunct Instructor, Freshman Programs
Sunny Wenger, M.Ed., Adjunct Instructor, Freshman Programs

In this chapter, you will:

- Gain an understanding of social and emotional intelligence.

- Explore relationships and learn how to foster positive connections with others.

- Increase awareness of your attitudes toward others.

- Recognize the importance of developing cultural competency and embracing differences.

"He who knows others is wise. He who knows himself is enlightened."

- Lao Tzu, Ancient Chinese Philosopher

Starting your first semester at OU marks the beginning of an exciting journey, filled with increased independence, expanded opportunities, and important life choices. During this time, students often experience changes in current relationships, while also building new ones. In addition, attending college can introduce new experiences of interacting with people from widely-varying backgrounds. With all of these changes, it is not unusual for students to feel an array of emotions. Developing emotional and social intelligence is key to successfully navigating this new chapter in your life.

Emotional Intelligence

Emotional intelligence is awareness and monitoring of one's emotions; awareness of the emotional cues of others; and, responding in a way that facilitates positive social interactions. According to Daniel Goleman (2003), emotional intelligence stems from five core components: self-awareness, self-regulation, motivation, empathy, and social skills.

Self-Awareness

Self-awareness is being conscious of your own emotions, thoughts, and behaviors, as well as their impact on others. Self-awareness also includes being honest about your strengths, weaknesses, values, and needs (Goleman, 1998). Some people tend to be naturally introspective, but for others, becoming self-aware is a challenge. The good news is that self-awareness can be developed. While there are many paths to increased self-awareness, journaling and asking others are two ways that we will discuss.

Journaling is one way of improving your self-awareness, especially if you focus on answering the following questions each time you write:

- What am I feeling in this moment? (Try to be as specific as possible.)
- Why am I feeling this emotion?
- What specific thoughts are impacting me today?
- How have I treated myself today?
- How have I behaved toward others today?
- How have others responded to me today?
- Were there specific behaviors of mine that contributed to the responses of others?

Another means of developing self-awareness is by asking others, particularly those you trust, to provide you with honest feedback about how you impact them and what they perceive to be your strengths and weaknesses. While it is natural to appreciate receiving positive feedback, hearing about areas of weakness may be incredibly valuable to you as well. Such feedback provides you with awareness of opportunities to make changes that may improve your relationships and may enhance your emotional intelligence. Therefore, when asking about your impact on others, it is important that you not become defensive. Remember, honest feedback from someone who cares about you is a gift and a means of increasing your emotional intelligence.

Self-Regulation

Self-regulation is the management of your thoughts, emotions, impulses, and energies (Goleman, 1998). Emotions, impulses, and urges – even negative ones – are a normal and healthy part of life. In fact, emotions serve an important adaptive function. For example, fear and anxiety motivate people to act in self-preserving ways (e.g. when you see a snake and feel afraid, that fear motivates you to move away from the danger). Even moderate anxiety over a test can be helpful because it can help motivate you to take steps to avoid the thing you fear (making a poor grade on the exam). Emotions only become problematic when they interfere with your ability to function well (e.g. if your anxiety over your test becomes so severe that you cannot focus on studying) or if they become harmful to your relationships.

Developing self-regulation is important to your success at OU, both academically and socially. It can help you develop self-control. Here are a few steps you can follow to aid in developing self-regulation:

Identify Your Emotions – Learn to reflect on what feelings you are experiencing.

Example:
"Am I feeling irritable? Is that irritability stemming from a deeper feeling of nervousness that I won't do well on my class presentation? Am I feeling fear that, if I mess up, everyone will look down on me?"

Identify the Thoughts behind the Emotions – Reflect on what dominant thoughts accompany your negative feelings. Remember that your thinking plays a large role in how you feel.

Example:
"If I stutter during my class presentation, everyone will laugh. So, I must not stutter, or I'll be a failure and people will make fun of me."

Evaluate Your Thoughts Realistically – Try to be as honest about your thoughts as though you were an objective outsider, assessing how realistic they are. Weigh your thoughts against the evidence.

Example:
"It is true to that some people might laugh if I stutter during my presentation. But, most people probably will not laugh. In fact, some of them might actually feel compassion for me since they may have fears of the same thing happening to them. Even if I do stutter, it doesn't mean I'm a failure. It just means that I was nervous, and everyone gets nervous at some point. And, it is not likely that anyone will even remember, a year from now, that I stuttered in one class presentation."

Replace Your Negative Thoughts with Logical, Reality-Based Thoughts - Training yourself to replace negative thoughts with realistic thoughts takes time and practice, but the benefits to successfully regulating your emotions are huge.

Example:

"There is a possibility that I will stutter during my presentation. If I do, it will be uncomfortable, but I can handle it. I suspect that other students in the class have the same fears, so they might be quietly feeling supportive of me. There is also the possibility that I will not stutter and that everyone will be impressed by my speaking abilities. Whatever the outcome, I can handle it."

Possible Selves

Thinking about who you want to become in the future can be a motivator to work hard today. *Possible selves are ideas of who you dream of becoming and who you fear you might become* (Markus & Nurius, 1986). Maybe you dream of being well-spoken, physically fit, and humorous. Your possible selves also include your fears of who you might become, such as becoming boring, lazy, or someone others do not like to be around. Your possible selves help by guiding your choices away from the person you do not want to become and toward the person you hope to be. As you begin your journey as a Sooner Citizen, let your possible selves motivate you to grow and develop academically, personally, and as a community member.

Possible Selves: Questions for Thought

1. Who do you fear you will become? – List as many traits as possible.

2. Who do you dream of becoming? – List as many qualities as possible.

Empathy

Empathy is the ability to connect with the feelings and perspectives of others. Essentially, empathy might be described as mentally and emotionally stepping outside yourself and "seeing a situation through another's eyes." Empathy is an important component of healthy relationships. By empathizing, you are better able to be open-minded about the needs of the other person, which can help you show support and reach compromises during conflict. Further, when others sense empathy from you, it is easier for them to trust and feel close to you.

Affective empathy refers to the sensations and feelings we get in response to others' emotions. This can include parallel affective empathy or mirroring another person's emotions such as feeling sad when someone else feels sad, or reactive affective empathy such as when one feels anger when another person feels fearful or sad from mistreatment.

One of the key components of intercultural communication is *cognitive empathy*, sometimes called "perspective taking," *which refers to our ability to identify and understand other people's' experiences and possible reasons for their emotions.* The process of cognitive empathy contributes to increases in cognitive complexity and the ability to think critically in complex social relationships and problem solving—something that employers value as this leads to innovative thinking across groups and in teams.

Cognitive empathy can be learned. Research shows that when people learn that empathy is a skill that can be improved rather than a fixed personal trait, they engaged in more effort to empathize with groups other than their own. Research also shows that even disfluent non-eloquent statements of empathy work to encourage perspective taking and understanding for the speaker, listener and those witnessing the perspective taking between people. Cognitive empathy or perspective taking reduces categorical thinking and the mechanisms of prejudice between people from different identity groups.

Social Skills

The obvious reason for attending OU is to improve your career possibilities through academic development. But, building a successful career requires more than earning a degree. Developing effective social skills is also important to your future career. Possessing quality social skills plays a significant role in whether you will do well in a job interview, whether you will climb the career ladder, and whether you will form social networks that build your career. On a personal level, well-developed social skills help you to establish a support system and a means of connecting with others.

Communication

Communication is often thought of as simply talking, but communication involves much more than the words you use. It involves the way you speak, your tone of voice, the

"HELLO, MY NAME IS" TIPS FOR REMEMBERING NAMES

Repeat: When you meet someone, you will generally hear their name within the first few seconds of introductions. Pause, and immediately ask them to repeat their name. When responding, you might say "'Nice to meet you Courtney. My name is Caleb." Finally, do not forget to repeat their name at the end of your conversation. For example, "Hey, it was really nice to meet you, Courtney. Maybe we'll run into each other later."

Label: Practice word association. If you enjoy books, TV shows, or movies, you might associate "Courtney" with a character or an actor (e.g. Courtney Cox from *Friends*). Maybe you learned that Courtney loves to play tennis, so you might associate her name with a tennis court. It has been said that Theodore Roosevelt had an impressive knack for remembering names. His trick was imagining people's names written on their foreheads, connecting their image with their name. You may also associate Courtney with your first impression of her, where you met, or even a distinguishing characteristic, such as her auburn hair.

Digitize: Once you know someone's name, you can use technology to keep a log of the people you have met. If you are serious about remembering people, keep a list on your computer or phone to help jog your memory. Social media sites can also help tremendously when trying to connect a name with a face.

Box 6.1

facial expressions you use, your eye contact, and your body language. It also involves your patterns of interacting with others. And, most importantly, communication involves listening.

Verbal communication - An important component of communicating is thinking about how your words will affect your listener and adjusting what you say and how you say it, in order to make your ideas clear to the unique person in front of you (e.g. taking into account their age, background, education level, emotional state, etc.). For example, you would use different words to talk with a child

than with a graduate student. Additionally, remember that the way you speak is shaped by the type of relationship you have with your listener. Your conversation with the Provost will be more professional, while conversations with your roommate will be more casual. Verbal communication also takes into account the emotional state of your listener. For example, if the person appears irritable, you will want to use calming language. Learning to adapt your choice of words to match the circumstances is a piece of social intelligence.

Listening - It is often said that listening is more important to communication than speaking. Listening allows you to better understand the needs, concerns, and feelings of the person with whom you are communicating. This awareness will help you to recognize what words and tones are most appropriate for the conversation.

Active listening is hearing with the goal of understanding what the speaker is trying to say and communicating that awareness to them. When actively listening, you are not trying to formulate a response in your mind while the other person is talking. Instead, you are fully devoted to grasping both the actual words and the nonverbal communication (facial expressions, tone of voice, body language, etc.) of the person speaking.

You may also check with the other person to ensure that you understood them correctly. You can use your body language to communicate this understanding and support (e.g. leaning forward and nodding your head). Talking to someone whom you can tell really hears what you have to say and cares about understanding is a precious gift.

Active listening helps speakers organize and prioritize their thoughts. By asking good questions of clarification (rather than rhetorical questions or persuasive questions), the active listener helps the speaker feel at ease and have a sense of voice and self when speaking. Active listeners also help their own memories and ability to recall information and focus on what is being said. Humans are socially cognitive creatures and active listening, even with minimal nodding and statements of "okay," and "hmm..." help both the speaker and listener think more clearly. This is why study groups are so effective and face-to-face teamwork in the work place are so commonplace. Active listening is also a skill necessary for developing cognitive empathy or perspective taking across groups. It is important to be open-minded and practice civility when actively listening, as you might occasionally disagree with something someone else says. Debating is a healthy part of learning, as long as both sides are willing to be open-minded and actively listen to what the other is saying.

Nonverbal Communication - When looking to begin new friendships and connections at OU, you may want to consider the nonverbal cues you are sending out to others. Smiling, maintaining open body posture, and engaging in eye contact are great ways to foster relationships on campus.

- Smile – Never underestimate the power of a smile. Individuals are more likely to approach someone who seems pleasant than someone who appears disinterested or detached.

- Body Language – Think about your posture. How are you standing? Are you arms crossed, or is your back to the crowd? You are going to be more approachable if your stance is open. Leaning in can also communicate that you are eager to make a connection and are interested in what the speaker has to say. If you lean away, you are sending the message that something is wrong, that you are uncomfortable, or that you are evaluating the other person in some way.

- Eye Contact – Look people in the eyes, and avoid gazing at the ground or away when you interact with them. Eye contact sends the message that you are interested, while avoiding eye contact is a social cue that you do not want to connect with the other person.

"I know that you believe you understand what you think I said, but I'm not sure you realize that what you heard is not what I meant."
-Robert McCloskey

Communication Styles

In addition to your verbal and nonverbal communication, you also have a communication style. There are four communication styles that people use: passive, aggressive, passive-aggressive, and assertive. As you read the following descriptions of each communication style, reflect on which communication style is typical for you.

Passive

People with a passive communication style have difficulty saying "no" to others. They often find it challenging to speak their opinions if there is a possibility that others will disagree, and they are not likely to speak up when someone is hurting or offending them.

Individuals with a passive communication style often feel silently frustrated or hurt that their feelings and needs are not being met. They often expect others to naturally "know" what they need, and they may feel betrayed when those needs are not met. Since they have difficulty saying "no," they frequently become over-committed, and feel used as a result.

Aggressive

Individuals with an aggressive communication style are prone to pushing their ideas on others in a forceful manner that is disrespectful of others' needs and/or feelings. They may make demeaning comments, yell, or engage in hurtful behaviors during conflicts.

People with an aggressive communication style often have difficulties in relationships because others find it difficult to work through conflicts with them and because others do not feel safe to be vulnerable around them. After all, no one wants to share an area of weakness with someone who may use that knowledge against them in a future conflict.

Passive-Aggressive

People with a passive-aggressive communication style use subtle actions (or inactions), rather than words, to communicate their negative feelings toward others. For example, they may invite everyone in a group to lunch except the person with whom they are angry. Or, they may intentionally not return phone calls in order to send a message that they are hurt. The "silent treatment" or the "cold shoulder" is a form of passive-aggressive communication. Sometimes, people with this communication style include little barbs in their jokes, and when the recipient feels hurt by the jab, they might respond with, "Don't be so sensitive. It was only a joke."

Individuals with a passive-aggressive communication style often create frustration in their relationships because others can sense that something is wrong, but find it hard to resolve the problem without an open discussion. This communication style is often distancing to others, since others may feel confused about how to work through difficulties with the passive-aggressive individual.

Assertive

Individuals who use an assertive communication style do not avoid difficult conversations. Instead, they approach such conversations with a willingness to demonstrate respect toward the other person. They openly discuss their needs, concerns, and desires, but without belittling or harming others. They do not avoid conflict, but they also refrain from becoming aggressive or passive-aggressive. They attempt to achieve communication that respects their own needs and the needs of others.

The assertive communication style is considered the healthiest approach to communication. It allows for difficulties to be addressed and needs to be acknowledged, and it does so in a manner that fosters supportive relationships.

"When asked the one statement of advice I might give students for their education and for living well, I have one standard answer: 'PAY ATTENTION!' This sounds simple enough, but it is the most difficult challenge of all. It requires that we be attentive to ourselves, the people around us, the systems of which we are part, and the world itself. To put it another way, I challenge students to 'be awake and aware.' Only by this means can we begin to order and direct ourselves to desired ends."

- Dr. Tom W. Boyd, David Ross Boyd Professor Emeritus of Philosophy and Professor of Religious Studies

Relationships

Changing Relationships

Beginning your journey at OU may introduce changes in your relationships. Although you may stay in touch with high school friends, the physical distance means much of your time will be spent away from those you know well. However, you also have the opportunity to build a new network of relationships at OU. Meeting new people and developing quality relationships provides you with a support system for achieving your goals and encourages a positive connection with the university.

Homesickness

Kelley is a freshman in his first week at OU, and even though he's excited about starting college, he is struggling with homesickness. When he walks across campus and does

---

Dealing with Homesickness

If you are dealing with homesickness, remember that any given emotion will eventually subside, and most of the time, the long-term impact of a situation is not nearly as bad as we imagine it. When impact bias is getting the best of you, it helps to step back and think about how the situation might look different and more positive in six months. Then, think of steps you can take, right now, to move toward that more positive place. You should also know that many of your peers are also going through the same thing. Take comfort in knowing that you are not alone. Flexibility and openness to new experiences will help you transition through homesickness. Getting involved, meeting new people, and interacting with others helps create connections to OU, and these connections are what will eventually make this university feel like home. If homesickness grows into anxiety or depression, talk to your Resident Adviser or a counselor at Goddard Health Center.

Goddard Health Center
University Counseling Center: 325-2911

University Housing
Adams Center Office: 325-4802
Cate Center Office: 325-2411
Couch Center Office: 325-0867
Walker Center Office: 325-1277

Box 6.2

---

not see anyone he knows, he feels deep sadness and misses his friends and family. Kelley is starting to think that he will never feel comfortable with living this far from home. When he thinks of the next four years at OU, all he can imagine is year after year of loneliness. He wonders if college is even the right choice for him.

In addition to feeling homesick, Kelley is also experiencing what social scientists call "impact bias." *Impact bias* is our tendency to overestimate how long and how deeply an event will affect us, when we are experiencing particularly intense emotions (Gilbert & Wilson, 2000). Impact bias can make painful or frustrating situations feel even more unbearable because it seems they will never end. In Kelley's case, he does not realize that, a year from now, he will have made great friends at OU and, while he will still miss home, he will have found many things he likes about living at OU.

Parents

Moving away to college will likely change your relationship with your parents. You, your parents, your siblings, and perhaps other family members each must transition, as everyone adapts to no longer living in the same home. This process of separation may bring about different emotions, and oftentimes, the parent-child relationship becomes strained. The move to college is often highlighted by excitement from your parents, as they celebrate this new phase, yet tinted with sadness about their sense of loss and an "empty nest." You may feel elated by your newfound freedom, but you may also feel homesickness as you miss your family, the conveniences of home, or the family pet. Successfully navigating this transition requires patience, support, and empathy with your family members, as each of you go through this time of change.

Roommates

A hallmark of emotional intelligence is the ability to know oneself and to see situations from another's perspective. Students are often tested in this area when it comes to roommate relationships.

Moving to college often means living in dorms. OU is a residential university, which means the university requires students to live on campus for the first year. There are two main reasons for this policy:

Sooners Ask for Consent

- Consent is the act of willingly agreeing, through words or actions, to engage in sexual conduct. Both of you are enthusiastic, equally engaged, and what is happening is mutual.
- Silence cannot be interpreted as consent. "No" always means "No," and the absence of "No" may not mean "Yes." When a person is silent, it usually means they aren't comfortable or they are unsure of what is happening.
- Saying "yes" to one activity doesn't imply consent to other sexual activities. Also, just because a person is okay with engaging in something with you once, doesn't mean they are required to do so again in the future.
- In order to give effective consent, one must have the capacity to consent. The most common cause of incapacity is through the use of alcohol or other drugs.
- Previous relationships or past consent does not imply consent to future sexual acts. A person has the right to change their mind about sexual activity at any time, whether in a relationship or not.
- You can't get consent by using physical force, compelling, threats, intimidating behavior, or coercion. Coercion is unreasonable pressure for sexual activity. Saying things to make the other person feel bad or guilty about not wanting to do something is not okay.

Box 6.3

Building and maintaining the right kind of relationships are important to success and wellbeing. At OU, there are numerous campus activities where you can meet people with similar interests, goals, or backgrounds. Consider the following questions:

- Who are the top 5 people I spend the most time with?
- How are these people positively or negatively impacting me?
- Do I take advantage of opportunities to meet new people?
- Who are my role models?

1. The residence halls provide a safe "next step" living environment that bridges the gap between living at home and being on your own.
2. Living in the dorms provides you with a shared experience that fosters bonds with other students and with OU.

Bonds between you, your roommate, and your hall-mates can be fun, rewarding, and long-lasting. Sometimes, however, lifestyles clash and tempers flare if students do not communicate effectively about problems in their living situation.

Opening the lines of communication with your roommate helps to avoid future disagreements. One way to assist in reducing conflict is to establish "room rules." Your resident adviser (RA) can give you a roommate contract, which you and your roommate may use as a framework for establishing rules for your space. One mistake freshmen routinely make is not talking to their roommate about issues that bother them early in the semester. If your roommate has a habit of sleeping through their alarm and waking you in the process, it is best that you address the issue immediately. If you wait until later in the semester to talk about it, you risk allowing your emotions to build up and experiencing a dispute that could have been resolved much earlier.

Friendships

When you left your hometown to come to OU, you may have left a strong network of supportive friends and family. Now, you may find yourself having to start over and build new friendships and sources of support on campus.

Creating interpersonal relationships is a way of bolstering your feelings of acceptance and connection with others, as well as your overall happiness. Over-exposure or under-exposure to new connections on campus can significantly affect your OU experience. Ask yourself these questions:

- Am I lonely, even though I am surrounded by thousands of students on campus?
- Am I meeting people at such a fast pace that I have trouble remembering names?
- Do I find that I am often sitting in my dorm room or going off campus when others seem to be getting together on campus?
- Am I hanging out and attending so many activities that my studies and schoolwork are suffering?

Whether you are connecting too much or not at all, strive to strike a healthy balance between the two. It is also important to ensure that the quality of your friendships is more of a focus than the quantity. Additionally, when looking to create new friends and connections, make sure you seek people who will support your goals, not sabotage them.

Finally, find others who share your interests. A good place to start is by exploring the list of student groups in your OU Planner or on the Student Life page at *studentlife.ou.edu.* Attending activities or joining groups within your interest areas will automatically give you topics to discuss with new acquaintances and will open avenues for connection. Your

Spoonholder
Named after OU President William Bennett Bizzell, the round concrete bench in the middle of the North Oval was crafted by the Class of 1910 to be their class gift. Its nickname comes from its shape – it resembles the item you place on a stovetop to hold your stirring spoon. According to legend, students who kiss in the Spoonholder are destined to marry.

floor or hall is another place to make friends. University Housing does an amazing job of creating opportunities for residents to gather, and sharing living space automatically creates common experiences.

If you are lonely on campus, ask yourself if you are putting forth enough effort to create new friendships or if something else is holding you back. Loneliness can spur you to make connections, or it can develop into even deeper loneliness and increased isolation. If you find yourself more and more isolated, talk to a counselor at Goddard Health Center, to your Gateway Instructor, or to your resident adviser.

Meeting and Connecting with Others

The size of the OU campus can be overwhelming when trying to meet new people, but opportunities to connect with others are everywhere. Start by reading the information all around you. Across campus, there are signs, posters, people at tables in the Student Union or on the South Oval, and chalking on the sidewalks, all asking you to come listen, experience, learn, and connect. When something piques your interest, follow through. Attend the activity, speaking event, fundraiser, or volunteer opportunity. If you walk by without ever interacting with others, you are missing wonderful opportunities to integrate with the University of Oklahoma.

Cultural Competence

An important component of developing personal awareness and fostering healthy relationships is assessing how you interact with others who are different from you. Learning to be open to differences, to make sensitive changes to your behavior that will positively impact those around you, and to celebrate the many textures and nuances of the human experience are important to your growth as a Sooner citizen.

Stereotypes are broad generalizations about groups of people that ignore the uniqueness of each individual within the group. Stereotypes may be based upon some trait that truly is often a characteristic of many (but not all) people in the group (e.g. "Southerners speak with a drawl."), but stereotypes often exaggerate those characteristics and carelessly paint everyone in the group as having that characteristic ("Italians are loud."). Sometimes, stereotypes have little or no basis in reality, but are actually perpetuated by myths in the society (e.g. "Blondes are dumb, but they like to have fun."), or they may be ingrained into us by media messages (e.g. "Beautiful women are thin."). Stereotypes may range from seemingly innocent and harmless (e.g. "Librarians are quiet, studious, and polite.") to hurtful and marginalizing (e.g. "Mexican immigrants are here illegally," or "Muslims hate America and are dangerous."). Stereotypes may be negative (e.g. "Poor people aren't motivated.") or positive (e.g. "Asian students are smart."). While it is relatively apparent that negative stereotypes may be hurtful, it is also important to note that even seemingly positive stereotypes may be undermining. For example, in regard to the stereotype listed above, what if you are an Asian student who has a learning disorder? How would it impact you if others were always expecting you to be smart, just because you are Asian? How much more discouraging would it be to cope with your learning disability, when everyone expects you to be academically gifted?

So, why do people use stereotypes? The answer is not simple, but we will look at a few reasons, including: 1) to conserve mental energy through use of cognitive schemas, 2) to make the world feel more predictable, and 3) to bring a false sense of superiority.

As we go through each day, our minds have to process large amounts of information in a short amount of time. Part of how our brains cope with these tasks is by forming mental shortcuts that help us rapidly identify and assimilate information. A cognitive schema provides us with one type of mental shortcut. *Cognitive schemas* are mental maps of what to expect of certain items, places, situations, or people. We use these schemas throughout each day. For example, your cognitive schema of how to checkout at a supermarket is probably that you will stand in line until your turn; the cashier will scan your items, put them in bags, and give you a total price; and, you will hand her/him your payment and leave with your purchases. Since this schema is engrained,

your brain does not have to figure out what each step should be, each time you go to the store. You already know what to expect with little thought. People carry these schemas about places, too. For example, your cognitive schema of a library is probably that it will contain long rows of books, will be a quiet place, and will have a counter at which you may checkout books. Because you have this schema, you do not stop to think about what a library is, each time you go to borrow books. Your brain already has a short-cut.

Sometimes, we form schemas about groups of people, too, and these schemas often become stereotypes. It takes much less mental effort to quickly peg people into quick groups than to process the information about the unique person standing in front of you. For example, when someone says "surfer" to you, your cognitive schema will probably kick in with a particular expectation of how a surfer talks, dresses, and behaves. Your brain is saving mental energy, by having a shortcut ready for you.

Another reason that people sometimes use stereotypes is to try to predict what other people will do to gain an element of control in an unpredictable world. This may

Ableism – Defining a person's worth based on their physical or mental abilities, with individuals who have reduced abilities being considered inferior.

Ageism - Discrimination based upon age. Ageism includes the belief that older people are not as desirable and valuable as younger individuals. Ageism may also manifest in the view that young people are inferior, based upon the perception that they are not as mature or as capable as older individuals.

Classism - The belief that people from lower socioeconomic levels are inferior or deficient and that individuals from higher socioeconomic levels are more desirable and more valuable.

Ethnocentrism - Judging another culture based on the values of one's own culture. Ethnocentrism also includes the belief that one's own ethnicity is superior to other ethnicities.

Homophobia - The belief that people who are lesbian, gay, or bisexual are inferior to, or less desirable, than heterosexual individuals.

Racism - The belief that other races are inferior to one's own race.

Sexism - Prejudice or discrimination based on a person's sex. Sexist attitudes may stem from traditional stereotypes or gender roles. Sexism may also be evident in "benevolent sexism," in which women are treated as helpless, frail, and/ or in need of male protection.

Box 6.4

be particularly true of people encountering others from a group with whom they have previously had little or no contact. For example, if I do not know you, stereotyping may help me to feel more of a sense of control and as though I am able to anticipate what will happen. After all, I have a stereotype that supposedly tells me who you are and what you are likely to do. The problem, however, is that, by forming an idea about who you are, based on some limited characteristic(s) (e.g. how you dress, where you are from, what your skin color is, what gender you are), I am not really getting to know you. Instead, I am trying to predict who you are, based on my own ideas. While this may reduce my feelings of uncertainty about you, how does it feel, from your perspective, to realize that I have already decided who you are, before you have even had a chance to show me who you are?

Finally, a reason that some people hold negative stereotypes is to allow them to feel a sense of superiority over other groups of people. Each of us wants to feel a sense of pride in who we are, but people who hold negative stereotypes sometimes arrive at that pride by viewing people from other groups as inferior. This demonstrates a lack of civility, fairness and open-mindedness. A sign of true maturity and personal integrity is when we are able to feel good about ourselves by looking at who we are, what we are achieving, and how we are growing, rather than by looking down on others. True maturity looks at experiences with others as a means of learning and growing, rather than as a means of developing a social hierarchy.

Prejudice refers to negative attitudes, thoughts, and emotions toward other people, based on their membership in a particular group. For example, someone who dislikes a classmate because she is lesbian is engaging in prejudice. Prejudice is often rooted in faulty or exaggerated stereotypes, and we typically learn prejudicial attitudes from our social circles, our families, groups to which we belong, and from the media.

Discrimination is acting on prejudicial attitudes by behaving in a manner that diminishes another, restricts their opportunities, deprives them of rights, and/or relegates them to an inferior position. For example, a fraternity or sorority intentionally excluding African American students from their membership would be exercising discrimination.

Discrimination is a serious legal violation when it occurs in the work force or in the educational system.

It can be painful to be the recipient of prejudicial attitudes and/or discriminatory behavior, and it may threaten one's sense of safety and belonging, along with undermining one's sense of worth. If you have experienced prejudicial attitudes and/or discriminatory behavior, it is important that you not suffer alone and not be silent in your pain and/or anger. Reach out to someone you trust or to someone who has walked through these types of experiences. You may also want to become active in a group that supports individuals who have had similar experiences. If you are unsure of where to begin, the University Counseling Center at Goddard Health Center and/or OU Student Life may be helpful starting points.

Implicit bias refers to ingrained bias against certain groups of individuals that exist outside of your personal awareness, but which impacts your perceptions and your attitudes. You may test to see what implicit biases you hold for or against particular groups by visiting *implicit.harvard.edu.*

Overcoming Prejudicial Attitudes

If, as you have been reading this chapter, you have become aware of prejudicial attitudes you carry or discriminatory behaviors in which you have engaged, it might feel uncomfortable and embarrassing to see these traits in yourself. Sometimes, people feel guilty or ashamed when they realize that they have been holding attitudes that are hurtful to others. However, by being honest with yourself about your attitude, you can change these attitudes and behaviors. The first step toward meaningful change is realizing that there is a problem area and striving to find

Becoming Your Best Possible Self

Do you think it's possible to change the trajectory of your own life?

If you could change one thing about yourself to achieve the goal of becoming your best possible self, what would you change?

ways to become more open-minded. A starting point for growth might be reading books or watching documentaries on the experiences of people from the group toward whom you feel prejudice. Also, actively seek opportunities to interact with people from the group toward whom you feel prejudice, while being open to learning about their experiences and about how you impact them. Growth can be uncomfortable – even painful – at times, but developing intellecutal humility means admitting that we all have areas in which we can grow. Living life with integrity and with embracing of humankind can be a rich and precious experience.

Intergroup Dialogues and Cultural Competence

Intergroup Dialogues are a curricular practice where students develop cognitive empathy skills or perspective taking skills by exercising active listening to discuss differences and similarities across groups that are different from one's own and also within one's own group. Intergroup dialogues help students develop perspective competency in face to face structured discussions which leads to reductions in categorical thinking in future interactions and also increases in cognitive complexity and the ability to engage in meaningful conflict that doesn't threaten one's identity. These skills and processes are key components of cultural competence necessary for innovation in problem solving while working in diverse teams.

Developing Cultural Competence

Your time at the University of Oklahoma provides an excellent opportunity to increase your cultural competence. Activities that may enhance your awareness of other cultural experiences include: participating in OU's Study Abroad program, taking foreign language courses, participating in cultural events hosted by student associations (visit *ou.edu/content/studentlife/diverse_communities* for a listing of diverse student associations), enrolling in courses through Women and Gender Studies, and/or becoming an OU Cousin.

Practicing Citizenship

As you grow in cultural competence, think of ways that you can apply your increasing awareness to issues facing the local, state, national, or global community. How might you use your personal abilities and your education to make a difference in the world? How might you impact individuals around you?

"Our lives begin to end the day we become silent about things that matter."
- Dr. Martin Luther King, Jr.

THE DIVERSITY EXPERIENCE AT OU

1. THE DIVERSE OU FAMILY
- Introduces you to the diverse make-up of the OU student body.
- Introduces you to various ways people form their identities, including race, ethnicity, color, national origin, sovereignty, class, sex, sexual orientation, genetic information, age, religion, ability, political beliefs, or status as a veteran.
- Shares stories of OU students and locates this generation of students within the ongoing project of building an inclusive community.
- Encourages you to consider your rights and responsibilities as part of the OU family.

2. BEING AWARE OF DIFFERENCE
- Helps you learn to identify the explicit but also subtle ways that group differences exist on campus and in society.
- Encourages you to understand that you are at a place that is welcoming and celebrates diversity and inclusion.
- Makes you aware of some of the ways that privilege and various forms of advantage can attach to differences.

3. UNDERSTANDING STEREOTYPES
- Introduces you to concepts such as implicit bias, stereotype threat, and attribution ambiguity.
- Helps you understand stereotypes, and how the resulting prejudice and discrimination can harm groups and individuals, even unintentionally.
- Explores the possible ways you experience the transition to the OU family.

4. LEARNING TO INTERACT
- Provides you with the opportunity to practice positive interaction in ways that recognize rather than repress identity issues.
- Provides you with templates and patterns for inclusive practice in the use of language and other forms of interaction.
- Introduces you to the dangers of aversive racism.

5. YOUR RESPONSIBILITIES
- Overview the rights and responsibilities of being a member of the diverse OU family.
- Provides you with effective techniques for active intervention in situations were the values of respect and diversity are being undermined.
- Introduces you to the many ways you can celebrate cultural diversity during your OU experience and learn more about the study of human difference through curriculum.

References

Andreatta, B. (2012). *Navigating the research university: A guide for first-year students*, third edition. Boston, MA: Wadsworth.

Gilbert, D.T., & Wilson, T.D. (2000). Miswanting: Some problems in the forecasting of future affective states. In J. Forgas (Ed.), *Feeling and thinking: The role of affect in social cognition*. Cambridge, England: Cambridge University Press.

Goleman, D. (1998). What makes a leader? *Harvard Business Review, 82,* 93-102.

Goleman, D. (2003). Maxed emotions. *Business Strategy Review, 14,* 26-32.

Hong, L., Page, S.E. (2004). Groups of diverse problem solvers can outperform groups of high-ability problem solvers. Proceedings of the National Academy of Sciences of the United States, 101(46), 16385–16389.

Markus, H., & Nurius, P. (1986). Possible selves. *American Psychologist, 41,* 954-969.

Page, S.E. (2007). The difference: How the power of diversity creates better groups, firms, schools and society. Princeton, NJ: Princeton University Press.

Schumann, K., Zaki, J., & Dweck, C. (2014). Addressing the empathy deficit: Beliefs about the malleability of empathy predict effortful responses when empathy is challenging. *Journal of Personality and Social Psychology* 107(3), 475-493.

Wong (Lau), K., Gurin, P., Nagda, B.A., Ford, A.C., Stephan, W.G., Maxwell, K., Perez, R., McCallum, C. (2013). Empathy in intergroup dialogues. In Gurin, P., Nagda, B.A., Zúñiga, X. (Eds.). *Dialogue Across Difference: Practice, Theory, and Research on Intergroup Dialogues*, 180-210. Russell Sage Foundation.

Chapter 6 REI

Understanding Self and Others

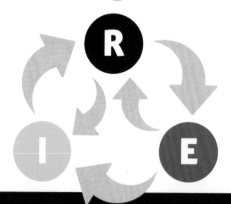

Reflect

Reflect on the words *empathy, communication,* and *self-awareness.* What do those words mean to you personally?

....

Engage

Review the communication styles discussed in Chapter 6 and watch the "Communication Styles" video on JANUX with Dean Damphousse (located in the Chapter 6: Overview section).

....

Impact

What is your primary communication style? Think of three specific things that you can do to challenge yourself to communicate better with people who might have different ideals, beliefs or backgrounds than you do.

....

Chapter 7
Getting Involved: *Campus Leadership and Involvement*

Ashley Sullivan, M.Ed., Student Programs Specialist, Freshman Programs
Courtnay Thomas, M.Ed., former Graduate Assistant, Freshman Programs

In this chapter, you will:

- Gain a better understanding of the concept of leadership.

- Be able to identify ways of developing leadership skills.

- Be able to recognize the benefits of campus leadership and student involvement.

- Learn about the leadership and involvement opportunities at OU.

- Understand the best ways to document your leadership and involvement.

"I suppose at one time leadership meant muscles; but today it means getting along with people."

- Commonly attributed to Mahatma Gandhi, Leader of Indian Nationalism

A leader has the role of inspiring and influencing others to achieve goals. (Recall the discussion of goal setting from Chapter 2). You may know someone on campus who is considered a "natural-born leader," but most leaders are made, not born. College is the perfect time to develop your leadership skills and to discover your own leadership style. While at OU, you will have opportunities to develop as a leader and as a Sooner citizen, through involvement in student organizations, by engaging in activities in clubs and organizations of the discipline you are studying, and even through interactions with friends where you live.

Leadership Styles

Leadership style is the overall approach one uses when leading others. Becoming aware of, and understanding, your personal leadership style can contribute to your effectiveness as a leader. There are four primary leadership styles: 1) Autocratic, 2) Participative, 3) Delegative, and 4) Transformational (Lewin, 1939; Northouse, 2001).

Autocratic leaders emphasize rules and discipline. In this leadership style, all tasks are directed, leaving little room for discussion. Further, there is a distinct divide between the leader and the rest of the group. Autocratic leaders generally do not solicit ideas from the group, but make all, or most, decisions themselves. The autocratic leadership style works best when decisions need to be made quickly and when the leader is the most knowledgeable about the task at hand.

Delegative leaders allow group members to have complete freedom over decisions regarding their work. In this leadership style, there is a high degree of member autonomy, but the leader is more than willing to help and to offer guidance. The delegative leader takes a hands-off approach and delegates all tasks to the group, with little-to-no direction. If those within the group are not expertly skilled, this can be the least productive style of leadership.

Transformational leaders do just what the name implies: they transform themselves and the organizations they lead. Transformational leaders focus on motivation, inspiration, and acting as role models for the group. These leaders make a point to understand the strengths and weaknesses of their group members, in order to challenge them and to enhance their performance.

Participative leadership is considered the most effective leadership style. *Participative leaders* motivate the groups they lead, and they allow others to contribute their ideas, thus promoting creativity within the group. These leaders provide guidance, but are also active participants within the group.

Developing Leadership Skills

Do you have to be in charge of a student group or organization to be considered a leader? Absolutely not! You can be a leader in your everyday life. In fact, it is quite possible that others already view you as a leader, even though you may have never considered yourself in that light. Being a leader is not reserved strictly for those in formal positions of power or in designated leadership positions. In fact, everyone can be, and at one time will be, a leader. You may be a leader as an older sibling, as a volunteer in your community, or as a motivated student in the classroom. You can demonstrate leadership qualities by acting as a role model in your everyday life and in your community.

In order to become a great leader, there are a number of skills, along with the nine virtues, that you should develop and refine throughout your time in college. While you do not have to possess all of these skills in order to lead, listed in Box 7.1 are some of the most common skills that great leaders possess.

Take some time to reflect on a leader whom you have come across or know of. Think about what kind of leadership style this person demonstrated? To get started, ask yourself the following questions:

- How were they selected for the position they are in?

- How do they implement change and growth?

- Does this person work with others when making decisions, or do they make decisions independently?

"A leader is best when people barely know he exists. When his work is done, his aim fulfilled, they will say: We did it ourselves."
-Lao Tzu

Benefits of Campus Involvement

There are many benefits of becoming involved on the OU campus. Campus involvement provides you with opportunities to develop leadership skills, to meet other students outside of the classroom, and to become familiar with faculty and staff across the university.

Characteristics of Leader: How the 9 Virtues Relate to Leadership

Honesty – It is imperative for effective leaders to maintain honesty and to uphold high moral standards. This involves being authentic and ethical.

Perseverence – Good leaders must be able to determine what they hope to achieve through their leadership and continue to press on to reach their goals in the face of opposition.

Civility – Successful leaders are effective communicators. They listen to others and are willing to engage in respectful dialogue.

Compassion – Effective leaders have learned the difference between empathy and feeling sorry for others and are able to show compassion when working with others.

Fairness – Leaders must be able to treat everyone fairly in order to foster teamwork and trust among group members.

Intellectual Humility – The intellectually humble leader does not deny their accomplishments but remains aware of the constant fact that one will continue to learn.

Self-Regulation – It is necessary for leaders to be able to regulate their thoughts, emotions and behaviors and to serve as examples to others in this area.

Love of Learning – A continuous desire to learn is an important trait for leaders who desire to make the world around them a better and more vibrant place.

Open-Mindedness – A true leader is willing to learn from others and take on the perspectives of others.

Box 7.1

Connections. OU is a large campus, but it feels much smaller to those who are involved. When you are engaged in campus activities, you have more opportunities to meet people with similar interests and aspirations. These connections can lead to a more meaningful experience at OU and can provide you with a more supportive environment for your personal and academic growth.

Better Grades. Research shows that college students who are involved in co-curricular, volunteer, or part-time

work outside of the classroom earn higher grades than students who are not involved in any out-of-class activities (Pascarella & Terenzini, 2005). This applies to students whose involvement totals no more than 15 hours per week.

Opportunities. The University of Oklahoma is home to world-renowned art, nationally-ranked athletic teams, original manuscripts of Galileo, and so much more. You may never again be in an environment where you have opportunities like these at your fingertips. While these opportunities are available to any student, you will probably be more likely to take advantage of them if you are involved on campus.

Skill Development. Becoming involved in campus organizations gives you the opportunity to cultivate the skills you need to be successful in your career. Engaging in student activities can help you develop skills such as event planning, strategic marketing, effective public speaking, and many other marketable skills.

Résumé Building. Employers look for students who are academically successful and who demonstrate leadership potential. Being involved outside of the classroom gives you the opportunity to apply your leadership abilities in new and different ways that strengthen your résumé.

Graduation. Students who are more involved in extracurricular activities, while in college, tend to have higher graduation rates than those who are not involved (Astin, 1999).

Student Involvement Theory

Dr. Alexander W. Astin (1999) noted that a significant element of student success is being involved on campus, both in academic experiences and in extracurricular activities. Astin explained, "student involvement refers to the amount of physical and psychological energy that the student devotes to the academic experience" (p. 518). He created a model of student involvement, which is composed of five pieces:

Involvement requires investment.

As a student, you must invest your time and energy into academics and into your social activities in order to reap the benefits. This investment can be specific, like studying for a final exam, or it can be more general, such as your

The Student Life Office provides resources to guide students in realizing academic, professional, and personal goals as they progress toward graduation and beyond. At Student Life, students can find programs dedicated to diverse communities, information for over four hundred student organizations, and a fun, welcoming environment. *ou.edu/studentlife*

The Leadership Development & Volunteerism Office provides educational programming and opportunities for students to make a difference in the world around them. Through numerous programs and activities, this office helps students further develop their leadership skills, assists with personal growth through student learning, and connects students to volunteer opportunities in the local community and beyond. *ou.edu/leadandvolunteer*

experience in a student organization.

Involvement occurs along a continuum.

You will have different degrees of involvement in your chosen activities. You may be more involved in your anthropology class than in your chemistry class, but both require investment of your time so that you can become a successful learner.

The amount of learning is related to the quality and quantity of the involvement.

You must be intentional with your time while in college. Therefore, you should carefully invest in campus involvement, with attention to the quality and quantity of time, effort, and energy you devote to your campus activities. You should also be mindful of your investment in relationships with friends, faculty, and those with whom you interact on a daily basis.

Involvement has both qualitative and quantitative features.

Quantitative features are aspects that can be accurately measured, while qualitative features have to do with the quality of a certain characteristic. For example, your involvement in academics can be measured quantitatively (how many hours you spent studying for an exam) and qualitatively (did you comprehend the material or were you going back and forth between the assignment and texting a friend?).

The educational effectiveness of an activity is related to the capacity of that practice to increase student involvement.

Choose activities that increase your involvement in areas that will help you grow toward your career goals. For example, if you are considering going into a career in advertising, take responsibility for the promotion of a campus organization. And, keep in mind that the more you are involved in both the academic and social aspects of college, the more you will learn as a student.

Listed below are a few additional benefits you can expect to receive from becoming involved with the OU community:

Leadership and Involvement Opportunities at OU

OU is a wonderful place for you to develop your leadership skills. In order to build these skills, you should consciously

The Pride

The official band of the University of Oklahoma actually started as an informal band that included Norman townsfolk. Beginning in 1901, they formed each football season and disbanded when the season was done. The first continuous student band was formed by Lloyd Curtis, a freshman in the Class of 1904. In 1929, the Pride gained its first full-time faculty member, William R. Wehrend, who in 1934 admitted women into the band and organized the new world record for longest drum roll – over ten hours! The Pride is currently led by a Drum Major who is famous among the Big 12 for his ability to lean so far back that his hat almost touches the green of the field.

choose to become an actively-involved member of the OU community. There are many ways to become involved, including joining student organizations and/or volunteering within the community. Engagement in these activities provides you with opportunities to meet individuals who share your interests, to work with a team, and to practice leading others.

Steps to becoming involved in a student organization:

Step 1: Find a student organization that interests you. You can do this by looking over the list of OU's registered student organizations (RSOs) at: *ou.edu/studentlife/get_involved/student_organizations.* If you see a group that interests you, send the president of the organization an e-mail telling her or him that you would like to get involved. Ask friends, roommates, and upperclassmen what organizations they have joined and why.

Step 2: Attend a meeting. Oftentimes, this can be the most intimidating aspect of getting involved.

Showing up at a meeting where you do not know anyone can be nerve-racking, but keep in mind that the organization wants you there. They are looking for new students to participate. Show up, introduce yourself to a few people, and listen. Does the mission of the organization fit with your interests? What is expected of members? Do the meetings and activities fit your schedule? If, after attending the meeting, you think this might not be the organization for you, do not give up. Start over at Step One.

Step 3: Participate. Being involved in an organization goes beyond attending a meeting once per semester. True involvement requires commitment. Sign up to participate in events, represent your organization at a table in the Union, or create a new program for your organization.

Remember, you will not become a leader in an organization without, first, putting in effort and bringing new ideas to the table.

Student Involvement Timeline

Although the exact timeline for every student varies, it is helpful to have a general idea of what involvement might look like for a student over the course of four years. You can also get a good idea of what your four years might look like by talking to an upperclassman who is involved in an organization in which you are interested.

Freshman Year
Fall Semester:
Use this time to gather information about the different types of organizations on campus. Find 2-4 organizations to join. Attend meetings, participate in events, and try to get an overall sense of the mission, impact, and expectations of each organization.

Spring Semester:
By now, you should have a better idea of the organizations that have captured your interest. Apply for a few leadership positions within those organizations.

Sophomore Year
Be active! Students have reported that this year is the busiest for campus involvement. Be as active as your schedule allows, and participate in as many events and programs as you can, while keeping your academics as your first priority.

Junior Year
By now, you should have narrowed down your activities to a couple of organizations about which you feel passionate. Pursue leadership roles in these areas, and stay consistently involved.

Senior Year
The senior year is usually different than previous years, in terms of student involvement. Focus often shifts from campus life to life beyond college (e.g. finding a job, gaining admission to graduate school, determining one's living situation, etc.). Most students find one primary leadership role on campus (chapter president, student organization chair, event executive, etc.) and devote all of their student involvement to that role. While it is important to remain a leader on campus during your senior year, do not overwhelm yourself with campus activities, as you will have many other priorities.

Your freshman year is a great time to gather information about different types of organizations on campus. Visit the comprehensive list of registered student organizations, find 2 that interest you, and answer the following questions:

- What is the purpose of the student organization?
- Who is the president?
- Who is eligible to join?

Find the full list of RSOs with contact information by visiting:
ou.edu/studentlife/get_involved/student_organizations.

Student Organizations at OU
There are over four hundred registered student organizations at the University of Oklahoma. With organizations connected to majors, cultural organizations, and service organizations, there is something for everyone. To view a complete list, visit the Student Life website at *ou.edu/studentlife*. Listed here, you will find some of the larger organizations on campus.

Student Government Association (SGA)
SGA's purpose is to serve and to advocate for the student

body, in order to continue improving the student experience. Each branch is aimed at representing student wants and needs through legislation, activities, or as a voice among the administration.

Union Programming Board (UPB)

The Union Programming Board (UPB) is a dynamic student-run organization dedicated to providing diverse programs in the Oklahoma Memorial Union for the University of Oklahoma community. Some signature programs include: Sooner Idol, Dancing with the Stars, and the Foam Party.

Campus Activities Council (CAC)

CAC is the programming branch of OU Student Government, presenting campus-wide traditions and events for all students. CAC programs some of the most exciting events on campus, including: Howdy Week, Homecoming, Dad's Day, and Sooner Scandals.

Housing Center Student Associations

The Housing Center Student Associations (HCSA) are organizations dedicated to programming, advocacy, and service for all students living in the residence halls or university apartments.

OU Cousins

The OU Cousins program was created in 1996 by President and Mrs. David Boren, as a way of developing understanding, friendship, and unity among U.S., international, and exchange students at the University of Oklahoma. Through this program, students are matched according to hobbies, majors, and countries of special interest. Each international or exchange student is matched with one or two American students and invited to participate in monthly programs.

The Big Event

OU held its first official Big Event in the spring of 1999. Since then, each year in early spring, thousands of OU students unite in this unparalleled effort to say "thank you" to the Norman-Oklahoma City area through this official day of community service. The Big Event strives to strengthen OU's friendship with the surrounding community.

Greek Organizations

There are 49 active fraternity and sorority chapters on the OU campus. These organizations provide students who

choose to join with opportunities for academic assistance, leadership development, and community involvement. Each chapter is a member of a larger Greek council.

Interfraternity Council

The Interfraternity Council (IFC) is made up of 19 fraternities. IFC organizes a formal recruitment week during the first week of fall classes and the third week of the spring semester. Men who are interested in participating in these recruitment events are encouraged to register online.

Multicultural Greek Council

The Multicultural Greek Council (MGC) is made up of 10 culturally-based fraternities and sororities. A couple of these chapters were founded right here at OU. Chapters host chapter-specific recruitment events (rush) during the first two weeks of the fall and spring semesters.

National Pan-Hellenic Council

The National Pan-Hellenic Council (NPHC) is made up of nine historically African-American fraternities and sororities. Individual chapters may host intake at various times throughout the year. Students interested in joining should contact individual chapters for more information about their intake processes.

Panhellenic Association

The University of Oklahoma Panhellenic Association is the umbrella organization for the 11 NPC sororities chartered at OU, and is responsible for organizing activities of mutual concern and interest to all the NPC sororities on campus. Each member group is autonomous as a social, Greek-letter society of college women and alumnae. Panhellenic Recruitment occurs the week prior to fall classes.

Other Leadership Opportunities

Class Council

The purpose of the Class Council is to connect students to in their class and to create a greater sense of class belonging through tradition, events, class-specific information, and class-branded items.

University College Student Advisory Board

The University College Student Advisory Board is composed of a select group of freshmen. The Student Advisory Board meets with and makes recommendations to University College Administration during the fall and spring semesters.

This board will also be invited to be recognized at the University College Awards Ceremony in the spring semester.

Camp IMPACT

Camp IMPACT is designed to provide OU students with an opportunity for an in-depth exploration of the role of character in their lives. It includes three main components: volunteer/service opportunities; personal, cultural and social experiences; and civic exposures. Students will engage in these purposeful experiences for four days over Spring Break in downtown Oklahoma City.

Leader Summit Leader Summit is a leadership conference that is held on OU's campus every spring. This is an exciting program for emerging and seasoned leaders across campus. Students are invited to attend to gain the leadership tools needed for today and for post-graduation.

Social media is a great way to get connected and stay involved with the various leadership and volunteer opportunities at the University of Oklahoma. You can check out the Facebook page for the Office of Leadership Development and Volunteerism here: *facebook.com/OULDV*

Student Recognition for Leadership on Campus

The university has many opportunities for recognition of campus involvement and leadership through campus awards. Outstanding students are recognized at various awards ceremonies during the spring semester. The following awards are open to freshmen only:

PACE Awards

PACE Awards are given to OU freshmen who demonstrate outstanding accomplishments in four areas (listed below) during the fall semester of the freshman year.

The PACE acronym represents:
- **Participation** in recognized campus clubs and activities,
- **Academic achievement**, as demonstrated by a minimum GPA of 3.25 in 14 credit hours,
- **Community service**, either on campus or in the Norman/Oklahoma City metro area, and
- **Excellence in leadership** positions on campus

Students may find application instructions for the PACE

awards on the University College website *uc.ou.edu*.

President's Award for Outstanding Freshmen

The President's Award for Outstanding Freshmen is presented to twelve (12) selected individuals who have excelled in the areas of scholarship, character, leadership, and service to the university community. This award is the highest honor bestowed to freshmen by the university. Application instructions for this award are available at the Leadership and Volunteerism website: *leadandvolunteer.ou.edu*.

Recognition of Academic Achievement

There are two university-recognized honor societies for students in their first and second years of college. Both of these organizations provide lifetime national membership to students based on their early achievements at OU.

Alpha Lambda Delta (ALD) is a national society that honors academic excellence during a student's first year at college. Founded in 1924, Alpha Lambda Delta is one of the most highly recognized and well-established honor societies in the United States. Alpha Lambda Delta provides local and national service, social, and scholarship opportunities.

National Society of Collegiate Scholars (NSCS) is an honors organization which recognizes first- and second-year students for outstanding scholastic ability. Members have the opportunity to become involved in a national organization that, not only recognizes outstanding students, but also provides opportunities to develop

BOX 7.2

Documenting Leadership and Involvement

As you become involved at OU, you will have opportunities to develop the creativity, teamwork abilities, and leadership skills that are a valuable part of our community. You will want to document these experiences on an engagement log until you are ready to transfer them to your résumé. Log all activities, big and small, because you never know how they will relate to future opportunities of interest to you. As you learned in Chapter 5, you can manage your résumé while at OU at *OptimalResume.com*. This will allow you to appropriately showcase your talents and strengths when you apply for future internship and job opportunities.

There are several types of résumés. When it comes time to apply for a position, choose the one that best highlights your strengths for the position in question. Among them are:

Chronological résumés show your job history, usually in reverse, with your most recent position first. Use these when you are highlighting your development through promotions and increasing skill sets.

Functional résumés focus on your skills and experience, rather than your employment experience. These will be particularly helpful to students and new graduates who do not yet have much work experience.

Targeted résumés focus on the requirements for the position being advertised and the ways you match them. This résumé highlights both work experience and skills relevant to the job you are applying for, and does not necessarily focus on chronology.

As you prepare your résumé for various opportunities, you will want to make sure to include a direct objective, so that your intentions are readily understood.

When submitting your résumé to a potential employer, you will also want to include a cover letter, tailored to the job for which you are applying. Draft this letter carefully, as it is your opportunity to create a positive first impression for the employer and is relative to how your skills and work experience fit with the job. Again, as you learned in Chapter 5, you can gain assistance with your cover letter in Career Services.

You always want your résumé to be a clear and honest representation of your experiences. Your past involvements will indicate your preparation for future opportunities, and you want to be sure to articulate these experiences as accurately as possible.

A Note on Personal References

When you apply for certain opportunities, you might also need to submit a personal reference. The purpose of a personal reference is for the selection committee or employer to gain a broader, more accurate picture of who you are and what you have to offer. When you choose someone to serve as a personal reference for you, it is important you are selecting someone who is appropriate. You want someone who can attest to your character, work ethic, and sense of responsibility. You should always ask that person's permission before listing them as a reference. They should be well prepared to speak on your behalf! If you need a reference letter, you should ask well before the deadline. It is always helpful when your references know what you are applying for and what the selection committee or employer is looking for in a strong candidate.

What Kind of Leader Will You Be?

What kind of leader do you hope to develop into during your time on campus?

In what areas do you see yourself stepping up to the challenge?

What method will you use to document your leadership on campus?

Cover Letters

A cover letter should accompany each resume you send to a prospective employer. This letter should not be a repetition of the information in your resume, although you may wish to expound upon one or two of the points you would like to emphasize for the reader. You can also highlight other aspects of yourself by including relevant achievements not listed in your resume. Some guidelines for writing cover letters:

- State why you are writing; identify the position or field of work for which you are applying. Tell how you heard of the opening or organization.

- Tell why you are particularly interested in the company, school, location, or type of work. Mention one or two of your qualifications that you believe would be of greatest interest to the employer. If you have had related experience, point out specific achievements and how these could benefit the organization. In sum, you want to make it clear that you can meet the needs of the position.

- Try to be concise; keep in mind that the reader will probably be skimming through multiple letters, so do not let yours drag on.

- Request the next step in the employment process: personal interview, further information, application forms, etc. Make sure your closing is not vague and elicits a response from the employer.

Sample Cover Letter

111 Olsen Drive
Norman, OK 73069

April 30, 2016

Figure 7.1

Mr. Jon Frederick
Senior Communications Officer
Oklahoma Young Journalist Press Association
420 Asp Avenue
Suite 2811
Oklahoma City, OK

Dear Mr. Frederick,

I am writing to express my interest in the Oklahoma Young Journalist Press Association internship position listed on your website. In May 2016, I will be graduating from the University of Oklahoma with a bachelor's degree in Journalism. Your organization's commitment to excellence and ethics in journalism align with the core values I hold myself accountable to professionally.

I have had several experiences working in the field that have helped qualify me for this internship. I have had the opportunity to serve as a video and communications intern for Discover Oklahoma where I was able to engage in many aspects of broadcast journalism including assisting videographer, shooting film for stories, and on-site interviewing. While I was working for News21 in Phoenix, Arizona, I had the honor of being published by the Washington Post and NBC News.

I am a goal-oriented, highly organized learner who is fast and efficient at developing new skills. I have strong written and verbal communication skills. I work well independently or in groups.

Thank you for taking the time to review my application materials. I appreciate your consideration for this position. I welcome the opportunity to meet with you in person to discuss this opportunity further.

Sincerely,

Sydney Sooner

Sydney Sooner

Sydney Sooner

(123) 456-7890
sydneysooner@ou.edu
1233 Boomer Lane
Norman, OK 73019

EMPLOYMENT/INTERNSHIPS

Discover Oklahoma
Video and Communications Intern
Oklahoma CIty, OK | 2016-Present
- Assist videographers with feature stories
- Transcribe interviews
- Shoot b-roll
- On-site interviewing

University of Oklahoma
Freshman Programs Teaching Assistant
Norman, OK | August 2013-August 2016
- Mentored and guided freshman
- Assisted instuctors with curriculum
- Led journalism students

News21 Fellowship
Ethics and Excellence in Journalsim Fellow
Phoenix, AZ | Summer 2015
- Conducted in-depth reporting
- Investigated gun control in the US
- Reported in five states
- Produced multimedia stories

EDUCATION

B.A. Journailsm
Minor in Criminology
Gaylord College of Journalism and Mass Communication
University of Oklahoma
Norman, Oklahoma
May 2016
GPA 3.63

British Media Study Abroad Program
England, France & Whales
Summer 2013

ACTIVITIES

Gaylord Ambassadors Chair - liason to college's donors and alumni

President's Leadership Class

Big Brothers Big Sisters of Oklahoma

Oklahoma College Broadcasters

Alpha Lambda Delta - National Honor Society

Young Life College

HONORS/AWARDS

- TSPJ Mark of Excellence Award, *2016*
- Gaylord College Council of Presidents, *2016*
- Gaylord College of Journalism and Mass Communication Dean's Honor Roll, *2012-2016*
- EPPY Award, *2015*
- Work Published by The Washington Post and NBC News, *2015*
- Outstanding University College Teaching Assistant, *2014-2015*
- President's 4.0 GPA Honor Roll, *2013-2015*
- Byron L. Abernathy Journalism Scholarship, *2014*

Sample Organizational Leadership Résumé

Current Address
101 Sooner Street
Norman, OK 73072

Joe A. Doe
jdoe@ou.edu
Current (405) 325-4020   Cell (405) 321-4567

Permananent Address
123 Lake Street
Happytown, OK 73072

° Figure 7.3

OBJECTIVE

To obtain a Service Co-chair position in the Alpha Lambda Delta Honor Society.

EDUCATION

University of Oklahoma
Management Major, Spanish Minor
Anticipated Graduation Month/Year: May 20XX

EMPLOYMENT/INTERNSHIPS

May, 20XX - Present   Food Service, Norman, OK, Student Food Service Worker

May, 20XX - August, 20XX   Hallmark, Inc., Kansas City, MO, Marketing Intern

ACTIVITIES

- Walker 12 Floor President
- Homecoming Volunteer with High School Bands
- University Sing and Sooner Scandal Participant
- Entrepreneurs Club Member

COMMUNITY INVOLVEMENT

- Spent three weekends constructing homes for Habitat for Humanity, November 20XX
- Participated in Big Event, March 20XX

HONORS, AWARDS & SCHOLARSHIPS

- University College Student Advisory Board
- Class of 20XX Council

APPLICANT HONOR STATEMENT

"To the best of my knowledge, the information provided on this résumé is truthful and accurate."

Signed _____

References

Astin, A. W. (1999). Student involvement: A developmental theory for higher education. *Journal of College Student Development, 40,* 518-29.

Lewin, K., Lippit, R., & White, R.K. (1939). Patterns of aggressive behavior in experimentally created social climates. *Journal of Social Psychology, 10,* 271-301.

Northouse, P. G. (2001). *Leadership theory and practice,* second edition. Thousand Oaks, CA: Sage Publications, Inc.

Pascarella, E., & Terenzini, P. (2005). *How college affects students: A third decade of research* (Vol. 2). San Francisco: Jossey- Bass.

Chapter 7 REI

Getting Involved

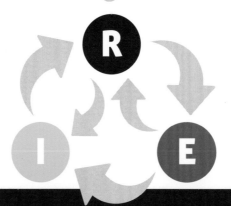

Reflect

Many students were heavily involved in various extracurricular activities while in high school, but struggle to get involved when they make the transition to college. What were some of the activities you were involved in during high school? Which do you believe benefitted you the most?

....

Engage

Watch the "Get Involved" video on JANUX (located in the Unit 7, Overview section). Next, go to the list of OU Registered Student Organizations (http://www.ou.edu/content/studentlife/get_involved/student_organizations/rsos.html) and identify three organizations that have purposes that align with your interests.

....

Impact

What are the three organizations you identified? What steps can you take to find out more about these organizations? How do you think these organizations can benefit you throughout your time in college?

....

Chapter 8

Maintaining a Healthy Lifestyle: *Health, Wellness, and Stress Management*

Nicole Kendrick, M.Ed., Assistant Director, Freshman Programs
former Health Educator, OU Health Services

In this chapter, you will:

- Become aware of OU departments that aid in student health and wellness.
- Learn about the top health concerns for college students.
- Recognize the connection between wellness and academic success.
- Learn techniques for enhancing personal health and wellness.
- Create individual strategies to achieve your personal health and wellness goals.

"Health is a state of complete physical, mental, and social well-being, and not merely the absence of disease or infirmity."

· World Health Organization

When we talk about health and wellness in this chapter, we are talking about the physical, mental, and social aspects of our lives that affect our health, happiness, and success in college. Wellness is about taking a holistic approach to taking care of yourself. The goal of wellness is achieving a balance in your life and making decisions to create the circumstances in which you are able to perform well and accomplish your goals.

College is a great time to begin developing personal health and wellness habits that you can continue for the rest of your life! For some of you, the first year of college is the first time you will be taking your personal health into your own hands. You will be the one determining when you need to see a doctor, what you will eat, and how often you will engage in physical activity. You will begin to make choices about your own health that will matter for the rest of your life. At the University of Oklahoma, our goal is to create a healthy campus community where everyone can thrive. When you can successfully achieve your personal health and wellness goals, it is likely that your academic success will follow!

Throughout this chapter, we are going to examine and discuss the top health concerns for college students.

Stress

Stress is the top impediment to academic success in college (American College Health Association [ACHA], 2009). This means the number one reason why students are leaving school or not doing as well academically as they potentially could is stress. Part of gaining emotional and social intelligence is learning how to identify, prevent, and manage the negative effects stress can have on you. When you learn how to deal with stress, you are likely to become a happier, more productive person. You can even lower your risk of developing serious health problems like heart disease, high blood pressure, and depression.

It is important to remember that stress is inevitable and not all stress is negative! Stress can help keep you moving in the direction of your goals and can help protect you in a dangerous situation. Being honest about the stress in your life and whether it is positive or negative is the first step toward managing it. See box 8.1 on the following page to look at the two main types of stress.

Acute stress can be a positive, short-term stress that keeps you motivated and moving in the direction of your goals. *Chronic stress*, on the other hand, is the persistent, negative stress that has long-term physical and mental health consequences. To identify which type of stress is present in your life, it is important to take time out of every day to examine your thoughts, feelings and attitudes.

Practicing relaxation is a great way to prevent stress from manifesting itself negatively in your life. Be open-minded about trying new techniques until you find what works best for you.

Pausing to reflect is not, however, as easy as it sounds. Self-reflection is something that you may have to practice before you perfect, but it is an important part of gaining social and emotional intelligence. If you are dealing with chronic stress, it is important to identify your stressors and to start taking steps toward a more balanced mental and emotional state by learning to manage your stress. You may want to consider seeking help through counseling.

Although experiencing some level of stress in life is inevitable, the good news is that there are things you can do to prevent it from getting out-of-control or becoming chronic stress. Here are some steps you can take:

1. Exercise – Engage in physical activity on a daily basis. Aim for 30 minutes a day! Even if you are unable to spare 30 minutes, remember a little exercise is better than none at all!

2. Eat a Nutritious and Healthy Diet – Eat a healthy and well-balanced diet, and try to include many fruits and vegetables in your meals.

3. Practice Relaxation Techniques – Personalize your relaxation time. Find something that you really enjoy and something that makes you feel at ease. Examples include: deep breathing, progressive muscle relaxation, and aromatherapy.

4. Change Negative Thoughts – Practice guiding your own thoughts. Replace them with positive, logical ones. Be a problem-solver!

5. Communicate – Talk to others about how you feel. When you find yourself feeling frustrated, take time to slow down. Listen and make a real effort to understand others.

6. Limit Caffeine – Excessive amounts of caffeine can cause anxiety, nervousness, and irritability.

7. Avoid Using Alcohol or Other Drugs – Drink in moderation or not at all.

8. Practice Time Management – Schedule to your advantage and use self-control to eliminate unnecessary and unimportant tasks. Prioritize and get organized!

9. Get Better Sleep – Think consistency, rather than quantity. Try to get into a consistent sleep routine, getting enough rest each night.

Figure 8.1

ACUTE STRESS	CHRONIC STRESS
Also known as the "fight or flight" response	Persistent, unending stress. Feelings of severe despondency and dejection
Immediate, short-term stress	May be more subtle than acute stress
Examples: the first day of class, skydiving	Examples: depression, severe anxiety
This type of stress can motivate and energize you	Chronic stress can lead to long-term mental and physical health problems

Taking Care of Your Mental Health: How to Know When You Need Help

You may be uncertain if you are living with a mental health problem. Experiecning one or more of the following feelings or behaviors might be an early warning sign. Reaching out for help is the first step toward recovery.

- Eating or sleeping too much or too little
- Pulling away from people and usual activities
- Having low or no energy
- Feeling numb or like nothing matters
- Having unexplained aches and pains
- Feeling helpless or hopeless
- Smoking, drinking, or using drugs
- Feeling unusually confused, forgetful, on edge, angry, upset, worried, or scared
- Yelling or fighting with family and friends
- Experiencing severe mood swings that cause problems in relationships
- Having persistent thoughts and memories you can't get out of your head
- Thinking of harming yourself or others
- Inability to perform daily tasks like going to work or school

information courtesy of Mental Health.gov

If you are unable to manage stress in your life, or if you are dealing with depression or severe anxiety, it may be a good time to seek professional help. *Depression* is a mood disorder that causes persistent feelings of sadness and loss of interest. It affects how you feel, think and behave. *Anxiety Disorders* are marked by an intense, excessive and persistent worry and fear about everyday situations that often involve repeated episodes of intense anxiety and fear or terror that reaches a peak within minutes.

As a college student, you may be experiencing many transitions, both positive and negative. It is common for college students to benefit from speaking to someone about the pressures and stress they are undergoing while dealing with these transitions. At The University of Oklahoma, we are fortunate to have a comprehensive counseling center for our campus community, located right on campus.

Staffed by psychologists, counselors, a psychiatrist, and a licensed drug and alcohol counselor, the University Counseling Center (UCC) is an important resource for students. UCC offers individual, couples, group, and career counseling to the OU campus community. UCC is equipped to handle crisis interventions and other emergencies. Additionally, UCC offers comprehensive assessments for a Attention Deficit Disorder and learning disabilities.

Any kind of transition can lead to stress, even if it's a positive transition like enrolling in college. Chances are you have already undergone many life changes since you've been here. Examples include: moving, finding a new job, making new friends, etc. Take a moment to reflect on the things that have changed in your life since you started at OU.

What changes have you made since you graduated from high-school?

What steps have you taken, if any, to ease the transition into becoming a college student?

Cold and Flu

Living in such a closely-knit community has many benefits; unfortunately, it also makes it easy to spread communal illnesses, like the cold and flu. Typically, as a student, you are living, eating, and going to class with hundreds of other students on a day-to-day basis, in very close proximity. Both the cold and the flu are spread by the air, by direct contact, or by indirect contact. For many students, a cold, flu or sore throat has the distinct potential to adversely affect academic performance. The good news is that you can take simple steps to help decrease your chances of getting sick. And, if you do get sick, there are steps you can take to alleviate discomfort, to get well faster, and to prevent illness from being spread further!

Frequent hand washing is your best defense against contagious illnesses, including the cold and the flu. Wash your hands often to stop transmission and to kill the most common germs that may make you sick. Here are a few other ways to prevent the spread of contagious illnesses:

• Eat a healthy diet and exercise regularly.
• Get enough sleep.
• Avoid sharing cups, plates, utensils, makeup, and other personal items.
• Avoid close, prolonged contact with an infected person.
• Avoid touching your face, eyes, nose, and mouth, unless your hands are washed.
• Frequently disinfect shared objects and areas (countertops, telephones, etc.).
• Stay home when you are sick.
• Get an annual flu shot.

Knowing whether you have a cold or the flu can help you seek the right kind of medical care and treatment, decreasing the time you spend sick. The common cold and flu are frequently mistaken for one another, which can lead to serious complications if you are treating yourself for the wrong illness. Both the cold and the flu affect the upper respiratory system and have similar symptoms, but they are not the same illness. Let's take a look at some of the identifying symptoms:

COMMON COLD:
Sneezing
Runny nose

Frequent hand washing is your best defense against contagious illnesses, including the cold and the flu. Wash your hands often to stop transmission and to kill the most common germs that may make you sick.

Sore throat
Head and body aches
Congestion of the ears, nose, and head
Mild fatigue
Low fever - less than 101 degrees F

FLU:
Rapid onset of symptoms
Chills and sweats
Dry cough
Severe head and body aches
Nasal congestion
Extreme fatigue and weakness
High fever - greater than 101 degrees F

Getting an annual flu shot is recommended for anyone who would like to decrease her/his chance of contracting the flu. When you get vaccinated, you are not only protecting yourself, but you are also helping protect the entire OU community. This may be especially important to first-year students living in dormitories. Flu shots are provided at no cost to students through OU Health Services (OUHS), as they become available.

Remember that the cold and the flu are viral infections. They should not be treated with antibiotics, like bacterial infections are, unless a secondary bacterial infection, such as pneumonia, occurs. Generally, cold and flu viruses must run their course. If you think you have a cold, there are some steps you can take to alleviate symptoms and discomfort at home:

Goddard Health Center

Situated just across Elm Avenue from the old infirmary at Ellison Hall, Goddard became the center for Health Services in 1971. It was named for Charles B. Goddard. Unlike many of the buildings on campus that were paid for by generous donations of philanthropic individuals, Goddard was paid for by students who in 1968 voted to increase their fees to help finance the building.

- Get plenty of rest.
- Drink plenty of fluids.
- Suck on ice or throat lozenges.
- Gargle with warm salt water (1/2 tsp. of salt per 8 oz. of warm water).
- Use a humidifier.
- Stop smoking and discontinue alcohol use.
- Try taking the following over-the-counter medications to relieve pain or to treat other symptoms:
    - o Acetaminophen (Tylenol)
    - o Ibuprofen (Advil, Motrin)
    - o Decongestant (Sudafed)
    - o Cough Medicine (Robitussin)

You should seek medical attention if flu symptoms are present; if your fever lasts longer than 72 hours; if you have difficulty breathing, a severe sore throat, or a cough that produces green or yellow mucus; or, if you have abdominal pain and/or excessive vomiting.

If you do seek medical care, OU Health Services, located at Goddard Health Center, is your healthcare source on campus. Health Services features a full-service clinic, offering primary care to the OU community. This includes visits for illness, injury, and prevention services. Almost everything you would go to your medical care provider for is available on campus through the clinic. Although walk-in appointments are available, making an appointment ahead of time, by calling the OUHS appointment line, is recommended.

As a student, you are eligible to be seen at OU Health Services at a student-discounted rate, even if you do not have health insurance. If you do have health insurance, no problem! Health Services accepts most major insurance plans. Just bring your insurance card or information to your appointment. Another convenient aspect of coming to OUHS is that most costs can be charged to your bursar account. Health Services also accepts cash, checks, and credit cards.

Sleep & Schedule

Your body needs sleep to properly function! Adequate rest not only helps you relieve stress and recover from illness faster, it also helps you perform better as a student. Lack of sleep negatively impacts physical performance, concentration, reaction time, coordination, and learning. Lack of sleep can cause memory lapses, injuries, and moodiness. Given the active and busy schedule most college students keep, it is no surprise that, for some, getting enough rest seems almost impossible. However, getting the right amount of sleep each and every night can have an enormous positive effect on your health and wellbeing and can dramatically improve the quality of your life. It is an important measure of self-control to be able to say no when needed and allow yourself enough time for adequate rest.

Remember, when we talk about sleep, consistency is more important than quantity. You do not "catch up" on sleep – in fact, oversleeping can negatively affect your health and life as well as under-sleeping. Although individuals need different amounts of sleep, as a general recommendation, most adults need 7-8 hours of sleep each night. One of

Know when to contact your doctor. It is not uncommon to have an occasional restless night, but if you consistently have trouble sleeping, make an appointment with a doctor. You may have underlying issues that are contributing to your restless nights, and it is important to seek treatment so that you can start enjoying the benefits of being well-rested.

the best ways to improve the quality of your health and your life is to begin developing habits that will lead you to getting consistent, restful sleep. To get started on your journey to a better night's rest, check out the following from the MayoClinic.com article, "Sleep Tips: 7 Steps to Better Sleep" (MayoClinic.com, 2011).

No. 1: Stick to a sleep schedule

Go to bed and get up at the same time every day, even on weekends, holidays and days off. Being consistent reinforces your body's sleep-wake cycle and helps promote better sleep at night. There's a caveat, though. If you don't fall asleep within about 15 minutes, get up and do something relaxing. Go back to bed when you're tired. If you agonize over falling asleep, you might find it even tougher to nod off.

No. 2: Pay attention to what you eat and drink

Don't go to bed either hungry or stuffed. Your discomfort might keep you up. Also, limit how much you drink before bed, to prevent disruptive middle-of-the-night trips to the toilet.

Nicotine, caffeine and alcohol deserve caution, too. The stimulating effects of nicotine and caffeine — which take hours to wear off — can wreak havoc with quality sleep. And even though alcohol might make you feel sleepy at first, it can disrupt sleep later in the night.

No. 3: Create a bedtime ritual

Do the same things each night to tell your body it's time to wind down. This might include taking a warm bath or shower, reading a book, or listening to soothing music, preferably with the lights dimmed. Relaxing activities can promote better sleep by easing the transition between wakefulness and drowsiness.

Be wary of using the TV or other electronic devices as part of your bedtime ritual. Some research suggests that screen time or other media use before bedtime interferes with sleep.

No. 4: Get comfortable

Create a room that's ideal for sleeping. Often, this means cool, dark and quiet. Consider using room-darkening shades, earplugs, a fan or other devices to create an environment that suits your needs.

Your mattress and pillow can contribute to better sleep, too. Since the features of good bedding are subjective, choose what feels most comfortable to you. If you share your bed, make sure there's enough room for two. If you have children or pets, set limits on how often they sleep with you — or insist on separate sleeping quarters.

No. 5: Limit daytime naps

Long daytime naps can interfere with nighttime sleep — especially if you're struggling with insomnia or poor sleep quality at night. If you choose to nap during the day, limit yourself to about 10 to 30 minutes and make it during the midafternoon.

If you work nights, you'll need to make an exception to the rules about daytime sleeping. In this case, keep your window coverings closed so that sunlight — which adjusts your internal clock — doesn't interrupt your daytime sleep.

No. 6: Include physical activity in your daily routine

Regular physical activity can promote better sleep, helping you to fall asleep faster and to enjoy deeper sleep. Timing is important, though. If you exercise too close to bedtime, you might be too energized to fall asleep. If this seems to be an issue for you, exercise earlier in the day.

No. 7: Manage stress

When you have too much to do — and too much to think about — your sleep is likely to suffer. To help restore peace to your life, consider healthy ways to manage stress. Start with the basics, such as getting organized, setting priorities and delegating tasks. Give yourself permission to take a break when you need one. Share a good laugh with an old friend. Before bed, jot down what's on your mind, and then, set it aside for tomorrow.

"It is a common experience that a problem difficult at night is resolved in the morning after the committee of sleep has worked on it." – John Steinbeck

Be aware of the campus resources available to help you achieve your health and wellness goals! Did you know there is a nutrition calculator where you can find nutritional information on foods from on-campus eateries like Crossroads and Couch Express?

Take a moment to find the nutrition facts of one of your recent meals on campus by visiting the following link: *ou.mynutritioncalculator.net*

Sexual Health & Responsibility

While in college, it is important to equip yourself with the right information, tools, and resources you need to be sexually healthy and responsible. If you have decided to become sexually active, it is important that you are aware of what it takes to remain healthy and sexually responsible.

No person is immune to contracting an STD! *Sexually transmitted diseases (STDs)*, also called sexually transmitted infections (STIs) are infections that spread by contact with infected skin or body fluids. Each year, nationwide, there are 20 million new sexually transmitted infections, and half of these cases occur among young people ages 15-24 (Centers for Disease Control [CDC], 2012). Many STDs have no signs or symptoms and, if untreated, can lead to serious health problems. Therefore, it is important to understand the risks associated with being sexually active. If you are sexually active, the only way to know for sure that you are STD-free is to get tested.

Getting tested, even if you do not have any symptoms, is an important part of being a sexually responsible adult. If you notice any of the following common symptoms, you should refrain from sexual activity until you have been diagnosed or treated:
• Unusual discharge
• Burning while urinating

• Pain in the genital or lower abdominal area
• Pain during intercourse
• Sores, ulcers, bumps, or rashes
• Itching

There are several local testing sites that are available in the Norman area. You may make an appointment through OU Health Services at Goddard Health Center by calling 325-4611.

If used consistently and correctly during every sexual act, male latex or male/female polyurethane condoms may be used to decrease the risk of certain types of STDs. It is important to remember that condoms do not protect you completely from contracting an STD, and even with their consistent use, you are still at risk. The only 100% effective way to prevent an STD infection is total abstinence.

Another consideration to take into account when you decide to become sexually active is the use of contraception, or birth control, to prevent unwanted pregnancy. Although no contraceptive method is perfect, you can choose one that best fits your lifestyle and your beliefs. It is best to choose a method with which both partners feel comfortable and which both partners will be able to use consistently and correctly each time.

Sexual Assault

Sexual assault is an issue that impacts all colleges and universities, including The University of Oklahoma. Nationally, 1 in 5 women and 1 in 71 men will experience sexual assault in their lifetime (Breiding, Chen, & Black, 2014). Further, college students are in the most vulnerable age range.

At The University of Oklahoma, we aim to challenge you to take a closer look at your social settings, personal relationships, and societal interactions, in order to help you to better recognize the risks of sexual assault. If you would like more information about sexual assault, there are several resources available on campus, including: the Women's Outreach Center (405-325-4929) and the Sexual Misconduct/Title IX Reporting Office (405-325-2215).

One Sooner Can Make a Difference

Are you outspoken? Are you resourceful? Are you creative? No matter who you are, you can always step in and speak out about sexual assault. Sexual assault is a human issue and when any student experiences sexual violence, our community suffers. If you hear someone make a joke about rape, speak up, and say it is not okay. When you see a risky situation, step in and ask if everything is okay. When someone says they've been a victim of sexual assault, believe them, and tell them there is help on campus. Be an active bystander, and help prevent sexual assault.

The Three D's of Being an Active Bystander
Imagine that you are at a house party with several friends. You see a girl from your hall, and she is very intoxicated. She's stumbling and having a hard time even standing. Then, a guy walks up to her and offers her more trashcan punch and is nudging her toward the stairs. You worry she could be in trouble. You think back to the Step In, Speak Out presentation you had in Gateway and think about which "D" to use.

- Distract-Interrupt a situation to change the direction of events "I think your car's getting towed".
- Direct-Interrupt by asking a pointed question about the situation OR make a statement that changes the direction of events "Hey, I don't think she needs any more to drink".
- Delegate-Involve someone else to interrupt a situation to change the direction of events (Find her friends and let them know they need to check in to make sure everything is okay).

Resources on and off campus

Sexual Assault Response Team:	405-615-0013
Rape Crisis Center:	405-701-5660
Sexual Misconduct Office:	405-325-2215
Gender + Equality Center:	405-325-4929
OUPD:	405-325-1911

Box 8.1

Figure 8.2

The Low Down on the Most Common STDs

	CHLAMYDIA	TRICHOMONIASIS (TRICH)	GONORRHEA	PAPILLOMAVIRUS (HPV)
WHAT IS IT?	A bacterial infection of the genital areas.	A parasitic infection of the genital areas.	A bacterial infection of the genital areas.	A viral infection with over 40 types that can infect the genital areas, including types that cause warts and cancer.
HOW MANY PEOPLE GET IT IN THE US?	About 1.2 million new cases reported each year. The highest rates are among adolescent women.	An estimated 5 million new cases each year.	About 650,000 new cases reported each year. The highest rates are among women aged 15 to 19 and men aged 20 to 24.	An estimated 6.2 million new cases each year, with at least 20 million people already infected.
SYMPTOMS	Often there are no symptoms. For women who do experience symptoms, they may have abnormal vaginal discharge, bleeding (not their period), and/or burning and pain during urination. For men who do experience symptoms, they may have discharge or pain during urination, and/or burning or itching around the opening of the penis.	Often there are no symptoms. For women who do experience symptoms, they may notice a frothy, smelly, yellowish-green vaginal discharge, and/or genital area discomfort. Men who have symptoms may temporarily have a discharge from the penis, slight burning after urination or ejaculation, and/or an irritation in the penis.	Most infected people have no symptoms. For those who do, it can cause a burning sensation while urinating, abnormal white, green, and/or yellowish vaginal or penile discharge. Women may also have abnormal vaginal bleeding and/or pelvic pain. Men may also have painful or swollen testicles.	Most infected people have no symptoms. But some HPV types can cause genital warts – small bumps in and around the genitals (vagina, vulva, penis, testicles, and anus, etc.). If they do occur, warts may appear within weeks or months of having sex with an infected partner. Cancer causing HPV types do not cause symptoms until the cancer is advanced.
HOW IT'S SPREAD	Through vaginal, oral, or anal sex. It can also be passed from mother to child during childbirth.	Through vaginal sex.	Through vaginal, oral, or anal sex. It can also be passed from mother to child during childbirth.	Through vaginal, oral, or anal sex. It can also be passed during skin-to-skin sexual contact, and in rare cases, from mother to child during childbirth.
TREATMENT	Oral antibiotics cure the infection. Both partners must be treated at the same time to prevent passing the infection back and forth. Both partners should abstain from sex until the infection is gone.	Antibiotics can cure the infection. Both partners must be treated at the same time to prevent passing the infection back and forth. Both partners should abstain from sex until the infection is gone. It is common for this infection to recur (come back again).	Oral antibiotics can cure the infection. Both partners must be treated at the same time to prevent passing the infection back and forth. Both partners should abstain from sex until the infection is gone.	There is no cure for HPV (a virus), but there are ways to treat HPV-related problems. For example, warts can be removed, frozen off, or treated through topical medicines. Even after treatment, the virus can remain and cause recurrences of warts.
POSSIBLE CONSEQUENCES (IF LEFT UNTREATED)	Increased risk for infection of other STDs, including HIV. In women, chlamydia can cause pelvic inflammatory disease (PID) which can lead to infertility and tubal (ectopic) pregnancy. Men may develop pain and swelling in the testicles, although this is rare. Babies born to infected women can develop eye or lung infections.	Increased risk for infection of other STDs, including HIV. In women, trich can cause complications during pregnancy.	Increased risk for infection of other STDs, including HIV. In women, gonorrhea can cause pelvic inflammatory disease (PID) which can lead to infertility and tubal (ectopic) pregnancy. Men may develop epididymitis, a painful condition which can lead to infertility. Babies born to infected women can develop eye infections.	Genital warts will not turn into cancer over time, even if they are not treated. Babies born to women with genital warts can develop warts in the throat. Cancer-causing HPV types can cause cervical cancer and other less common cancers (like anal cancer) if the infection lasts for years. Cervical cancer is rare in women who get regular Pap tests.

	GENITAL HERPES	SYPHILIS	HEPATITUS B VIRUS (HBV)	HIV
WHAT IS IT?	A viral infection of the genital areas. It can also infect the area around the mouth.	An infection caused by bacteria that can spread throughout the body.	A viral infection affecting the liver- can be acute (mild illness lasting for a short time) or chronic (a serious life-long illness).	The human immunodeficiency virus (HIV) is the virus that causes AIDS.
HOW MANY PEOPLE GET IT IN THE US?	An estimated 1 million new infections each year, with about 45 million people already infected.	About 46,000 new cases reported each year.	An estimated 40,000 new cases each year (most of which are acquired through sex). Up to 1.2 million people are already infected with chronic HBV.	About 56,000 new infections each year, with an estimated 1.1 million people already living with HIV.
SYMPTOMS	Most people have no symptoms. Herpes 1 typically causes cold sores and fever blisters on the mouth. Herpes 2 typically causes genital sores or blisters. But both viruses can cause sores in either area. A herpes outbreak can start as red bumps and then turn into painful blisters or sores. During the first outbreak, it can also lead to flu-like symptoms (like a fever, headaches, and swollen glands).	Symptoms vary based on the course (timing) of infection— beginning with a single, painless sore (called a chancre) on the genitals, anus, or mouth Other symptoms may appear up to 6 months after the first sore has disappeared, including a rash. However, there may be no noticeable symptoms until syphilis has progressed to more serious problems (see below).	Many people don't have any symptoms, especially adults. People may experience tiredness, aches, nausea and vomiting, loss of appetite, darkening of urine, tenderness in the stomach, or yellowing of the skin and the whites of the eyes (called jaundice). Symptoms of acute HBV may appear 1 to 6 months after exposure. Symptoms of chronic HBV can take up to 30 years to appear, although liver damage can occur silently.	Many people who are infected with HIV do not have any symptoms and feel healthy. Symptoms don't usually develop until a person's immune system has been weakened. The symptoms people experience are usually related to infections and cancers they get due to a weakened immune system. On average, it takes about 10 years from initial HIV infection to develop AIDS.
HOW IT'S SPREAD	Through vaginal, oral, or anal sex. It can also be passed through skin-to-skin sexual contact, kissing, and rarely, from mother to child during childbirth.	Through vaginal, oral, or anal sex. It can also be passed through kissing, if there is a lesion (sore) on the mouth, and from mother to child during childbirth.	Through vaginal, oral, or anal sex. Also through childbirth if the baby does not get vaccinated against HBV; sharing contaminated needles or razors; or exposure to the blood, bodily fluids (like cum) or saliva of an infected person.	Through vaginal, oral, or anal sex. Also by sharing contaminated needles or drugs; and from mother-to-child during pregnancy or breast-feeding. The chance of getting it through kissing is very low.
TREATMENT	There is no cure for herpes—the virus stays in the body and may cause recurrent outbreaks. Medications can help treat symptoms, reduce the frequency of outbreaks, and reduce the likelihood of spreading it to partners.	Antibiotic treatment can cure syphilis if it's caught early, but medication can't undo damage already done. Both partners must be treated and avoid sexual contact until the sores are completely healed.	Most often, acute HBV is treated with rest, eating well, and lots of fluids. Chronic HBV is treated through close monitoring by a doctor and anti-retroviral medications.	There is no cure for HIV or AIDS. Anti-retroviral treatment can slow the progression of HIV disease and delay the onset of AIDS. Early diagnosis and treatment can improve a person's chances of living a longer, healthier life.
POSSIBLE CONSEQUENCES (IF LEFT UNTREATED)	Increased risk for infection of other STDs, including HIV. Some people with herpes may get recurrent sores. Passing herpes from mother to newborn is rare, but an infant with herpes can become very ill.	Increased risk for infection of other STDs, including HIV. Untreated, the symptoms will disappear, but the infection stays in the body and can cause damage to the brain, heart, and nervous system, and can even cause death. Syphilis in women can seriously harm a developing fetus during pregnancy.	Increased risk for infection of other STDs, including HIV. Chronic, persistent inflammation of the liver, and later, cirrhosis or cancer of the liver. Babies born to infected women are likely to develop chronic HBV infection if they don't get needed immunizations at birth (including HBV vaccination).	Increased risk for other life-threatening infections and certain cancers. By weakening the body's ability to fight disease, HIV makes an infected person more vulnerable to infections that they wouldn't otherwise get. HIV can also cause infections that anyone can get, such as other STDs and pneumonia, to be much worse. Left untreated, HIV infection is a fatal disease.

Alcohol and Drug Use

Whether you choose to drink alcohol or not, you are likely to be exposed to alcohol use in some way during your time in college. It is important to get the information, the tools, and the resources needed, in order to potentially prevent yourself or someone else from getting into a risky situation.

Alcohol is the most widely used and abused drug on campus. Not everyone is drinking, though despite how it may seem. If you choose not to drink, you are not alone! In fact, 27% of students choose not to drink alcohol at all, and the majority of students who choose to drink, choose to drink responsibly (NCHA-11, 2009). A small percentage of students are drinking the majority of the alcohol consumed, or engaging in binge drinking. Your first semester of freshman year can be an especially risky time, when it comes to drinking and alcohol-related consequences. This may stem from pre-conceived expectations that alcohol plays a major role in the life of a college student, from little or no previous exposure to alcohol, and from dealing with the freedoms that come with moving out on your own for the first time. Along with the health consequences that are associated with risky drinking, students who consume alcohol also make themselves vulnerable to academic and social consequences (National Institute on Alcohol Abuse and Alcoholism [NIAAA], 2012).

One of the most detrimental outcomes of binge drinking is alcohol poisoning. Alcohol is toxic to humans, when consumed in large quantities. At a certain level, alcohol is poisonous enough to cause brain damage, induce a coma, or lead to death. In small amounts, the human body can handle alcohol because the liver processes it at a constant rate of approximately 1 standard drink per hour. This means that if you have had 3 drinks over a span of 2 hours, your body has processed about 2 drinks, and you still have about 1 drink that is affecting your blood alcohol content. When you drink too quickly for your body to respond to the amount of alcohol consumed, you are putting yourself at risk for alcohol poisoning. If you are drinking standard drinks, it is easy to have an idea of where your blood alcohol content is.

> Blood Alcohol Concentration, or BAC, refers to the amount of your blood volume that is alcohol.

Your BAC can be measured by a breath analysis, a blood test, or a urine test. At a .03 BAC (about 1 drink), you may be feeling mild relaxation, warmth, or a buzz. As your BAC climbs, the other depressive effects of alcohol kick in. If you are going to be driving, the legal BAC limit is .08. At a BAC of about .10, you may start to experience impairment in balance, reaction time, and judgment. Of course, if you are drinking mixed drinks, there is no way of knowing how much you have had to drink or how fast your BAC is climbing.

In addition to the speed and the quantity of your alcohol consumption, other factors may contribute to your BAC. For example, your body weight and your gender are contributing factors. Also, if you are drinking on an empty stomach, the alcohol will affect your BAC much faster than if you have eaten. One factor that is frequently overlooked is the combination of drugs and medication with alcohol. It is important to find out if it is safe to drink while on certain medications. Many times, people will have unexpected reactions to even a small amount of alcohol, due to a prescription they are taking.

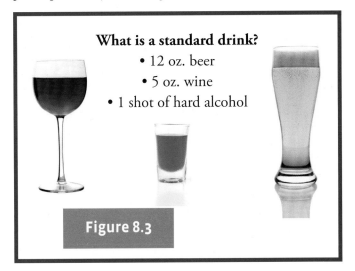

What is a standard drink?
- 12 oz. beer
- 5 oz. wine
- 1 shot of hard alcohol

Figure 8.3

There are several things you can do to avoid putting yourself in dangerous situations. Avoiding trashcan punch, or mystery drinks, is one way of protecting yourself. "Trashcan punch" refers to a mixed alcoholic beverage that may contain a very high percentage of alcohol and is often mixed with a sweetening ingredient. In any given cup of mystery drink, there could be 5 or more shots of alcohol. This means, if you are a 120-pound female and you have one cup, your BAC will already be at a dangerous level, at approximately .15. When you are drinking at this rate, your body does not have a chance to respond, or even give you signals, that you are poisoning yourself. Not only is it impossible to know the alcohol content of your drink, when you consume trashcan punch, but unknown ingredients, such as prescription medications and sedatives like rohypnol (also known as the date rape drug), could be mixed in the drink. Simply put, anything could be in trashcan punch. If you do not know who made your drink or what is in it, or if your drink has been left unattended, your best option is not to drink it.

If you suspect someone is at risk of alcohol poisoning, the best thing you can do for them is to respond quickly and call 911. You should stay with the person and monitor the situation until emergency responders arrive. It is a good idea to turn the person on her or his side, in case they vomit on their own (to prevent them from inhaling their own vomit), but you should NEVER induce vomiting. It is also important to remember that, even if a person has stopped drinking, it does not mean their BAC will not continue to rise. A person could potentially have had their last drink and be only a "little sick," but they could continue to become dangerously ill as their BAC climbs. You should never leave a person alone to "sleep it off," if you suspect they have had too much drink. Further, be aware that the alcohol "strike policy" at The University of Oklahoma is in place to protect you, and you will not be issued a strike for seeking help for yourself or for someone else whom you suspect has had too much to drink.

If you are going out, there are strategies you can utilize to reduce alcohol consumption and to drink more safely.

1. Plan Ahead - Know how much you will drink while you are out, and do not exceed the limit you set for yourself. Also, know where you are going and how you are going to get home.

2. Go out with a Designated Thinker - We all understand the importance of having a designated driver, but having a designated thinker can be just as important. Drinking alcohol affects your judgment and decision-making. It is a good idea to be with at least one friend who is not consuming alcohol. Go out with people you know and trust.

3. Drink Slowly - Give your body a chance to respond to alcohol consumption. Alternate every alcohol beverage with a non-alcoholic beverage, and eat before and during drinking. Binge drinking displays an obvious lack of personal self-control that leads to harmful and dangerous side effects.

4. Avoid Drinking Games - Alcohol poisoning occurs when you are quickly consuming alcohol in a short amount of time.

5. Choose not to Drink - You are not alone if you choose not to drink. It does not mean you have to avoid your friends or social interactions. You just might be that designated thinker that helps someone else stay out of harm's way.

Alcohol is not the only dangerous substance that you may encounter at college. There are other drugs which are illegal for anyone of any age to use and that should be avoided. Typically, students who use drugs believe that there will not be any long-term effects – to their health or otherwise. However, many drugs have negative side effects, cause lifelong consequences, and can lead to addiction. Becoming addicted or relying on any drug (including alcohol) can stop you from achieving academic success. All drugs, especially illegal substances, are likely to prevent you from achieving your goals.

Here are a few of the most common illegal drugs:

• Marijuana
• Ecstasy
• Cocaine
• Amphetamines
• Hallucinogens
• Narcotics

Controlled substances can also be misused or abused, and their use may lead to negative consequences. You should only take medications that a doctor prescribed to you, and you should pay attention to the dosing recommendations. Do not share medications. Abusing prescription medication, or even over-the-counter medications, can have serious consequences. Medication abuse may lead to addiction, overdose, health complications, or death. If any drugs have affected your health or someone else's, please seek medical attention immediately.

Nutrition

With busy schedules and little time, focusing on nutrition and on eating the right kinds of foods is sometimes a low priority for college students. Convenience and available time often determine the food you eat. Unfortunately, convenient eating is not always the best type of eating. There is, however, good news! If you take time to learn about proper nutrition, to plan your meals, and to discover on-campus resources aimed at helping you lead a healthy life, proper nutrition can be yours! Nutrition is about eating the right foods and getting the right nutrients to fuel your

life. It takes self-control to refrain from over-indulging and perseverance to maintain your health. Maintaining a healthy diet and a healthy body weight can reduce your risk of many diseases and has many other overarching benefits!

Remember to get adequate vitamins, minerals, proteins, carbohydrates, and healthy fats, while staying within your calorie needs. Choose nutrient-dense foods and beverages. Nutrient-dense foods are foods that are rich in nutrients, when compared to their calorie level. Try to minimize intake of "empty-calorie" foods or foods that have a high calorie-to-nutrient ratio.

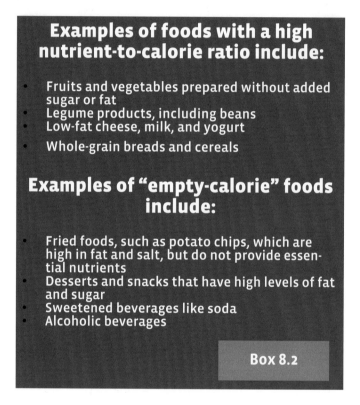

Examples of foods with a high nutrient-to-calorie ratio include:

- Fruits and vegetables prepared without added sugar or fat
- Legume products, including beans
- Low-fat cheese, milk, and yogurt
- Whole-grain breads and cereals

Examples of "empty-calorie" foods include:

- Fried foods, such as potato chips, which are high in fat and salt, but do not provide essential nutrients
- Desserts and snacks that have high levels of fat and sugar
- Sweetened beverages like soda
- Alcoholic beverages

Box 8.2

If you need to lose weight, aim for slow, steady weight loss by eating nutrient-dense foods, staying within your calorie goals, and increasing your physical activity. If you need to gain weight, increase your intake of healthy fats, whole-grain products, low-fat dairy foods, and lean meats. Engage in strength-training exercises, like weight-lifting, to build muscle mass.

OU Housing and Food Services is committed to helping you make nutritious choices. You have many healthy dining options on campus, and you may view the menus of all on-campus restaurants online! The Fitter Foods initiative from OU Food Services aims to help you identify food

items on campus that contain less than or equal to 500 calories, 15 grams of fat, and lower sodium, by placing a Fitter Foods logo next to menu items. Fitter Foods items are available at Crossroads Restaurant, The Laughing Tomato at the Oklahoma Memorial Union, and at the Flying Cow Café in the National Weather Center.

OU Health Service's registered dietitian, Mary Montgomery, MS, RD/LD, offers 9 general tips for college students:

1. Eat breakfast - Breakfast really is the most important meal of the day. It is a great way to start your day and jump-start your metabolism. Beginning your day with protein (i.e. milk, an egg, or Greek yogurt) can help prevent cravings for sweets and other carbohydrates later in the day.

2. Avoid skipping meals - Having a regulated meal pattern, with at least 3 meals per day, is a great way to keep your metabolism going all day long. Not skipping meals helps to control hunger and prevents overeating at the next meal. Avoiding skipping meals is also a way to stabilize blood sugar levels.

3. Smart snacking - Snacking can be a way to maintain energy levels and to prevent the body's metabolism from slowing down. Healthy snack options include: nuts, fruits, vegetables, or cheeses. Be sure not to snack out of boredom or due to emotional hunger, for that type of snacking can result in excess calorie intake and weight gain. Instead, go for a walk, or read your favorite magazine.

4. Do not eat when distracted - Common distractions include watching TV, using the computer, talking on the phone, and reading/studying. Eating while distracted can lead to unconscious eating, where you are unaware of how much food and how many calories have been consumed. Distracted eating may result in weight gain.

5. Increase fruits and veggies - Fruits and vegetables make great snacks. They are loaded with vitamins and minerals, which promote bone, muscle, brain, and immune health. They also contain fiber, which can help you feel full longer.

6. Fill up on fiber - It is recommended to have 25-35g of fiber daily. Eating fiber will make you feel full faster and stay full longer. It can also help lower cholesterol and stabilize blood sugars. Foods that are good sources of fiber include: whole grain cereals and breads, brown rice, beans, raspberries, broccoli, bananas, carrots, and almonds.

7. Drink plenty of water - Try to drink half of your body weight in ounces of water daily. For example, if you weigh 150 pounds, you should drink 75 oz. of water every day. Getting enough water is important because it flushes toxins out of the body, promotes good digestion, and can even suppress appetite.

8. Avoid alcohol - Besides the health risks, alcohol provides a lot of extra calories. One light beer typically contains 100 calories. So, if a person drinks one light beer a night, the calories from the beer, alone, can cause over a 10-pound weight gain in a year. Alcohol can also lead to dehydration, which can cause headaches, confusion, lack of concentration, and dizziness.

9. Get moving - Exercise will help increase your metabolism, which allows you to burn more calories. It can help suppress appetite, control blood sugar levels, and improve your mood. Exercise can also be used, instead of food, as a great stress reliever.

To schedule an appointment with a dietitian through OU Health Services, you may call (405) 325-4441 or stop by the reception desk at Goddard Health Center.

Eating Disorders

Eating disorders involve the emotions, attitudes, and behaviors that surround what you eat and when you eat it. Eating disorders are serious and have life-threatening consequences. Males and females of any age may be affected

Huston Huffman Fitness Center

Named for OU Regent Huston Huffman, the fitness center was completed in 1981. Hosting Intramural Sports, individual fitness opportunities, and fitness classes, the Huston Huffman Fitness Center is a great place to burn off stress. The facility includes courts for basketball, racquetball, and badminton, an indoor track, a rock wall, and workout rooms that can be reserved by student organizations. To use the facility, bring your valid SoonerCard.

by eating disorders. A serious problem may begin with simply dieting and counting calories, and may quickly escalate to a preoccupation with food, weight, and body image. There are three main types of eating disorders:

Anorexia Nervosa – characterized by starving oneself and denying nutrients to oneself in an attempt to decrease body weight.

Bulimia Nervosa – characterized by cycles of binge eating, followed by purging, in an attempt to maintain or lose weight.

Binge Eating Disorder – characterized by compulsive, excessive, or binge eating.

People with eating disorders should seek professional help. Getting early treatment increases the likelihood of recovery. If eating disorders are not identified in the early stages, they can become extremely difficult to identify and treat. The most effective treatment involves some form of counseling, paired with medical and nutritional care. It is important for individuals to start treatment where they feel most comfortable – whether that be with a medical doctor, a dietitian, a counselor, or a psychologist.

If you feel concerned about a friend or a family member whom you believe may have an eating disorder, remember that you cannot force someone to seek professional help. Making the decision to start treatment is an important part of the individual recovery process. The best thing you can do for a friend whom you suspect has an eating disorder is to share your concern, offer them information, and provide support. To learn more about eating disorders and what you can do to help, visit *NationalEatingDisorders.org*.

Physical Activity & Fitness

Being active every day is not just for those who would like to lose weight. It is for everyone! Physical fitness is an important part of your overall health and wellbeing. As a busy college student, you can include activities that are easy to fit into your schedule, such as walking or riding your bike. *A little physical activity is better than none at all, but it is best to aim for 30-60 minutes each day, in order to help you build strength, reduce stress, gain energy, and improve your sleep.* The benefits of staying active are vast, including decreased risk of heart disease and other conditions, such as some cancers, diabetes, osteoporosis, and high blood pressure.

Body Composition is the makeup of the body in terms of lean mass and fat mass. The right types of exercises will help you decrease your body fat while increasing or maintaining your muscle mass.

Aerobic Exercise: This type of exercise increases the health and function of your heart, lungs, and circulatory system. Jogging, swimming, and cycling are among the methods used to achieve this component.

Strength Training: This is the process of building resistance using progressively heavier weights to build or retain muscle. An increase in muscle mass can lead to an increase in the amount of calories your body burns.

Flexibility: Flexibility is an important component of physical fitness. Stretching increases your physical performance, decreases risk of injury, increases blood supply, and reduces stress- just to name a few benefits of stretching.

To avoid dehydration, drink plenty of fluids before feeling thirsty, especially when engaging in physical activity. Muscle contractions produce heat, which leads to perspiration in an effort to cool the body. Dehydration can cause nausea, dizziness, and other complications.

At The University of Oklahoma, it is convenient to stay physically fit with the help of Fitness + Recreation, located at the Huston Huffman Fitness Center. Fit+Rec features a 150,000 square-foot indoor fitness facility, 10 outdoor tennis courts, and intramural fields. Additionally, Fit+Rec provides an indoor and outdoor pool, available to the campus community at the Murray Case Sells Swim Complex. Programs and services are offered year-round to keep the campus community active and engaged in physical activity.

Get Moving – What Fit+Rec Offers:

- 8 basketball/volleyball/badminton courts
- 5 racquetball courts
- Climbing wall
- Squash court
- 1/6th mile indoor track
- 2 large multipurpose rooms
- 2 weight rooms
- Cardio room with flat-screen TV's
- Massage therapy
- Outdoor pursuits
- Group fitness & personal training
- Aquatics lessons
- Intramurals

Whether you are interested in the great outdoors, group fitness classes, or rock climbing, Fit+Rec has something for you – no matter your fitness level!

Plan for Health

Everyone is at a different place in their health and wellness journey. Start where you are and set goals for a healthier and happier you.

Discuss one health and wellness goal you have for your first year as a college student.

Determine 2-3 immediate steps you can take to start on the pathway that will help you achieve this goal successfully.

References

American College Health Association (2009). *American College Health Association National College Health Assessment II: Reference group executive summary fall 2008*. Baltimore: American College Health Association.

Breiding, M.J., Chen J., & Black, M.C. (2014). *Intimate partner violence in the United States — 2010*. Atlanta, GA: National Center for Injury Prevention and Control, Centers for Disease Control and Prevention.

Centers for Disease Control and Prevention (2012). *Sexually transmitted disease surveillance 2011*. Atlanta: U.S. Department of Health and Human Services. Retrieved from: http://www.cdc.gov/std/stats11/surv2011.pdf.

Mayo Clinic (2011). Sleep tips: 7 steps to better sleep. Retrieved from: http://www.mayoclinic.com/health/sleep/HQ01387.

National Institutes on Alcohol Abuse and Alcoholism (2012). *College drinking fact sheet*. Atlanta: U.S. Department of Health and Human Services. Retrieved from: http://pubs.niaaa.nih.gov/publications/CollegeFactSheet/CollegeFactSheet.pdf.

Public Educational Partnerships: MTV (2013). Get yourself tested campaign toolkit. The low down on the most common STDs. Retrieved from: http://www.itsyoursexlife.com/toolkit/materials?category=20.

Chapter 8 REI

Maintaining a Healthy Lifestyle

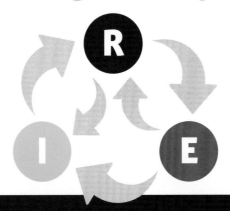

R Reflect

Mid-semester and finals are two times in the semester in which student health issues commonly develop, especially stress. Have you experienced any health concerns since you have been here?

....

E Engage

Make a list the top 6 stressors in your life at this moment. Take a look at Figure 8.1 (on page 134) and determine what kind of stress you have been experiencing.

....

I Impact

Are more of the stressors you are experiencing acute or chronic? How do you think this is affecting your overall health? What are three action steps you can take to ensure that your health stays at its maximum potential?

....

Chapter 9

Managing Your Money: *Finances for College and Beyond*

Jeff Provine, MPW, Adjunct Instructor, Freshman Programs

In this chapter, you will:

- Gain an understanding of the concepts of income and expense.
- Be aware of the responsibilities of debt.
- Understand the importance of budgeting to financial health.
- Identify ways to maximize income and minimize expense.
- Develop a plan for your financial goals.

"The habit of saving is itself an education; it fosters every virtue, teaches self-denial, cultivates the sense of order, trains to forethought, and so broadens the mind."

- T.T. Munger, Research Scientist

Money management is important to college students, who are often leaving the protective nest of home where someone else took care of living expenses. For the first time in their lives, many freshmen are faced with bills, rent, debt, and budgeting. Some become reckless with their spending and find themselves in dire financial positions as a result.

According to a recent poll by the University of California Los Angeles, 85.9% of first-year college students said that landing a good job was a very important reason for going to college (Gordon, 2012). Indeed, learning, networking, and earning a degree from a university are important steps to gaining financial security. However, no matter how much money you earn, if you do not have the skills to manage your money, it will be difficult to go far financially. Learning to manage your money is vital to gaining and maintaining financial security after graduation.

Overview of Budgeting

The foundation of good money management is budgeting. The word "budget" comes from the Middle French word "*bougette*", which means a leather pouch often used to carry money. The term was first applied in politics as a representation of the treasury. In essence, a person's **budget** is the balance between money coming in (income) and money going out (expenses).

Thinking of a budget as a physical bag reminds us that money is a measurable unit. Money, itself, is symbolic (the paper on which currency is printed is of little worth), but what it represents is very real: value. Money does not grow on trees, and ATM's are not magic. In order to have money, a person needs to earn it by contributing value to society. In exchange, society gives value, in the form of money, to the person.

When looking toward your financial goals, remember that you will need to display value (i.e. have a job that contributes something of merit) to achieve income. Having a great deal of value to offer typically provides for a great deal more income. Attending college and achieving a degree typically make a person more valuable to society, and as a result, society returns a higher wage to them.

According to the Bureau of Labor Statistics (2013), an individual with a bachelor's degree earned an average of

"Spending is quick. Earning is slow."

-Russian proverb

$1,066 per week in 2012. Meanwhile, someone with merely a high school diploma yielded only $652 per week, a difference of $414. Imagine what you could do with an extra $400 per week: you could buy a new tablet or phone, take awesome weekend trips, live in a nicer home, or stow away a nest egg of savings for emergencies. On the other hand, imagine what you would have to cut from your lifestyle to live on $400 less each week. Additionally, for those considering a graduate degree, income was found to go up an average of $300 more weekly for master's degrees and an additional $300 weekly for doctoral degrees (Bureau of Labor Statistics, 2013). Further, the unemployment rate of those with bachelor's degrees is 4.5%, which is substantially lower than the high school diploma average of 8.3%. Clearly, education pays.

Earning a degree to land a high-paying job is a great idea, but what can college citizens do until then? Before finding yourself fresh out of college, with student loans hanging over your head, live a well-managed life with a balanced budget that maximizes income and minimizes expenses.

Needs and Wants

When you consider your spending habits, what do you think the difference is between needs and wants?

Think about your spending habits in the past.

Do you think you will need to change the way you spend your money as a college student? If so, how? If not, why not?

Income

The image of "the poor college student" is a classic: eating Ramen noodles on top of a pile of textbooks, while wearing clothes inside-out because there are no quarters for the washer. Some students have additional income through gifts from their parents or grandparents, but not all are so fortunate. Even if you do receive contributions from your family, you need to be mindful of your budget. The trick to avoiding the picture of a student eating Ramen noodles is achieving a reasonable income, even while in college, through scholarships, grants, loans, and working.

Scholarships and Grants

Scholarships and grants are essentially "free money" for your education, as they do not have to be repaid. Scholarships often carry specific academic requirements, such as achieving minimum ACT scores, taking classes in certain fields of study, or maintaining a minimum GPA. Scholarships may also be need-based or may be awarded in an effort to encourage individuals to enter a particular field. Grants are targeted to any number of recipients, from academically-gifted individuals to students with learning disorders, from individuals of a particular gender to children of service members, etc.. Grants may also be awarded based upon a particular set of skills or involvement in certain activities. Federal Pell Grants from the U.S. government are distributed to undergraduate students with financial need.

For both scholarships and grants, you must complete applications. If you have not already done so, complete the Free Application for Federal Student Aid (FAFSA) to learn if you qualify for need-based educational funding from the U.S. government (*www.fafsa.ed.gov*). Also, visit the OU Financial Aid Office (*www.ou.edu/financialaid*) for lists of potential scholarships and grants, as well as information on deadlines for applications. Individual colleges and departments at OU often have their own scholarships available, such as funding for students majoring in architecture, journalism, engineering, and other majors.

In addition to OU's resources, be sure to look for additional scholarships and grants. State, tribal, and local groups often offer grants of their own. The requirements are varied, and applications are free. So, why not apply?

As a note of caution, in your quest for college funding, you should be alert for scams that pose as scholarships, but actually charge for an application and then run with your money. Be aware that scholarship applications should not include a fee. If you have any questions on a potential scholarship, contact the Financial Aid Office.

When you have free time, you should scroll through potential scholarships and grants on OU web sites and other web sources, to see what is available. Completing these applications is good practice for applying to internships and jobs down the road, and you might get money for college as a result of your efforts.

Work

Many students choose to work while in school, in order to generate income. This is a great strategy for bolstering your résumé and for learning job skills, while also earning a paycheck. Even short-term sources of income can make a difference in your financial situation. Be careful, however, that work does not take control of your life, rather only supplements it. Full-time students should always be students first.

There are numerous opportunities for student employment at OU and in the surrounding community. Look into applying for jobs that interest you whenever you see a "Help Wanted" sign. Alternatively, you might begin your own lawn-mowing business in the summer or help friends and acquaintances with babysitting. In addition to off-campus jobs, be sure to check OU's Office of Human Resources' listings at jobs.ou.edu for employment opportunities on-campus. On-campus positions at OU generally work around your class schedule, minimizing the stress of trying to find work hours during the week. Some campus jobs, such as resident adviser positions through OU's Housing and Food, pay in the form of room-and-board waivers and monthly stipends - all for only a few hours per week. With room-and-board expenses resolved, you can use the additional stipend money on something fun or save it for the future.

As a college student, you have options in addition to conventional employment. Internships are an excellent way to get your foot in the door of your career field. While some internships are unpaid, they may still offer class credits. Further, internships sometimes develop into full-time jobs, and such an opportunity may save you the job hunt after graduation.

Loans

A popular source of college funding is borrowing student loans. With student loans, money is granted at a special rate to enable students to pay the steep costs of college. Once you graduate, you are expected to pay back the investment the lender made.

Student loans are not gifts like scholarships. These funds will have to be repaid, along with interest. Repayment of student loans typically begins six (6) months after you graduate,

although you should confirm this information with your respective lender(s). Some students treat their loans like free money, only to find that they are in an enormous debt crunch later. According to the Institute for College Access and Success' Project on Student Debt (2012), the average U.S. graduate of the Class of 2011 owed $26,600 in debt, which translates into hundreds of dollars in repayment each month.

There are two types of student loans: subsidized loans and unsubsidized loans. With subsidized student loans, the government pays the interest until you graduate, giving you a chance to increase your value as a citizen without as much financial burden. Just as public schools are established so that communities may have an educated populace with skills such as reading and writing, the U.S. government also invests in students pursuing higher education, in order to enable the public to reach a higher status. With unsubsidized loans, the interest adds up, even while you are in school, making your loan amount much larger than what you initially borrowed. If at all possible, you should minimize the amount of loans you borrow. This will make your transition from college to post-grad life much easier.

Expenses

Attending college has become increasingly expensive. Tuition and fees are necessary, as the university must have funds to pay for professors' salaries, for the maintenance of campus, and for student services, such as computers in the library, access to health facilities, and more. If you believe fees are too high, you may want to become active in student government, through the University of Oklahoma Student Association (UOSA). Participation in the UOSA gives you an avenue to petition for cost reductions. Just as with federal taxes and the like, simply grumbling is not likely to get you what you want. Also, similar to taxes in government, fees provide great advantages to students, and investigating them may actually lead you to wish there were more fees, in order to have even better facilities, such as another parking garage or a new swim complex.

In addition to tuition and fees, students also need to purchase textbooks. A college myth is that you do not ever use the text, so there is no reason to buy it. Many professors, however, use the textbook as a supplement to lecture material, since they are only able to cover a limited amount of material in each class period. This means that you will be required to know subject matter that is not mentioned in class. This may seem unfair, but it is important that OU students are as knowledgeable about their topic as possible, in order to demonstrate the value of an OU degree.

Fortunately, for students who are shocked at the bookstore prices, there are ways to avoid paying full price. Buying used textbooks allows you to obtain a book at a discounted rate, much like purchasing a used car. Selling books back at the end of the semester may sometimes recoup a little of the expense, but the store has costs to cover, so you will never recover the full amount you originally paid. Some bookstores, including the OU bookstore, have also begun renting textbooks for a semester, which results in lower costs than buying texts new.

Another option is for students to purchase their books online, often through auctions or discount sites. If you opt for this route, bear in mind that many textbooks keep the same title but have updated editions. Because of this, it is important that you ensure that the edition you order is the same as the one required for your course. Buying the textbook's 7th edition is unhelpful if your professor uses the 10th edition. If you choose to purchase online, you should also be sure that the delivery date is as soon as possible, so you do not miss required material. When buying and selling online through any means, always use good judgment and maintain your security. Sellers are usually willing to mail your book after you have paid through a trusted online site, such as PayPal exchange. Bear in mind that meeting in person may be dangerous and should never take place at your home.

The "Got Textbooks?" program through the OU Libraries provides another alternative for borrowing textbooks. Thanks to a $200,000 fund established by President David L. Boren, the library has created a reserve of textbooks for many common courses. Using your student ID, you may borrow a textbook for two hours at a time, which is often sufficient time to study or to complete assignments. You may visit *www.libraries.ou.edu* for more information.

In addition to the costs of college, students face ordinary living expenses. Living expenses include: rent for somewhere to sleep and keep belongings, bills for such services as cell phones, food, toiletries, entertainment, and perhaps even a car. While tuition and fees are essentially locked-in, each person may choose their own lifestyle, and thus, can determine a certain extent of their living expenses.

Rent

As a freshman, you likely live in the residence halls or commute from home, but you will eventually need to make a decision about where to live next year. Everyone is different, so consider your needs. Options for housing include: remaining on-campus in student housing (check *www.ou.edu/housingandfood* for room rates and meal plans) or moving into a sorority or fraternity house, an apartment, or an independent house. Each option comes with its own benefits and drawbacks, so it is important to know what you require to feel comfortable in your home.

Questions to ask yourself:

"How much room do I need?"
Living in a small space is not necessarily a bad thing. If you do not need a walk-in closet and your own parking space, then do not pay extra for them.

"How much privacy do I need?"
If you need a quiet environment to study, a house full of roommates may not be the best option. If your cleaning habits are very particular, having your own bathroom may save a lot of stress. On the other hand, if you can live with roommates and share a bathroom, you may save money.

"What amenities do I need?"
An apartment complex may have a pool, a workout room, and basketball and volleyball courts, but if you do not actually use them, they are needless expenses. Check your budget, and see what you can afford.

"How often will I be here?"
Many people with busy lifestyles use their apartments primarily for storage and sleeping. In such instances, a studio apartment or an apartment with a small bedroom and kitchen makes more sense than paying for a place with a dining room you will never use.

"How does this place make me feel?"
An apartment may be incredibly affordable, but if the environment does not feel safe to you, it probably is not worth the savings. College can be very stressful, so bear

in mind that the way your home makes you feel can be important to your wellbeing.

Ways to minimize expenses:

Find roommates to split expenses. Remember that living in an apartment, rather than a house, usually cuts down on utility bills and lawn care. Keep in mind that a first-floor apartment generally has lower heating/cooling costs, due to the extra insulation provided by the upper floor(s).

Bills

Living in student housing or in a fraternity or sorority house can be an effective way to save money. This may seem unlikely, when staring at bills for thousands of dollars, but remember that those bills include electricity, water, internet, and amenities. Also, living on-campus may save in gas costs and in commuting fees, as well as making getting to class easier. If, however, you determine that you can live more happily elsewhere, it may be your best option to share a place with a roommate or two.

Ways to minimize expenses:

Shop around. Use ads in newspapers and magazines, online listings, posters, and word-of-mouth recommendations to find a variety of options in different price ranges. Save on electricity by turning off lights and by flipping off power supplies to any appliance when not using it. "Vampire" appliances such as televisions (and practically anything with a clock in it) continue to sap electricity even when turned "off."

Raise the thermostat in the summer and lower it in the winter, while dressing accordingly for comfort. According to the U.S. Department of Energy (2012), heating and cooling expenses are typically half of the average utility bill. Ask yourself, "What can I live without?" Do you need that extra bandwidth and those movie channels, or could you live as happily with a smaller plan? These extra luxuries might even be a detriment if you constantly get caught up in social media discussions or in watching games, when you should be studying.

Food & Supplies

Even the thriftiest person has to eat, and items such as toilet paper, clothing, etc., are necessities for maintaining a normal life. While living on campus, your food is locked-in with your meal plan, but later on, you will have to furnish your own groceries. It is a good idea to shop around, in order to learn where you can buy the items you need at the most reasonable prices. When stocking a first apartment, a set of dishware from a dollar store might be a good option, rather than purchasing nice dishes that you will replace later.

Ways to minimize expenses:

Cook dinners at home, and pack lunches whenever possible. Keep in mind that the costs of eating out add up quickly - in dollars as well as calories. Use a refillable water bottle instead of purchasing and throwing away individual plastic water bottles. Buy generic brands, when possible. Compare the labels between the more expensive, colorfully-marketed items and the less expensive ones. Often, the two are essentially the same, and you may be paying more for the appealing packaging when you buy the more expensive brands.

Look for sales and coupons for items you plan to buy. Watch out, however, for purchasing something that you are not going to use, just because "it's a good deal." If you do not need it, do not buy it. Watch out for social pressures that may lead you to purchase items that, deep down, you do not even want.

Amenities

While in an ideal world people might spend only what they need to spend, this is the real world, and most people will want more than the basic necessities. Plan to set aside some of your money for activities that bring you stress relief, adventure, interesting experiences, and fun.

Ways to minimize expenses:

Some expenses arise from boredom. Keep yourself entertained with free activities, such as a round of Frisbee golf, instead of buying amusement park tickets. Go by the library to check out DVD's, or scan through Netflix, instead of going to the movie theater. If bored, go jogging, rather than flicking through online stores to see what purchases are recommended for you. Wait to watch big-screen blockbuster movies in the Oklahoma Memorial Union on Friday nights, rather than spending full price for a theater ticket.

The OU campus has many events that offer free food. To find these activities, visit #freefood@OU on Twitter.

Join a club, or start one yourself. After a semester of probation, new OU clubs can obtain funds from UOSA for food purchases. Further, clubs may choose their own menus.

Dates and outings can be expensive, but even free activities can be enjoyable. See priceless works of art by Monet, Van Gogh, and Picasso on campus for no charge at the Fred Jones Jr. Museum of Art. Or, enjoy an afternoon picnic with a date at the Duck Pond on campus. Also, visit the Norman Convention and Visitors Center web site at *www.visitnorman.com* for listings of free events taking place in the community.

For those who enjoy recreational shopping, rather than visiting boutiques or the mall, check out local flea markets at the Cleveland County Fairgrounds, thrift stores on Main Street, and estate sales listed in the Norman Transcript. The thrill of the hunt can be the same, but at remarkable savings.

For book-lovers, borrow books from the library. This saves on costs, as well as eliminating the need to store the books after you have read them. Increasingly, DVDs and e-books are also available for loan from libraries. If the book you would like to read is not in stock, you may request an interlibrary loan through the library web site. Both the Bizell Memorial Library on campus and the Norman Public Library participate in interlibrary loan programs, in which the library obtains the requested book for you from another library.

Vehicle Ownership

In Oklahoma, owning a vehicle seems to be a necessity. Vehicles can, however, be deceptively expensive. In addition to the cost of the purchase, there will also be finance charges and interest expenses on your loan. Plus, there will be costs associated with insurance, gas, regular maintenance, and emergency repairs. Think about whether you actually need

Sam Noble Oklahoma Museum of Natural History

Situated south of main campus beside the OU Law School, the Sam Noble Museum was opened in 2000. It features permanent exhibits of Native American artifacts, Oklahoma wildlife, and the famed Hall of Ancient life, which holds some of the best displays of prehistoric creatures in the world. In addition, the museum has numerous programs that bring exhibits from all over the world to Oklahoma, ranging from paleontological finds, to kachina dancers, to chocolate. The museum is free to OU students and a great place for dates.

a car or if it will typically sit in the parking lot while you have to make payments.

Ways to minimize expenses:

Ride a bicycle. In addition to providing transportation, bike riding is also healthy exercise and an excellent means of reducing your impact on the environment. Bear in mind that the OU police department has an annual bike sale, where students can purchase a bike at a discounted rate.

Ride the bus. OU collaborates with the Norman CART bus to provide transportation all over town and even to Oklahoma City. Students often ride free with an OU ID. Visit ou.edu/cart for routes and times. For long-distance travel, such as a weekend trip to Dallas, take the train from Norman, ride the Megabus, or utilize other discount travel services. Save on a commuter pass by parking for free at Lloyd Noble and riding the shuttle bus to the South Oval.

"We'll hold the distinction of being the only nation in the history of the world that ever went to the poor house in an automobile." -Will Rogers

Debt

For most first-year students, debt seems far away, but it will become very real, very fast. Debt is a complex issue in modern America.

British economist John Maynard Keynes (1883-1946), writing at the time of the Great Depression, saw the potential for economic recovery in spending (Library of Economics and Liberty, 2008b). He proposed that the government borrowing money and creating jobs allows people who would otherwise be unemployed to gain income that they, then, might spend. He suggested that this spending fosters a stronger economy, by allowing debts to be repaid later. For individuals, this could mean borrowing money to start a successful business, or it could mean living in a home and building equity by paying a mortgage, instead of renting and saving. Friedrich Hayek (1899-1992) countered Keynes' idea, by stating that creating debts only causes more complicated problems down the road (Library of Economics and Liberty, 2008a). He believed that too much debt would cause the economy to falter and, upon the eventual next recession, to fall even further. On an individual level, Hayek

noted that people lose much of their income, due to steep monthly credit card payments.

As a college student, you may act as a Keynesian, taking student loans to invest in your future career, while trusting that your future profession will enable you to repay those loans. Or, you may be of the Hayek mindset, working and hoping to leave school without any debt. In either case, it is important to be mindful of how much debt you have and of your future capacity to repay it.

Another point to consider is that taking out and repaying loans improves your credit score, a rating by which potential lenders gauge whether loaning money to you is a worthwhile investment. Credit bureaus track the financial worthiness of an individual, and give the individual a rating that lenders use to determine whether they should offer that person a loan. Factors such as on-time payments, use of credit lines, length of credit history, and types of credit used are calculated to determine the score.

College can be a crucial time to build your credit score, as many institutions are eager to work with college students who are just starting out. While it might not seem important at the moment, a credit score may be requested for an apartment application, a job application, and, especially, a loan application for a car or a house. If you intend to have a mortgage someday, beginning to build your credit score with a credit card and ensuring that all of your payments are made in a timely manner can be a good way to establish a solid score.

Credit cards are a means to build your credit, if used carefully, but they may also be a trap. College students, fresh from home and without adequate money sense, usually treat credit cards as "free money." However, that is hardly the case. Everything has to be paid back and, often, with interest.

Thanks to the Credit Card Act of 2009, companies are less able to prey on college students (White House, 2009). You should, however, still be mindful of lending policies, and do not allow yourself to get stuck in a bad financial situation. For example, do not sign up for cards that charge application fees or membership fees. Also, be mindful of the Annual Percentage Rates (APR) which dictate the interest charged on your purchases. Further, always pay your monthly bill on time, or you may accrue expensive late fees.

Credit cards operate on what is called revolving credit. *Revolving credit* is a type of credit that does not have a fixed number of payments. This credit is automatically renewed as debts are paid off. Whereas some debts, such as mortgages or student loans, have a set number of standardized payments, credit cards have a small minimum payment that often fluctuates according to your balance. While it may look like you are saving money with a small payment, the credit card company is able to charge interest on the leftover debt, as well as on the interest it has accrued. The next month, you will owe practically the same amount, despite your payment, and the credit card company will happily send you another statement asking for more. After interest accrual, a $40 tank of gas, paid with a minimum of $25 over the course of several months, could cost you $60 or $70 in the end.

Budgeting During College

Be mindful of your income and your expenses. Plan to sit down and write out all of your incoming funds for a semester, whether they come through scholarships, student loans, and/or working. Then, write down all of your potential expenses, such as rent, bills, groceries, etc. If you are factoring in scholarship funds, student loans, or other money that comes only once per semester, break the expenses into monthly blocks to ensure that you save some for December, rather than spending it all by the end of October. Also, make sure that your expenses do not exceed your income. Otherwise, you may be in a major crunch when the money runs out. It is also important that you always pace yourself and frequently update your budget. Maybe $150 per month is not enough for groceries, and you need to allocate more to that. Maybe you decide to go to the dollar theater instead of the regular theater and, thereby, save $19 dollars per week. Do your best not to "borrow" from yourself, saying "I'll spend next month's date night money this month, and then, I'll eat Ramen all next month instead of real groceries." Showing responsibility with your money in the short term by saying "no" to an unnecessary expense will save you a lot of pain later.

Budgeting After College

After graduating college and finding a well-paying job, you will begin to make progress toward your financial goals. Each person will have her/his own goals, whether it involves home ownership, early retirement, investing in college funds for children and grandchildren, or all of the above. If you believe you will need increased income to meet your desires, a good strategy is to further your education. While a bachelor's degree provides an average of $1,066 a week, a master's degree raises the amount to $1,300 per week. A professional degree in medicine or law raises the weekly income to $1,735. In addition, achieving certifications can be a great way to increase your value as an employee and, thereby, your salary. Even after school, you should continue your education to continue to grow your income potential.

When evaluating salaries, be mindful of gross versus net income. Gross income is the total value of your income before taxes and deductions are withheld, whereas net income is what is left after withholdings. The most notorious distinction is in taxes, which take about 24.7% of national income to provide government services (Porter, 2012).

While making $4,000 a month sounds like a lot, consider the following budget: $1,000 to taxes; $500 in student loans; $700 in a mortgage or rent; $300 in bills; $500 in groceries and eating out; $300 in a car payment; and $100 in gas and car upkeep. This budget leaves only $600 after expenses. Just like in college, if you minimize your expenses, you can live on less money and dedicate the money you have saved to a nest egg or investments. As Benjamin Franklin wrote, "A penny saved is a penny earned."

The earlier you begin saving money, the more quickly you will establish a responsible lifestyle. Make careful investments with your income. Rather than buying heavily marked-up clothes that will be out of style the next season, wear what you have and accessorize. Rather than blowing all of your money on a wild weekend in Vegas, invest in something you will enjoy for years to come. You may have an urge to buy a DVD box set right now for $89, but if you wait a few months, you could pick it up on sale for half of that price. Study after study has shown the benefits of a lifestyle of delayed gratification (University of Rochester, 2012). Consume less now in order to secure a comfortable

retirement free from worry. Those who invest poorly burn through their money quickly on expensive purchases, like concert tickets, and when they are elderly, they live on very limited retirements. That same money, well-invested, will allow for more and better choices later on, such as travel or entertainment. Further, it is important to be mindful that medical costs increase with age, meaning that treatments you may someday wish you could afford may be financially out-of-reach in old age.

In addition to minimizing consumption, the money you save may be invested in a bank through a savings account or a retirement fund. Saving early allows more interest to accrue, giving you more money in the end. The Rule of 72 gives a formula for predicting interest growth: divide 72 by the interest return rate. An investment at 6% will double in twelve (72/6) years. If you begin investing at age 22, instead of age 34, you will have twice the retirement fund.

Finally, remember that the definition of "poor" is highly relative. People with six-figure incomes often do not consider themselves rich as they look toward millionaires, but the average person on the planet makes only about $7,000 a year (Boston Globe, 2007). A "poor" college freshman in name-brand clothes with a smart phone and keys to a car is really doing quite well, compared to people in other parts of the world. Appreciate what you have, and work toward attaining what you would like to have in your future.

Where will your money go?

One of the advantages of a college education is the opportunity you will have to increase your spending power. How you spend your money impacts not only you, but your community as well.

Think forward about how you will spend your money as your income grows. Imagine you live in a community with a large corporate chain grocer, an employee-owned multi-location store, and an independent locally-sourced grocer. Where will you choose to buy your produce?

COLLEGE BUDGET WORKSHEET

Take some time to create your personal budget by using this worksheet to list your income and expenses for the month, semester, and school year. Determine if you have more income than expenses for each time frame. If not, consider areas where you will need to cut back to maintain a more balanced budget. Also, consider how to distribute the funds you receive in order to best meet your needs over time.

INCOME CATEGORY	MONTHLY	SEMESTER	SCHOOL YEAR
Job(s)			
Parents			
Scholarships			
Grants			
Loans			
Other			
TOTAL:			

EXPENSE CATEGORY	MONTHLY	SEMESTER	SCHOOL YEAR
Rent or Room & Board			
Utilities (water, electric, gas, garbage)			
Groceries			
Clothing/Personal			
Medical/Healthcare			
Donations/Gifts to Charity			
Savings			
Entertainment (cable, cell phone, internet, eating out)			
Transportation (car payment, insurance, and gas)			
Debt Payments			
Other (books, tuition & fees, computer expenses)			
TOTAL:			

Adapted from:
9 Things Every College Student Should Know About Money
Copyright 2006 Brad Burnett

1. Have a Plan

Do you want to know the secret of financial success? Spend less than you make! In creating your financial plan, first determine what money you have coming in (revenue). Then, ask, "Where's the money going out (debt)?" Determine what you need versus what you want. Once that has been determined, pay for the things you need first, and then, go after what you want.

2. Hey, Gotta Dollar I Can Borrow?

Companies let you borrow because they make a profit from loaning you money—by charging interest. With that in mind, it is almost always best to pay cash when making a purchase. Interest not paid equals money saved. The majority of people, though, are not walking around with enough cash to buy a house or pay for college. Car loans, student loans, and home loans are all "installment" loans. ("Installment" means that the loan has a beginning and an end.)

A car loan is typically a bad investment. This is because a vehicle depreciates (loses value) dramatically once it is purchased. A new vehicle may lose up to 20 percent of its value simple by being driven off the lot. So, a vehicle purchased for $22,000 is only worth $17,600 immediately after purchase. It may be a better financial move to buy a used car.

One of the best ways to start creating wealth is by purchasing a home. A home is one of the few tangible items you can purchase where the value actually appreciates (goes up) after you buy it. A home located in an area where prices are going up, provided it is well-maintained, will increase in value.

A student loan is more like an investment in you. One goal every college student should have is to graduate. That should be your "end game," and achievement of that goal has a dollar figure attached to it. The latest Census Bureau information reports that, nationwide, the median yearly income for a high school graduate is $33,904. But, if you graduate college, the median yearly income is $55,432. That is a difference of $21,528 a year, or when multiplied over a 40-year career, $861,120! So, on average nationwide, a bachelor's degree has the potential to increase earnings more than $860,000 over a high school diploma. Get a master's degree, and the figure is more than $1 million!

Student borrowers, on average nationwide, graduate $26,600 in debt. But, let's keep this in perspective: $26,600 is about the cost of a new automobile. You are presented with an opportunity to invest $26,600 in yourself now to create an earning opportunity of more than $750,000 over your lifetime. However, I strongly suggest you research all your funding options before you borrow. Your OU Financial Aid Office can help!

3. Charge

Another type of credit is revolving credit, such as is used in credit cards. As the word "revolving" implies, there is no end. You make payments at the interest rate offered, in an open-ended financial relationship. If you pay your balance in full every month, there are no penalty or interest charges, and it's just like using cash.

The problem comes when you don't pay your balance in full. Let's say you obtain a credit card at 18 percent interest and purchase an iPad for $500. Approximately 30 days later, you will get a bill from the credit card company, indicating that you have a balance of $500 and that the minimum payment due is $10. So, you mail a check for $10 to the credit card company. They get your check, smile because you didn't pay them in full, then go back to the beginning of the billing period, and charge you 18 percent interest (1.5 percent monthly) on $500 from the first day of the month to the last day of the month. That comes to $7.50 of interest off the top and will only apply $2.50 to your balance! Thirty days later, you will get another statement in the mail, showing a balance due of $497.50. You send them another $10 minimum payment. They get the $10, go back to the beginning of the billing period, and once again charge you 18 percent interest on $497.50. You have now sent them $20, and you still owe them $494.96! By making only the minimum monthly payment, it is actually costing you more than $1,000 for your iPad – more than twice what it is worth! Plus, it will take you more than nine years to pay off the card/iPad! You will have graduated and be years out of college and still sending the credit card company the minimum payment for that iPad, which you will probably no longer own.

Credit cards are not evil, but they are the single most dangerous financial tool a college student can have in possession. Students are being financially devastated by them on a regular basis.

4. They Are Watching

"They" are the credit bureaus, and they're watching how you handle money. They know your personal information, if you have a checking account, if you have a credit card in your name, if you have a car loan, and if you make a mistake. A FICO score (a type of credit score) ranges from 300 to 850. The higher your score, the more willing people are to loan you money and the better the terms they will offer. If you "pay as agreed"(which means that you pay on time), your score will go up. But, if you are late on a payment or if your account is sent to collections, your score will drop, and the blemish will stay on your record for seven years.

There's a rumor that the only way to build a credit score is to have a credit card and carry a balance. That is not true. It is true that, if you get a credit card and pay the balance in full every month, your score will go up. Actually, if you get a credit card and only make the minimum payment every month, your score will go down.

5. If it Sounds Too Good To Be True, It Probably Is

There's an old saying that goes, "If it sounds too good to be true, it probably is." If you're watching television at 3 a.m. and somebody is screaming at you, "Send me your money and I'll give you the secret to getting rich," don't listen. The only person getting rich in that scenario is the person who gets your money. "Make $50,000 a year stuffing envelopes." If you could make $50,000 stuffing envelopes, everyone who has a job making less than fifty grand would quit and go stuff envelopes. Don't be hustled.

6. Appearances Can Be Deceiving

Remember, you typically bring home 65 to 70 percent of your earned salary. If your gross amount is $1,000, you're only going to bring home $650 to $700, after taxes and deductions. That is the amount you should consider when creating your financial plan.

7. Pay Yourself

Pay yourself first. Consider yourself as an expense. Take a percentage of your income—many use 10 percent—and put it into an account that earns interest (e.g. a savings account). Then, decide how you define an "emergency," and only touch that money if an emergency occurs. If your emergency threshold is too low, you will never save money because you will constantly be dipping into these funds. On the other hand, it is comforting to know that you have funds available if something unforeseen happens.

8. Time

Each of you has going for you the single greatest factor in the creation of wealth: time. The fact that you're young puts you in a position to create tremendous amounts of wealth. It's called The Rule of 72.

9. The Rule Of 72

The Rule of 72 is this: You put money into some type of account that earns interest, and then, you take the amount of interest being earned on that money and divide into 72.

# of years to double your money = 72/interest rate earned

If your money is earning 10 percent interest, divide 10 into 72 to determine how long it will take for your money to double. At 10 percent, your money doubles every 7.2 years. The more doubling you do will depend on when you start saving. The earlier you start to save, the more times your money will double.

If you put away $400 a month, starting at age 23, and your money earns 8 percent interest, by the time you turn age 60, you will be a millionaire. Now, let's say you decide you just can't afford to save right now, so you put it off. You would have to save $2,500 a month starting at age 44, if your money is earning 8 percent, to be a millionaire by 60. It is so important to start saving young.

References

Boston Globe (2007). Average income worldwide. Retrieved from http://www.boston.com/news/world/articles/2007/10/07/average_earnings_worldwide/.

Bureau of Labor Statistics (2013). Education pays. Retrieved from http://www.bls.gov/emp/ep_chart_001.htm.

College Board (2012). New college board trends reports: Public college tuition increases slow; Rapid growth in federal grant aid ends [Press release]. Retrieved from http://press.collegeboard.org/releases/2012/new-college-board-trends-reports-public-college- tuition-increases-slow.

Gordon, L. (2012). More college freshmen see getting good job as key goal, poll finds. *Los Angeles Times.* Retrieved from http://articles.latimes.com/2012/jan/26/local/la-me-0126-freshman-20120126.

The Institute for College Access & Success (2012). Average student debt climbs to $26,600 for class of 2011 [Press release]. Retrieved from http://www.ticas.org/files/pub//Release_SDR12_101812.pdf.

Library of Economics and Liberty (2008). John Maynard Keynes: The concise encyclopedia of economics. Retrieved from http://www.econlib.org/library/Enc/bios/Keynes.html.

Library of Economics and Liberty (2008). Friedrich August Hayek: The concise encyclopedia of economics. Retrieved from http://www.econlib.org/library/Enc/bios/Hayek.html.

Porter, E. (2012). America's aversion to taxes. *New York Times.* Retrieved from http://www.nytimes.com/2012/08/15/business/economy/slipping-behind-because-of-an- aversion-to-taxes.html?_r=2&src=recg&.

University of Rochester (2012). The marshmallow study revisited. Retrieved from http://www.rochester.edu/news/show.php?id=4622.

US Department of Energy (2012). Tips: Heating and cooling. Retrieved from http://energy.gov/energysaver/articles/tips-heating-and-cooling.

White House (2009). Fact sheet: Reforms to protect American credit card holders [Press Release]. Retrieved from http://www.whitehouse.gov/the_press_office/Fact- Sheet-Reforms-to-Protect-American-Credit-Card-Holders.

Chapter 9 REI

Managing Your Money

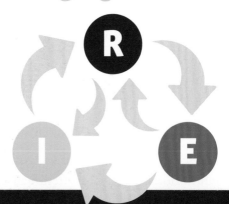

R

Reflect

Think about your past experience handling finances? Did you have a job in high school? Did you receive an allowance? How did you handle your money decisions?

....

Engage

Review the College Budget Worksheet on page 162. Fill it out or create a similar budget based on your own personal financial considerations.

....

Impact

Did anything about your budget surprise you once you saw it on paper? What can you do to improve your financial habits? Specifically, list three practical ways you can economize now as a student.

....

Chapter 10

Impacting Your World: *Civic and Community Engagement*

Kyle Harper, Ph.D., Senior Vice President and Provost and Professor of Classics and Letters

In this chapter, you will:

- Learn the meaning of civic education.
- Gain a greater understanding of the spheres of influence.
- Learn how you can impact your various communities.
- Learn how your education can prepare you for life.

"You are a citizen, and citizenship carries responsibilities."

- Paul Collier, Author

The years you spend at OU will be among the most formative years of your life. The person who walks across the stage at graduation will still be you, but older, a little wiser, and certainly better prepared to enter the workforce.

The Opportunity of a Lifetime

You came to college wanting a degree, because you need a job. So you'll work to acquire the knowledge and skills – whether in Accounting or Meteorology, Journalism or Dance – that will launch you on the career you seek to have. But, the person who walks across the stage at graduation won't just be older and more knowledgeable. You will be a different person. The experiences and the relationships – and the intellectual journey – that you will have at OU will shape you into the person you will be for the rest of your life. That is the root meaning of education – from the Latin *ex* (out of) + *ducere* (to lead forth) – to bring out of you the person who you truly are. The college years are a unique phase of life, beyond the adolescent experiences of high school, before all of the responsibilities of work and family begin to intrude. Never again will you be so free to decide what you want to become, to explore your values and ambitions. Never again will you have the opportunities to meet people who are different from you across all types of meaningful identities through student clubs, participating in intercultural activities, study abroad and everyday relationships from all walks of life all over the state, our nation and the globe. And never again will you have such a community around you designed to help you – even provoke you – into that process of exploration where

you can challenge yourself to learn, extend your view of the world, make mistakes, ask for help and support, and learn from your mistakes with the support of an entire university community interested in your growth and success.

The seal of the University of Oklahoma features a seed sower – a symbol of the fact that an education plants the seeds of future growth and development as a person. Around the seed sower are the words, in Latin, *CIVI ET REIPUBLICAE*, the motto of the University. The phrase means "For the Citizen and for the Country." It expresses the values of the University, which exists to send its graduates off into the world prepared for the duties of citizenship.

Civic education, the education that is necessary for good citizenship, is a fundamental mission of the university. Civic education shapes the curriculum. It influences the priorities of the University. It fosters many virtues including love of learning, intellectual humility and open-mindedness. It determines what sorts of events and speakers and clubs are supported on campus. Civic education has three goals. First, it should provide you with the basic knowledge you need to function as a citizen. For instance, if you don't have some basic understanding of how the Constitution works, then it is impossible to be an effective part of our democratic system. Second, it should provide you with the essential tools you need to participate as a citizen. You need to be able to think critically and to communicate clearly to be an effective participant in American life. Third, a civic education should give you the inspiration you need to develop as a citizen and to care about your responsibilities within your community. Ideally, your education should make you informed, aware and engaged. An essential part of this civic education is learning to engage in a diverse world that is interconnected culturally, economically, politically and socially. The basic knowledge to function well in society requires an ability to work in diverse teams, to recognize your own diversity and to responsibly facilitate diverse intellectual thought in organizations.

One of the most important skills of living in a society and working side by side with others, supervising others and reporting to others is self-reflection. *Self-Reflection*, or the ability to understand oneself as one moves into adulthood is an incredible life skill. You need to learn when you need help. Having the understanding of your relative strengths and weaknesses and knowing that you need to seek out someone who can help you or support you is an important tool for success. Helping others to self-reflect is also an important adult skill that will serve you well in leadership and your future work life.

This chapter explores the values that animate the University and identifies some of the opportunities that you have for development and for engagement. It is meant to encourage you to use the full resources of the campus community to become the type of person – and the type of citizen – you want to be.

Beyond the Classroom

There are 168 hours in a week. You will spend 15 of them in class. But don't think of those hours, and the time you spend studying, as "school," and the rest as "free time." At OU, you are surrounded with opportunities for cultural enrichment, spiritual community, and political engagement. Inevitably, you will be encouraged by a professor to attend an evening lecture or visit a museum, probably for "extra credit." This is a way to incitivize you to expand your horizons and to recognize the richness of the campus life around you. You should seize on these opportunities, but you should also be proactive and take advantage of the riches all around

you. Go to a lecture – when it's not for extra credit. Visit a museum – for yourself. Go to a symphony – on a date! You might be surprised at how much you will enjoy it, and keep in mind that never again will you be surrounded by so much free culture. It's easy to feel that there's so much going on that you have no idea where to start (how do you jump on a moving carousel that never stops?). But the earlier you take the leap into involvement, the more time you'll have to discover what you're passionate about and how you can make a difference.

Some ways to accelerate your engagement, include:

- **Ask** - Never, ever, ever be afraid to ask someone how to get involved with something. Go to your professor's office hours and ask how to be involved in a project or a lab. Ask people – faculty, staff, other students – how they got involved in what they're doing.

- **Friends and Others** - It's always easiest to follow your friends and to learn about what they're involved in. But, widen your circle in any way you can. You will rarely have the chance in post-university life to explore the diversity of interests, cultures, activities, and purpose driven organizations than you will here at OU.

- **Look for opportunity where it's advertised** - Pay attention to the events listed or advertised in *The Oklahoma Daily*. It's the central spot for notifying the campus community of what's going on.

- **Get your foot in the door** - If you find a business or a cause or a campaign that you care about, do what it takes to get your foot in the door. Ask about internships, and if they don't have internships, ask if they'll consider creating one. Sometimes, getting your foot in the door means being willing to do basic jobs. For instance, the way into a political campaign may be stuffing envelopes or handing out stickers at a football game – it's not glamorous, but it gives you an inside view and fosters relationships that will open doors for you down the road.

Ready for Impact

You might find yourself thinking about how you might

be able to impact your community in the future. But, what about now? There is no need to wait until you have graduated college and your career is in place to begin making an impact. You can start today!

As you reflect on ways to impact your world as a student, you may recall our discussion of Spheres of Influence in Chapter 1. Again, these spheres of influence radiate outward from each learner in the following manner: 1) campus community, 2) local community, 3) national community, and 4) global community. We will discuss a few examples of how you might choose to impact each of these spheres while

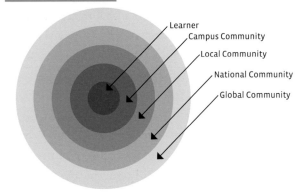

| Figure 10.1 | **Spheres of Influence** |

Learner - Learners bring their individual backgrounds, experiences and talents that have been influenced by their families, schools, and communities. As learners grow and mature, they increase their ability to influence, contribute to, and improve their various communities.

Campus Community - The campus community creates opportunities for the exchange of knowledge and creativity among diverse members of the university. It is the expectation that each member will exude respect, openness, and honesty in this environment.

Local Community - The local community entails the neighborhoods, cities, and states in which individuals live. This local community offers direct engagement to its members by providing opportunities for participation in various social and civic activities.

National Community - Within the national community, individuals share the freedoms and practices that come with living in a particular country. As part of these commonalities, members take part in mandatory and voluntary responsibilites such as paying taxes, obeying laws, and voting. Citizens of a national community help shape the future of the country in which they live.

Global Community - As members of the global community, individuals should be knowledgeable of political, social and economic factors that impact others around the world. Members should seek to understand and respect people from all cultures and strive to preserve the planet's other life forms and resources.

you are at OU. Keep in mind that this is not an exhaustive list, and no doubt, there are many wonderful ideas that you and your classmates can add to these suggestions.

Campus Community

During your time at OU, you will likely encounter many opportunities to impact your campus community. As discussed in Chapter 7, the University is bursting with campus programs and events that are seeking student volunteers to assist in the excellent work they do for the OU community. As a Sooner Citizen, impacting your campus community can be a rewarding experience, both in the benefits to others and in the strengthened ties to your university.

Follow Your Passions

As you consider ways to impact your campus community, one of the best guides you can have is to follow your passions. When you are passionate about a cause, you are more likely to give your most devoted and invested efforts. There are numerous ways to follow your passions on the OU campus. For example, if you care deeply about integrity and are concerned about the impact of cheating, plagiarism, and other forms of academic dishonesty on the university's reputation, you might volunteer to become a student representative for the Academic Integrity Council (*integrity.ou.edu*). If you are concerned with issues surrounding sexual violence on campus, you might volunteer to be a peer educator in the "Step In, Speak Out" Program or become involved in one of the many other activities sponsored by the Gender + Equality Center. If you are motivated to advocate for changes to OU policies or to find solutions to campus challenges, consider participating in the OU Student Government Association (*ou.edu/sga*). Or, maybe you care about our campus staying beautiful and want to participate in OU's Adopt-an-Area program, in which students sign up to care for a section of campus each week. You may be interested in joining any one of the numerous racial and ethnic student organizations on campus to mentor or be mentored. Or you may want to have an impact by working across groups and join programs or volunteer at the Southwest Center for Human Relations Studies. Whatever your passion, you can find opportunities to use that energy to impact your campus community.

Be Alert for Daily Opportunities

On a daily basis, you can impact your campus community by

helping someone who appears lost, by giving an encouraging word to a classmate who is struggling, by picking up litter, and by showing kindness and consideration for your classmates, roommates, and professors. As you can see, in little ways, you can make a difference each day in your campus community.

Local Community

There are also opportunities for you to make a positive impact on the Norman community, the wider Oklahoma City metro area, and the state of Oklahoma during your time as a student. You can become engaged by participating in campus charitable activities that positively impact the local community, by offering your time to local volunteer organizations, and by becoming involved in national programs that make a difference in the local community.

Share Your Specialized Abilities

Consider using your specialized skills to impact the local community, as well. For example, if you are adept at rock wall climbing, ziplining, canoeing, or fishing, consider becoming a camp counselor for Camp Fire Heart of Oklahoma. Camp Fire Heart of Oklahoma provides an opportunity for young men and women to learn and develop their character through various programs, including day camps, after-school programming, and teen service and leadership activities ("Camp Fire Heart," n.d.). If you have hands-on skills for building, painting, etc., you might volunteer to help build homes for the less fortunate through Habitat for Humanity (*cchfh.org*). Or, if you are a photographer, Habitat for Humanity also seeks out photography volunteers to document the community work they are accomplishing. If you are a musician or performer, you might volunteer to work with the Arts Council of Oklahoma City (*artscouncilokc.com*). Or, if you are skilled with using computers, the Arts Council of Oklahoma City – along with many other non-profit charitable organizations – seeks volunteers to assist with their computer projects. For those of you with a knack for managing finances, handling accounting-type procedures, etc., you might volunteer with Consumer Credit Counseling Service, a non-profit organization that offers services to individuals struggling with debt challenges by providing services to families that include bankruptcy, resolving delinquent mortgages, debt management, and financial counseling ("Consumer Credit Counseling," n.d.). For a list of numerous local volunteer

sites to which you can contribute your specialized abilities, visit:

vccentralok.force.com

Pay Attention to the Needs Around You

You can also impact your local community by paying attention to the needs around you. For example, you might take food and a movie to someone who is sick, pick up trash at a city park, donate used clothing to Goodwill, give blood, or countless other caring deeds that can positively impact the people of our local community. Each day, in little ways, you can make a difference.

National Community

In thinking of ways to impact your national community, once again reflect on the issues that are important to you. For example, if the wellbeing of U.S. military children who have a parent deployed concerns you, you might volunteer to work with these children through Tinker Air Force Base's KUDOS (Kids Understanding Deployment Operations) Program (*tinkerfamilyreadinessfund.org*). Or, maybe there are health issues impacting our nation toward which you would like to devote time and energy in order to make a difference. If so, you might consider contacting organizations such as the American Heart Association (*americanheart.org*), the American Lung Association (*breathehealthy.org*), the Alzheimer's Association (*alzokar.org*), or others.

Use Your Voice

One of the powerful ways you can impact your national community is by using your voice to advocate for positive change. You may do this in many ways, but one is by contacting national leadership about matters that you believe to be important to the nation's wellbeing. To access contact information for representatives in the U.S. Congress, visit *www.house.gov*. To find contact information for members of the U.S. Senate, visit *www.senate.gov*. Both web sites provide search engines to obtain contact information for specific national representatives. Alternatively, if you wish to express your views to the President, you may visit *whitehouse.gov* for contact information.

Sometimes, people minimize the importance of contacting national leaders and expressing opinions, but keep in mind that these leaders are elected by the public and maintaining a pulse on the opinions and desires of their constituents is how many of these individuals stay in office. When you care about an issue, use your voice!

Another way that you can use your voice is to join with other OU students who share your passions and, together, be a collective voice that impacts the national community. A few examples of student associations at OU that focus on national issues include:

CONSTITUTIONAL STUDIES STUDENT ASSOCIATION: A group for students who are interested in law and politics. Meetings occur frequently and include debates and discussions of constitutional issues. See *www.facebook.com/OUCSSA.*

COLLEGE REPUBLICANS: A group for Republicans, which brings in conservative speakers and connects students to party politics and campaigns. See *psc.ou.edu/student-organizations.*

YOUNG DEMOCRATS: A group for Democrats, which brings in liberal speakers and connects students to party politics and campaigns. See *psc.ou.edu/student-organizations.*

POLITICAL SCIENCE CLUB: A group for students interested in politics or political science. See *psc.ou.edu/student-organizations.*

Register to Vote

One of the greatest opportunities you have to impact your national community is by voting. Keep in mind that, in order to vote in an election, you must be registered in advance. To learn more about registering to vote, visit: *ok.gov/elections/.* Opportunities to impact your national community are around you. Keep your eyes open for them!

Global Community

Being a Sooner Citizen also includes having an awareness of issues impacting the broader global community, behaving responsibly toward our planet's resources, demonstrating sensitivity and respect for cultural differences, and recognizing ways in which you might make a positive impact.

One way you can increase your awareness of these areas, while at OU, is by studying abroad. Immersing yourself in another culture is not only fun and exciting, but it is also a wonderful way to gain deeper appreciation for diversity and to increase sensitivity for cultural differences. To find a study abroad opportunity, visit the OU Education Abroad Office at *ou.edu/ea.* Other opportunities for increasing your consciousness of the global community include joining cultural organizations, attending lectures on issues affecting the global community, staying abreast of news stories from around the world, and taking language and culture courses.

Raise Awareness and Take Action

After you have gained more knowledge of issues affecting the global community, take action to impact your global community and to raise the awareness of others. For example, help preserve the planet and its ecosystems by recycling and by encouraging your friends and neighbors to recycle. Also, through social media, you might endeavor to raise awareness of human rights concerns across the planet and to educate the general public about issues of global concern. After all, the more aware society becomes of problems, the more likely that change will occur. Additionally, you might utilize social media to share donation links for groups who are engaged in bringing positive change to the global community.

For example, you might want to post a donation link to your social media page for a non-profit that is endeavoring to bring clean water to areas with unsanitary drinking sources or to a fund that helps refugees. Or raise money to put together birthing kits to reduce maternal mortality in regions of the world where there are no available health services.

There are many other ways to contribute to global change. If you care about issues of hunger, poverty, and disease around the world, consider volunteering at the Oklahoma City office of World Neighbors. In addition to ongoing volunteer opportunities, World Neighbors also offers a World Fest International Shopping Market in Oklahoma City each fall, as one of its fundraisers, and you might choose to assist with that event ("World Neighbors," n.d.).

Preserve Resources

Be sure not to overlook daily opportunities to positively impact your global community. For example, you can choose to walk, ride a bicycle, or take public transportation, in order to preserve the planet that we share with our global community. You can also choose to recycle, to "shop green," and to reduce your consumption of nonrenewable resources. When you turn off a light as you leave a room, or when you open the windows to let breezes cool your room, rather than turning on your air conditioner, you are impacting your global community by conserving valuable energy resources. Each day, you can choose to make choices that will benefit the global community.

Ready for Life

When you walk across the stage at graduation, you will be a person with four years of college education – and four years of experiences and relationships. The activities you experience and the friendships you make will have the most

Ada Louis Sipuel Fisher Garden

Born in Chickasha, Oklahoma, in 1924, Ada Sipuel Fisher challenged the segregationist policies typical of the day by applying to the OU School of Law in 1946. She was refused on grounds of race, and her suit was appealed to the Supreme Court where it was decided that a state must provide the same education for black citizens as white. Her efforts contributed to the Civil Rights Movement as she braved school, forced to sit in a chair marked "colored" and to eat in a chained off section of the cafeteria under guard. Fellow students and faculty rejected the segregation and crawled under the chain to eat with her. Thanks to the work of Sipuel Fisher and men and women like her, OU is today a more diverse community.

lasting impact on you. The purpose of your education at OU is to give you a deeper understanding of your place in the world, to prepare you with the knowledge and skills you need to succeed after college and to continue to contribute to your community, and to inspire in you a love of learning that will stay with you for the rest of your life. Therefore, your experiences and education will help you develop the tools neccessary to advance as an individual and to improve the lives of others.

As part of this development, our hope is that you will be motivated to make philanthropy a part of your life. **Philanthropy** is the desire to promote the welfare of others expressed by the donation of time or money. When you serve or give to others, you are investing in your community and the people who live in it.

William Butler Yeats said, "Education is not the filling of a pail, but the lighting of a fire." You are not at OU to acquire information. You are here to become the kind of person you want to become. You belong to the most prosperous generation of human beings who have ever walked the planet. You have more access to knowledge than any previous generation ever to have lived. You have these opportunities because others before you have worked hard to create them. Use your education to understand this inheritance and to ask yourself: what do I owe the world?

"The only limit to your impact is your imagination and commitment."
- Tony Robbins

References

Camp Fire Heart of Oklahoma (2013). Welcome to Camp Fire Camp DaKaNi. Retrieved from http://campdakani.org/.

Consumer Credit Counseling Services of Oklahoma (2014). About us. Retrieved from http://cccsok.org/about/.

World Neighbors (2013). Get involved in global issues. Retrieved from http://www.wn.org/site/c.buITJ7NRKsLaG/b.6248435/k.34E3/Get_Involved_in_Global_Issues.htm.

Chapter 10 REI

Impacting Your World

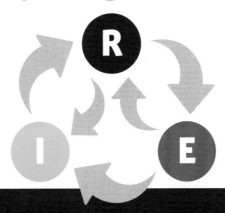

Reflect

Reflect on one way you have evolved during your first semester of college.

....

Engage

Take a look at the Spheres of Influence discussed throughout this chapter.

....

Impact

What is one sphere that you have had an influence on this semester? What sphere would you like to influence more in the future? Consider how you might make an impact on a specific issue in this community and discuss.

....

INDEX

A

D

E

F

G

L

M

N

O

P

T

U

V

W